REBEL MUSICS

in memoriam

Violet Fenton Carlson (1903-2002)
and
Dr. Girijabai Heble (1900-1990)

REBEL MUSICS

Human Rights, Resistant Sounds, and the Politics of Music Making

Daniel Fischlin, Ajay Heble, editors

Montréal/New York/London

BLACK
ROSE
BOOKS

Black Rose Books No. GG321

National Library of Canada Cataloguing in Publication Data
Daniel Fischlin, 1957-
Rebel musics : human rights, resistant sounds, and the politics of music making /
Daniel Fischlin, Ajay Heble, editors

Includes bibliographical references and index.
Hardcover ISBN: 1-55164-231-X (bound) Paperback ISBN: 1-55164-230-1 (pbk.)

1. Music--Political aspects. 2. Popular music--Political aspects. 3. Social justice--Songs and music--History and criticism. I. Title. II. Title: Human rights, resistant sounds, and the politics of music making.

ML3916.F529 2003   306.4'84   C2003-904156-5

Although every effort has been made to secure permission for materials reproduced herein, in some cases we have been unable to locate a copyright holder.

Cover design: Associés libres

BLACK ROSE BOOKS

C.P. 1258	2250 Military Road	99 Wallis Road
Succ. Place du Parc	Tonawanda, NY	London, E9 5LN
Montréal, H2X 4A7	14150	England
Canada	USA	UK

To order books:

In Canada: (phone) 1-800-565-9523 (fax) 1-800-221-9985
email: utpbooks@utpress.utoronto.ca

In United States: (phone) 1-800-283-3572 (fax) 1-651-917-6406

In the UK & Europe: (phone) London 44 (0)20 8986-4854 (fax) 44 (0)20 8533-5821
email: order@centralbooks.com

Our Web Site address: http://www.web.net/blackrosebooks

A publication of the Institute of Policy Alternatives of Montréal (IPAM)

Printed in Canada

The Canada Council | Le Conseil des Arts
for the Arts | du Canada

Table of Contents

Image and Photo Credits

Title Page Ink Drawing and Chapter Icons Courtesy of Artist Eric Drooker
Take One and Take Two Chapter Icons Courtesy of Lusmore Productions

Acknowledgements

We thank the many musicians with whom we have worked over the years and who have fed into the ideas developed in this book.

We thank our supportive colleagues in the School of English and Theatre Studies (SETS) at the University of Guelph, and especially Dean Jacqueline Murray and School Director, Alan Shepard. The unique research atmosphere in our School has played a significant role in allowing us to pursue this work. Thanks also to the University's Centre for Cultural Studies / Centre d'études sur la culture, and to the Social Sciences and Humanities Research Council of Canada for supporting this project.

We thank the research assistants without whom this book would have been impossible, especially Dorothy Hadfield, Cory Legassic, and Bart Vautour—all dreams to work with.

We thank Linda Barton and Dimitri Roussopoulos at Black Rose Books for their enthusiasm and professionalism.

We thank our colleagues at the Guelph Jazz Festival for their commitment to the music.

We thank our contributors—from whom we have learned a great deal—for their patience, generosity, and diligence in responding to our editorial suggestions as we worked to a very tight timeline.

And we thank our families, immediate and otherwise, for their discrepant engagement with the sounds we make, the reciprocities they continue to share with us.

We dedicate this book to the memory of our grandmothers, strong women through whose example we learned the linked virtues of music, community, and activism.

Preface

From Thomas Mapfumo to Bob Marley. William Parker to Frank Zappa. Edgard Varèse to Ice-T. *Negativland* to *Rage Against the Machine*. Plunderphonics to Chilean *canto nuevo*. Blues to West African drumming. Abbey Lincoln to Ani DiFranco. Paul Robeson to Gil Scott-Heron. Hip hop to *son*. Chicano punk to Zorn and Braxton. Gospel singing to rock 'n roll cabaret. Screaming panic noise to folk lyricism. Free jazz to diasporic, intercultural mix-ups.

Rebel musics are aligned with some of the most trenchant critiques of global politics, colonialism, neoliberalism, and degrading democracy. And their expressive powers speak directly to the worldwide struggles for civil rights and meaningful justice that remain the most pertinent of human concerns in the here and now.

What does it mean to practice political resistance through music making? What sounds animate liberatory, solidary discourses? How has music come to be the "weapon of the future"? How are human rights and music making explicitly linked? How do rebel musics, in spite of forces that seek to either commodify or marginalize them, continue to activate diverse energies of critique and inspiration? Why are truly rebel musics so often a function of intercultural collisions? What kinds of concrete models for alternative community practices and political organization do rebel musics provide? How does musical activism resonate in practical, political terms?

Rebel Musics examines some of these questions in relation to a diverse range of musical practices and performers. Written with a wide audience in mind, the book is one of the first to juxtapose human rights issues with different forms of music making. If rights discourses are founded on expressive freedoms, then surely music making, the most universal form of human expression besides language, must play a key role in imagining what it means to achieve social justice, freedom, and meaningful community.

Little work has been written on the specific relations between different forms of music making and human rights theory and practice. *Rebel Musics* foregrounds musical discourses of resistance in relation to pertinent issues of human rights, globalization, political theory, identity politics, cultural critique, and the development of new networks of social interaction and responsibility.

Bringing together leading voices on the topic of music and human rights, *Rebel Musics* represents an original and needed contribution to discourses of resistance that seek to effect social change via non-traditional means. The book focuses its attention on the ways in which musical resistance is enacted and informs the social movements that oppose neoliberalism, globalization, and transnational corporatism. Essayists examine the meaning of oppositional musics in relation to specific political, cultural, and theoretical issues and provide a unique glimpse into the stunning array of resistant social formations in which musical expression is a key feature.

Loosely based on both Ron Sakolsky's and Fred Wei-han Ho's seminal *Sounding Off!: Music as Subversion/Resistance/Revolution* and the film *Musiques rebelles Québec* produced by Productions Multi-Monde, and released in concert with the 10th annual Guelph Jazz Festival—a festival long-recognized for the way in which it programs rebel musicians—this book provides, we hope, a fascinating entry into the contentious arena where music, politics, and cultural theory meet.

A final note to readers: we have deliberately tried not to produce a comprehensive approach to rebel musics and have structured the book to represent interventions into a range of areas, from personal reflections by artists through to major pieces on jazz, blues, Chilean protest music, and youth culture. Moreover, we have avoided the trap of using the introduction to summarize the individual essays, instead opting for what we think is a more innovative structure in which issues taken up in the introduction and in the contributors' various essays are re-examined in a critical postlude. Readers are invited to free-fall through the materials presented here, a sampling of a much larger palette of musickings that envision alternate possibilities of engagement with the social and political practices that shape lives around the globe.

Daniel Fischlin and *Ajay Heble*

Daniel Fischlin

Take One / Rebel Musics: Human Rights, Resistant Sounds, and the Politics of Music Making

"What Decent People Don't Want to Hear": Sound as Contradiction

Sound as dissident practice, commentary, critique. Sound as rebellion, resistance, and revolution. Sound as the base element in the alchemy that enables human expression. Sound as possibility, potential, power. Sound as the contradiction of silence. Musicking as the contradiction of silencing, of *being* silenced.

DANIEL FISCHLIN is Professor of English at the University of Guelph and co-author with Martha Nandorfy of *Eduardo Galeano: Through the Looking Glass* (Black Rose Books, 2002). He has been active as a musician for most of his life. This is his fourth book devoted to the interdisciplinary study of music.

In this book we seek to map out the beginnings of a much larger story, a much bigger picture. And we acknowledge that this book is incomplete: so many sounds to document and articulate, so many musical practices to account for, celebrate, reflect upon. So few pages. And always, the threat that the written word will somehow evacuate the potency of the sonic forces to which it refers. Or, the threat that music will be seen in isolation from the many other sites in which resistance is produced and multiplied, something we wish to caution our readers about from the start. This book, then, does not envision music as a singular force in the complicated and emergent scenario that is the global struggle for equitable rights and social justice. Rather it shows how a wide variety of musickings play an important and often neglected role in that struggle—a role that must be understood in conjunction with multiple other sites in which the same battles are being waged.

The diverse ways in which sonic projections, multiple musickings, have produced an impact on human rights and social justice issues is the subject of this book. And this book also interrogates the question of the degree to which so called rebel musics actually have had an impact on rights issues, either through (among others) the expression and consolidation of solidarity with rights initiatives, through playing a key role in the pedagogy of rights culture in the dissemination of pertinent information, through the activation of the emotive powers that are all too often detached from the actual instruments of rights legislation, through the raising of money for rights causes, and through participation in the development of the kinds of critical consciousness without which rights discourses would be impossible.[1]

We begin by acknowledging that nothing in sound is intrinsically revolutionary, rebellious, or political. But, simultaneously, we acknowledge that to say as much is to dream a nightmare world in which sound is pure and essential, divorced from its social and political contexts, meaningful in its abstract and metaphysical potential but irrelevant in what it has to say to the *here and now* of daily life. We don't live in that abstract space and neither, we think, do you.

Instead, we live in communities permeated by the sounds they give shape to and that correspondingly give shape to them. We define communities by the sounds they make—and the sounds they refuse. We generate sound and ideas about sound as extensions (reflections) of our political cultures, but also as critiques thereof. And the sounds we call music haunt our daily lives at their seemingly most trivial moments, and also at their moments of apocalypse and cataclysm.

> [T]he only unchanging, essential characteristics of music are those which are written into the physics of sound, and those which are wired into our nervous system or our primal experiences: sudden loud sounds startle us, sounds that remind us of adults cooing over an infant have the opposite effect. Beyond that sort of nearly involuntary analogy, the use to which people are putting a given music will gradually decide its nature.
>
> Military bugle calls once effectively allowed synchronized advances and retreats on confused battlefields: here is a function so simple that it's really only a signal, and some might not want to call it musical at all. But after the fight, the same person picks up the same instrument and plays taps over the graves of his comrades. He plays slowly and well, people are moved: have we entered the realm of art yet? (Johnson 47)

The same instrument that summons to battle, plays a requiem in the name of peace. The instrument is the same, the political context of the sound it emits completely different. Sound and music are always produced in social and political contexts, some of which seek to occlude music as a pure distillation of "our" essential humanity that has nothing to do with or to say to the multiple contexts that allow for its creation and dissemination. But the aesthetics of the depoliticization of music is really for another book. Here, we propose something different: a peek into the ways in which politically committed music-making represents a crucial, if barely understood, vein in the ways in which music has always been made in different places and in different times.

•   The sounds of Bob Dylan's electric guitar first heard publicly at the Newport folk festival in July of 1965, Igor Stravinsky's driving polyrhythms in *Le Sacre du Printemps* (*The Rite of Spring*, 1913), and Edgard Varèse's sonic non-pitch textures have all incited outraged responses or criticism because they announced the arrival of revolutionary sounds in contexts unwilling to accept them.[2] Insofar as they pushed the generic limits and expectations of their audiences, those sounds represented resistance to orthodoxies and conventions. But could it be that those sounds, so ill-received then, so quotidian today, had much further-reaching implications? Could it be that the introjection of new sonic textures, unheard of instrumentations, unimagined sonic possibilities have anything to do with opening up spaces of resistance and renewal that have an important connection with emergent rights discourses? Our argument posits a qualified "yes" as an answer to both these questions, echoing George Lipsitz's observation that "African nationalists, reformers, and revolutionaries, Australian indigenous and Native American activists, and Québécois separatists have all used popular music as part of their strategies for securing, shaping, or stunting the power of the state" (151).

Musicians themselves have railed against how quickly generic stereotypes are formed and are reinforced by the commercial interests that seek to use expression for profit. This is the case for Frank Zappa, who despised the linkages between foundation monies and musical vogues like serial/electronic music or minimalism, suggesting that in the latter case all that gets produced is, in a memorable pun, monochromonotony. Zappa's extraordinary ability to parody generic stereotypes, transforming them into biting social commentary (for example, his brutal take-off *We're Only In It For the Money*, on the Beatles' *Sergeant Pepper* album and 60s so-called "countercultures") is one response to the limits imposed on audiences through the mediations of the musical marketplace, in which stable genres equal stable cash-flows.[3] Parody and de-composition (or what some might prefer to call deconstruction) gave Zappa strategies to produce his music as a social practice with persistent social consciousness and relevance all the while sustaining his focus on the expressive power and potential of music.

Similarly, American composer Scott Johnson paints a picture of the kind of confluence of marketing concerns and expressive strategies that neuter the musician's relation to the public sphere:

> Artistic specialization, along with its cousin in marketing, tightly focused demographic targeting, has reached such extremes that serious composers live in a sort of internal exile, playing virtually no part in their parent culture. When the most gifted converse only among themselves, their complaints about a debased public sphere become a self-fulfilling prophecy. At some point it ceases to matter whether they withdrew first, or were driven away by Philistines; the end result is identical. (57)

Hamid Drake and William Parker, Guelph Jazz Festival, 2002

When musicians either pander to or seek to disengage from the social contexts in which they produce their work it becomes extraordinarily difficult to sustain the potential and integrity of music as a socially relevant practice. And, further, socially relevant music measures itself in relation to how far it goes in affronting orthodoxies. Or, as Greil Marcus puts it in *Ranters & Crowd Pleasers: Punk in Pop Music, 1977-92*, "To make true political music, you have to say what decent people don't want to hear."[4] But even to say as much is to pigeon-hole the complex cultural phenomena generated by music into categories where social relevance is equated unthinkingly with political resistance at the expense of other forms of expressive power produced by music and linked with, for instance, community affirmation and celebration.

Like the music he created, which so carefully avoided any simplistic reduction of its complexities to academic categories, Zappa's unique and courageous voice took many forms. His life in music poses many of the central questions that are congruent with this book's ends, especially relating to the ways in which the commercialization and globalization of music effectively problematize its capacity to sustain those qualities that are most critical and resistant to any form of totalitarian thinking. Think of virtually any popular musical form associated with "rebellion" over the latter half of the twentieth century and think of how it has been commodified: blues, rock, punk, hip-hop, rave. And of course, to say as much is to essentialize complex musics into their commercialized forms, and to ignore the many ways musicians continue to resist this conformity and commercialization. And further, to say as much is to evacuate the potential that even straitjacketed forms of rebel music, duly packaged and sold to large audiences, have for transmitting the sounds and ideas that produce resistance, critique, and a differential relation to hegemony.

Kevin Courrier uses an article Zappa published in *Life Magazine* entitled ("The Oracle Has It all Psyched Out," June 28, 1968) to demonstrate how Zappa "traced the evolution of rock as a rebellious art form, but proficiently described how the business of rock would render its own rebellion superfluous. 'It is something of a paradox that companies which manufacture and distribute this art form (strictly for profit) might one day be changed or controlled by young people who were motivated to action by the products these companies sell,' Zappa wrote prophetically" (165). Zappa's unflinching critical attitude to the ways in which music is used caused him no small degree of difficulty, the least of which entailed his being stereotyped into the genius / eccentric / iconoclast category as a way of diminishing the rebellious force of his musickings. In "Oh No," from *Weasels Ripped My Flesh*, he "[responds] to John Lennon's 'All you Need is Love' and the Beatles' simplistic cry for universal brotherhood. Zappa didn't see how positive anthems trumpeting the virtues of love could change the volatile political climate around him:

Oh no, I don't believe it
You say you think you know the meaning of love

You say love is all we need
You say with your love you can change
All of the fools, all of the hate
I think you're probably out to lunch.

Zappa's dismissal of the privileged Lennon's plea for peace is more than a simple act of cynicism, it's a recognition that self-righteous bromides—even well-intentioned ones—won't plumb the depths of human iniquity" (Courrier 211).[5] Difficult as this may be for some to swallow, Zappa clearly envisioned the dangers in any music that permitted a trivializing distortion of complex material realities in which power, the capacity for great evil, and the shameless pursuit of corporate or state self-interest had all too often produced astonishing misery and suffering in violation of the spirit of the post-Universal Declaration of Human Rights (1948) world.

The great free jazz improviser/composer William Parker, someone we will meet again later in this book, suggests that in his music "I am more concerned with restoring life, with keeping the fire of human compassion burning. The fire of flowers as well as the fire of revolution" (liner notes, *Sunrise in the Tone World*). How to reconcile Zappa's critique of Lennon's bromides with this sort of intent and philosophy of music? How to sustain the spirit of Parker's appeal to compassion and revolution as a key ideological undercurrent in his music while at the same time sustaining the spirit of Zappa's relentlessly critical insights into musical and ideological cliché?

Musical sounds are interwoven into the warp and weft of virtually everything. They mediate the world as we know it through being linked in astonishingly diverse ways with images, words, and the formation of community. From the "riot grrrl" phenomenon—which attacks everything from rampant masculinism in the rock star industry to sexual abuse, racism, and homophobia—through to the persistent sounds of AfroCuba de Matanzas—a group that conserves and renews the astonishingly rich musical heritage of the Afrocuban diaspora by playing monthly *peñas* on the broken streets of the La Marina barrio in which its members live—music as a protean, dynamic, and forceful expression of cultural memory and resistance refuses to be ignored.[6]

AfroCuba de Matanzas, Street Peña, 2003

And yet it has been, like so many other disciplines in the so-called arts, where marginality is the price paid— or extorted—for critical countervoicings. And yet.

And yet, musical artists in virtually every genre have produced work of incisive relevance to human rights discourses as a function of their art, their commitment to variant forms of social justice, their belief in the communicative power of music, their compulsion to articulate the dissidence that grounds their worldview. Fela Kuti's courageous attacks on "neocolonialism and the control of the African economy by multinational corporations, especially in Nigeria" (Tenaille 70), for instance, led to the persistent state and police pressures he and his extended family faced. And as he persisted in offering his trenchant critiques of corrupt dictatorships, corporate thievery, and colonial oppression, he proffered the position that "Music is the weapon of the future / music is the weapon of the progressives / music is the weapon of the givers of life" (Tenaille 76). When "Sandra Smith (now Sandra Isidore), a woman active in the Black Panther Party, gave Fela a copy of *The Autobiography of Malcom X*," the book introduced him to ideas about Pan-Africanism that had been censored in Nigeria," (Lipsitz 39) and marked a turning point in the politics of Kuti's music making. American black revolutionary consciousness, so profoundly associated with the civil rights movement, then, fed into the radical politics of Kuti's music, which was based on the realization that "I had no country. I decided to come back [from the United States] and try to make my country African" (cited in Lipsitz 40).

And in the United States, Nina Simone's musical contributions to the civil rights movement were exemplified in the sarcastically upbeat and incendiary show tune "Mississippi Goddam." The song attacks entrenched racism, responds (as did Dylan) to the murder of Medgar Evers and, as well, to a church bombing in Mississippi, and bitterly frames the dilemma of race in America: "I don't belong here. I don't belong there. I've even stopped believing in prayer...Oh this whole country is full of lies. You're all gonna die and die like flies. I don't trust you anymore. You keep on saying go slow...You don't have to live next to me. Just give me my equality." These sort of sentiments find their echo in Public Enemy's "Hitler Day," which blasts out the lyric: "Remember the dead and it makes me curse / when they don't include 100 million / of us black folks / that died in the bottom of boats / I can carry on 'bout killin' till dusk and dawn / and war ain't the reason they gone" (Chuck D 153). Chuck D's lyrics and music here, like Simone's, carry out the role of producing alternative narratives that foster communities of resistance with ongoing civil rights dimensions. Rap and resistant musical strategies, as Tricia Rose argues, can provide a kind of nexus for imagining alternative knowledges and cultural formations associated with resistant politics:

> Under social conditions in which sustained frontal attacks on powerful groups are strategically unwise or successfully contained, oppressed people use language, dance, and music to mock those in power, express rage, and produce fantasies of subversion...

these cultural responses to oppression are not safety valves that protect and sustain the machines of oppression. Quite to the contrary, these dances, languages, and musics produce communal bases of knowledge about social conditions, communal interpretations of them and quite often serve as the cultural glue that fosters communal resistance. (99-100)[7]

It is impossible to underestimate the importance of such "fantasies of subversion" in producing the sites where alternative political realities and discourses that address social justice issues are configured and given emotive articulation.

For instance, consider the linkage between music and liberatory politics in Kenya, where a song called "Who Can Bwogo Me" became a campaign anthem for presidential frontrunner Mwai Kibaki's National Rainbow Coalition in September 2002, in an election he eventually won. The song, as detailed by Matthew Rosenberg, "bridge[d] tribal divides with a message of resistance to corruption and oppression. 'Bwogo' means 'scare' in the language of the Luo tribe of western Kenya, and the tune is about somebody 'who doesn't want to be oppressed, to be kept down—to be harassed,' said Julius Owino, one half of the Gidi Gidi Maji Maji, the duo who wrote and recorded the song." Consider, too, the work of Norman Nawrocki and Rhythm Activism, discussed at length elsewhere in this book, who attribute their brand of rock 'n roll cabaret activism to the "late 19th century bars and bistros of Paris" that gave birth to cabaret as a

stage for political and social criticism…These first cabaret artists aimed to entertain, inform and agitate, and blended their artistry with political commitment…In time the cabaret movement both attracted and produced some of the continent's most celebrated political poets, actors, performance artists, and playwrights. Bertolt Brecht first performed as a cabaret artist accompanying himself on guitar as he sang his radical poems off key. Later, some cabaret artists in Germany were named 'enemies of Nazism' and not permitted to perform during Hitler's reign. (Nawrocki 6-7)

More Kick!, a 1995 Rhythm Activism album uses, among others, lyrics from Brecht as well as lyrics sung by Italian Partisans during World War II—all part of its project to reclaim the lost history of musical activism. Rhythm Activism's commitment to a range of rights issues is remarkable and they have gone out of their way to associate their music with the political movements with which they align themselves—from attacking religious fundamentalism that restricts women's rights through to support for the rights of the homeless and indigenous land claims. An earlier album, *Blood & Mud*, was released in 1994, the same year that the Zapatistas in Mexico began their public struggle for land rights and social justice in Chiapas. The album contains a scathing denunciation of the North American Free Trade Agreement [NAFTA] and liner notes explicitly and repeatedly mention rights issues, as in this citation that accompanies "NAFTA Love Song":

As for concerns about human rights violations & environmental abuses in Mexico & the possibility that the bank's presence (the National Bank of Canada/Banque Nationale) & actions could help siphon Canadian jobs to that nation, Leon Courville (bank president) was quite candid: "We don't have a moral responsibility to pass judgement on how business is done in Mexico," he said. "It's not our country. —*Montréal Gazette,* March 1994.

Rhythm Activism's denunciation of economic globalization that refuses any ethical linkage to the effects it creates gives voice to the hypocrisies of strategic globalization, which seeks to benefit the very few at the expense of the majority all the while doing so by refusing to acknowledge that economic realities are inseparable from rights realities.[8]

Rhythm Activism, Vienna, (left to right) Luc Bonin, Norman Nawrocki, Wilf Plum, Sylvain Côté

This refusal parallels the general separation that exists between the actual legal and juridical instruments associated with rights (and how they are given shape in treaty and constitutional form) and the discourses generated in the arts. A telling example of this separation occurs in a chapter in *Crimes Against Humanity: The Struggle for Global Justice,* written by prominent British barrister Geoffrey Robertson who has a long and distinguished career in international rights law. In "Twenty-first Century Blues," Robertson opens with an articulate account of how "Human rights standards are becoming rules of international law because a campaigning mass movement is putting pressure on democratic governments to practice what they preach when they ratify treaties which embody these standards" (131). Robertson, in work he metaphorically (perhaps even intuitively) associates with the "Blues" sensibility, does not once mention music (or any other art for that matter) as a crucial element in the "campaigning mass movement" that is actually creating the political pressure he describes—a problem in how the different sites in which rights get articulated are all too often (and wrongly) dissociated from each other by disciplinary boundaries. The chapter is important because it crystallizes Robertson's legal focus on rights issues in which battles worldwide remain to be won, rights battles that are at the thematic core of many of the musicians (like Nawrocki and Rhythm Activism) we mention in this chapter: freedom from execution, minority rights including the "right to exist" and the "right to be different," indigenous rights, self-determination rights, economic and social rights, and the right to democracy.

The latter issue addresses how rights doctrines have traditionally been formulated to be (supposedly) "profoundly apolitical, in the sense that its rules have been carefully tailored to suit sovereign states irrespective of whether that sovereignty inheres in a monarch or a military dictator or a popularly elected president" (Robertson 174). This highly problematic and illusory purity of rights law from the politics of their creation let alone of their enactment is strangely parallel to what apologists for music's essential purity argue for as well—a kind of depoliticization that suits quietist and oppressive polities or the ideological aim of those who deny that music is always mediated by context.

And yet, for Joe Strummer [John Graham Mellor] of The Clash, perhaps the most important punk rock band of the late 70s and early 80s, this purity and disciplinary separation was nonsense. Strummer clearly linked the band's music with "a world of troubles and insurgencies," stating in a 1988 interview that if "you ain't thinkin' about man and God and law, then you ain't thinkin' about nothin' " (Pareles). The Clash's politics, so different from the anarchic, bleak "everything is fucked" nihilism of the Sex Pistols, made it a band to listen to because they so articulately "railed against apathy, powerlessness, police brutality, American cultural domination and poseurs of all sorts" (Pareles).[9] Moreover, the band recognized the dangers of the musical commodification of rebellion in lyrics sung by Strummer: "You think it's funny turning rebellion into money" ("White Man in Hammersmith Palais," 1977). Further, Strummer who was heavily influenced by Woody Guthrie, reggae, and soul music, among others, saw the influence of reggae on the band as a "badge of interracial solidarity" (Pareles) and such albums as Sandinista! and Combat Rock gave vent to a critical, internationalist politics in opposition to repression, political quietism, and political and disciplinary isolation. And examples such as these could be proliferated for music specifically associated with protest over a range of issues with pertinence to rights discourses—from anti-racism through to militarism, government corruption, censorship, freedom of association, personal security, access to education, hunger, queerphobia, and so on.

In the case of queer culture, the example of Matt Wobensmith, Outpunk label owner, publisher of the short-lived Outpunk zine (both of which are dedicated to articulating the connection between punk and queer cultures), and originator of the term queercore, illustrates how "art gets transformed by long-term intimacy with radical politics" (Sinker 315). Wobensmith, in an interview with Daniel Sinker, expresses his frustration with how the tag "radical" gets used to turn the material realities of his day-to-day life into abstract theory: "I don't make Queer Theory, I live it. I don't want theory. I want facts. I'm around too many people who know nothing but theories. Theories don't feed me, they don't pay my rent or do anything for me. I'm just running a business and disseminating information" (318). Wobensmith articulates the long-standing imaginary divide between doing and theorizing, materiality and abstraction, making and imagining. This divide frames any consideration of what rebel musics actually accomplish in relation to advancing rights agendas as opposed to what they may think they accomplish. In response to this problem Wobensmith suggests that "the most important things to happen to punk in the '90s were the riot girl phenomenon and, feeding off that, the queercore thing…[both] brought punk full-circle back to its original political roots. What riot girl was doing was relating punk to feminism, to shit that was really going on, not some system of government you didn't understand, but the life being lived by your mother. For so long all the politics in punk were so theoretical. Riot girl redirected punk to recognize the human element. Queercore did that, too" (318). While Wobensmith expresses admiration for how these genres redirect political energy to daily, lived experience he blasts traditional punk cultism and insularity that diminish these experiences, arguing that "Punk will never be anything but a middle-class phenomenon because it's all about fantasy—a liberal fantasy that thinks it knows how to run the world" (321). Wobensmith states how he's "heard people equate punk's musical purity with California's Prop 187 laws enacted against 'aliens' and immigrants. People don't like contamination. I say contaminate" (322).

The contradiction between punk's "musical purity" and the queer politics that challenge that purity from "within" points to the road ahead as we examine the ways in which rebel musics confront their own fragmentation and failures of imagination in the face of material realities that complicate their politics.[10] Wobensmith's experiences in this struggle are instructive when understood in relation to aspects of human rights theory. Rhoda E. Howard, for example, argues that:

> The activist liberal citizen, translating private reflection about the common good into public action, protects his own and other people's human rights. In so doing, he simultaneously contributes to his community and protects his own integrity as an individuated human being. Protection of his human rights is protection of everyone's rights. Protection of everyone's human rights permits retention and formation of humane, socially satisfying communities. (222)

Howard's assumptions about liberalism and the translation of the private into the communal good assume far too much about the homogeneity of purpose and action that exist in contradiction to the multiple "contaminations" envisioned by Wobensmith. The equation of activism with liberalism, where liberalism has become a form of mild-mannered conservatism, may actually do little to promote the kinds of rights agendas in which socially satisfied communities get produced and all people's rights are respected. Moreover, the kind of social satisfaction envisioned as the end result of such liberalism signals precisely the kind of smug, uncritical stasis of which queercore activists like Wobensmith are so suspicious. And the reliance on "private reflection" as a sort of decontextualized, non-community related activity assumes a kind of essentialist liberal capacity to generate abstractions that become the social will, a very dangerous form of detachment that Wobensmith's critical musical politics decry. Our juxtaposition of Howard's and Wobensmith's views suggests two very different imaginings of community: community is not so much defined through homogeneity and overlap as through its constructive, progressive ability to encounter differences and "contaminations" that challenge that homogeneity.

Far beyond the boardrooms of corporate and state power, the very places to which rights talk has been relegated for far too long, musical artists have produced an astonishing body of work with direct relevance to the vast spectrum of issues most pertinent to the establishment of a worldwide, equitable, and implementable system of rights: colonialism and its aftermath, racism, the oppression of women, aboriginal rights, intercultural exchange, human health, environment, species extinction, worker exploitation, police brutality, catastrophic militarization, land rights, gay, lesbian, and queer rights—and on and on.

And musicians have paid the price, as many of the examples in this introduction show and as many essays in this volume document. And they have borne witness to the inherent contradictions that make "music" the contested site of meanings and social practices in which larger issues of human freedom and expressivity are simultaneously at stake. Theodor W. Adorno, a controversial twentieth-century figure in articulating what and how music means, notes "The contradiction between the freedom of art and the gloomy diagnoses regarding the use of such freedom—this contradiction is one of reality, not just of the consciousness that analyzes reality so as to make some small contribution to change" (20). The cold truth Adorno envisages here is that a split exists between the freedom to make art and how that art gets used to make freedom.

No necessary connection exists between art created in a "free" context and how that art gets used to further enable freedom. The recent situation at the United Nations in which Picasso's magnificent anti-war painting *Guernica* (1937) was covered over by a curtain "so that such disagreeable scenery would not distract from Colin Powell's clarion call" (Galeano 35) to war in Iraq attests to Adorno's cautionary insight. Silencing art is a form of negative use with obvious connections to censorship and repression. Silencing *Guernica* in this way, ironically, only paid even more tribute to the actual expressive power to which it gives vent. The contradictions between the artistic freedoms that produce liberatory works of art and how those works get used must be a determining factor in any attempt to understand how music of any sort gets aligned with liberatory, civil rights discourses. And many such contradictions abound. Exemplary of this would be the split in the 1960s between "the folk music of predominantly White anti-war protest and the predominantly Black Civil Rights movement. It is a division that suggests a deep division of commitment and purpose in the two cataclysmic affronts to the American social and political system during the 1960s" (Gonczy 14). Daniel Gonczy, in a wide-ranging discussion of folk music and civil rights, suggests that:

> Two aspects of the music of the Civil Rights movement must be emphasized. First, music was integral to any activity, be it a small local gathering of people to discuss the need for further desegregation or a massive demonstration to call attention to the need for unrestricted use of voting rights…the second aspect to stress must be the fundamental contribution of religious fervour and spirit. Even those indifferent to religion were caught up in the effect and the enthusiasm these songs were capable of producing. Conviction and a sense of community were all-pervasive in the movement. In short 'History has never known a protest movement so rich in song as the Civil Rights movement. Nor a movement in which songs are as important.' (14-15)[11]

Even as these comments point to the importance of music in producing resistance, they participate in the myth of an American-centric universe in which the American civil rights movement takes on a trans-historical importance while ignoring the many other sites in which oppressive forces and music have come into conflict with authority. How far, in other words, does such an analysis go toward appropriating music to a use that is contrary to the social context in which the music is being made?

Another example of such a contradiction occurs in that icon of liberated music-making and freedom-fighting, Bob Marley, who experienced extreme disillusion upon seeing, on his first visit to Africa in 1978, a continent that mirrored the shantytowns of a Jamaica whose own poverty and violence had contributed to making his voice such a powerful catalyst for Pan-Africanism, black independence, and disaffected youth all over the world. Marley's allegiances to anti- colonial and anti-racist movements are well-known. Marley was influenced by, among others, music entrepreneur Danny Sims, whose radical politics had an effect on the music Marley made: "They had Garveyism and the struggle against oppression as a meeting point, but Danny's Stateside Civil Rights and Black Power experiences were an education for Bob, expanding his radical consciousness beyond Kingston's ghettos. Just as what Bob had to tell about colonialism and how that worked would be edification for the Americans" (Bradley 411). But, as told in Timothy White's controversial biography (which used "invented conversations and thoughts combined with actual interview material" [Barrow and Dalton 463]), when Marley finally did go to Africa for the first time in December 1978, he saw the same slums and hungry faces he'd left behind in Jamaica, the same corrupt, strong-arm governments towering over the misery. This Africa was the sole continent where virtually no modern political leader had ever been peacefully voted out of office. He entered war-torn Ethiopia from Kenya to discover that his beloved Haile Selassie, the man he worshipped as God, had died in disgrace and had been buried in an unmarked grave. The absence of any memorial to the man, coupled with the open contempt with which Ethiopians recalled their former emperor, had left Marley severely shaken. (3)

Marley's voice, long-associated with resistance in music and politics had then to face up to the material realities that did not coincide with his musical ideology in which the freedom to create had not necessarily created freedom. The term "rebel music" has clear historical associations with the "seismic shift" that had transformed mainstream reggae in the first half of the 1970s.[12] Rebel music referred to the "social discontent often expressed in the music of [the] artists—many of whom were committed Rastafarians. The Wailers exemplified the changes in youth music, having evolved from representatives of West Kingston's rude boys into more conscious 'soul re-bels'" (Barrow and Dalton 135). But the dilemma Marley confronted in the years immediately following upon this phenomenon asked the implicit question: how had his music actually changed the lived circumstances of the people to whom it was addressed, whether in Africa or in Jamaica? And worse, how had such a rebel, freedom movement evolved from an ideology aligned so clearly with a reviled dictator?

Further examples of contradictions that problematize any discussion of rebel musics abound. Chuck D, lead singer for the seminal rap group Public Enemy, recognizes that "For many young people who are a part of the Hip-Hop Nation today, the Vietnam War and the turbulent 1960s is a period that they read about in history books—not for me. I actually lived through that and was personally affected and shaped by the pervasive antiwar, civil rights, and Black-Power sentiments as a child" (25). But how many of Public Enemy's listeners make absolutely no such connections, having been overtaken by the commercial, dehistoricizing forces that fuel the music industry's rela-tions to its youth market? Similarly, the Chicano punk band Los Illegals struggled with the market-ing of its 1980 album *Internal Exile* by A&M Records and worried over how the politics of their music was being mapped onto corporate profit. A&M clearly sought to use the "connections/as-sociations Los Illegals had already made with Chicano community-based and political organiza-tions" (Reyes and Waldman 137), itself an instance in which the radical politics of the music were aligned with commercial interests even as the release of Los Illegals's bilingual single ("El Lay") was largely ignored by the Chicano community outside of East LA.[13]

World music, too, produces contradictions that make any simplistic and well-intentioned denomination of music simply as a "form of intercultural communication and information"

(Negus 172) worth thinking through carefully. Keith Negus's work in this area suggests that asymmetrical relations of power are always at stake in how world music circulates as both an exoticized commodity and a form of alternative community formation and solidarity across traditional cultural and state boundaries: "world music travels an ambiguous route, between the mythical search for authentic redemption and a quest for purity, and a type of reflexive post-exotic listening which is aware of the territorializing strategies of the music industry, media and the way in which the musical identity has been constructed. The same sounds take both routes simultaneously and cannot be reduced to one or the other" (169).

The ideological content of music, then, is not always the same as the ideological context in which that music is used. Adorno argues that:

> The function of music is ideological not only because it hoodwinks people with an irrationality that allegedly has no power over the discipline of their existence. It is ideological also because it makes that irrationality resemble the models of rationalized labour. What people hope to escape from will not let them go. Their free time is spent dozing, merely reproducing their working energies; it is a time overshadowed by that reproduction. The consumed music indicates that there is no exit from the total immanence of society. (52)

In this view, music is consumed precisely because it "hoodwinks" people into thinking of it as vacant of ideology, a quietist belief with which many educated musicians and performers would have no trouble aligning themselves. And at the same time, music recapitulates the structures and forces that subject people to their discipline. Feel like you need order in your life? Listen to a classic Mozart sonata. Feel like you need a dose of chaos? Buy up the Sex Pistols. Feel like your life isn't exotic enough? Well, there's any number of world music artists to choose from. But the minute you consume any of these you become subject to the logic that exchanges your labour for the music you consume, and you replicate inexorably the logic that Adorno analyzes so forensically: consumption, in this context equated with leisure, merely reinforces the logic of capital, and leisure becomes work as surely as work becomes leisure.

If music plays into this capital logic and reinforces what Adorno identifies as the lack of "exit from the total immanence of society" what room is left for musickings that purport to resist such forces, that catalyze and focus aspects of the resistant social formations that have produced the so called "rights revolution?" Further, how to reconcile this question with the extension of Adorno's argument that "If the function of music is really one with the ideological trend of society at large, it is inconceivable that its spirit, that of the institutional power as well as the people themselves, would tolerate another public function of music" (53). How to differentiate between music so purely aligned with the institutional "power" of self-replicating social forces whose self-interest negates and absorbs alternatives that seek to undermine it, and music that defines itself as resistant? Is it not possible that Adorno's position is itself indicative of how social criticism reproduces a capital logic that denies meaning to those indefinable strains of resistant sound and text that have meaning precisely because they can signify in ways that no criticism can appropriate, however much it seeks to?

"A Prime Cause of Unwanted Mass Behavior": Music and Resistance

Though we have already given numerous examples of the kinds of musickings that produce resistance, in this section we want to proliferate these. Many, if not most, resistant musics emerge from effects of the African diaspora. Popular music in North America, itself a huge cultural machine with enormous influence, is unthinkable without the influence of the Black musicians who gave it its distinctive forms. In this book several authors examine some of the strands of the complex story that links resistant music to the African diaspora and then back again to the struggles for social justice and civil rights. Racism, then, has played a key role in music that generates resistance. In Ray Pratt's work on this topic he shows how:

> In the United Kingdom the Rock Against Racism movement, which began in 1976, prefigured most organizational efforts over the next decade. Created not long after reported apparent racist comments by Eric Clapton, it involved such groups as Steel Pulse, the Specials AKA, UB40, and the Beat...and brought together over 80,000 to a concert in Victoria Park, London in 1977. Its success and significance lay in its explicit merging of music and politics, providing a model for new forms of involvement for musicians in political causes that would emerge repeatedly in a variety of ways over the next dozen years, from the MUSE "No Nukes" concerts of 1978 through Live Aid and Band Aid, the Artists United against Apartheid "We Are the World" video and record, the Farm Aid concerts, the "Sun City" record and educational project, and various other efforts to support South African resistance to apartheid and to free imprisoned black leader Nelson Mandela, through the Amnesty International Human Rights Now! Tour of Bruce Springsteen, Sting, Tracy Chapman, Peter Gabriel, and others in 1988. (211-12)

Pratt's summary of key events in the history of bringing together mass spectacle with political support for human rights initiatives hints at the tip of a much larger iceberg. For every one of these large-scale and highly problematic events, numerous artists without marquee names were fighting it out in a variety of formats and cultural contexts for similar causes. Pratt is rightly sceptical of the actual effects of these hugely publicized events suggesting that "Although hundreds of millions of dollars, perhaps even billions, were raised, the total amounts provide only small portions of the vast sums needed to make a transforming impact on any of the problems addressed" (212).[14]

But things had gotten to such a state that global political inertia among the most powerful and self-interested states had created historic inequities with profound rights consequences for the majority of people on the planet, who lived without access to adequate education, without sufficient food or potable water, and without recourse to justice when exploitative and oppressive forces sought to violate further their rights in the name of corrupt dictatorships and scandalously vacuous and unethical state and corporate apparatuses. Pratt recognizes that these spectacles were not without "important impacts on the consciousness of audiences or participants…This is so even though proponents boasted of raising more money than the foreign aid budgets of some countries, a statement itself indicative of the naivete of participants in failing to recognize the historically complementary role of most national foreign aid programs in facilitating profoundly unequal and exploitative trade relations between developed and underdeveloped worlds" (212). Courrier echoes this sentiment, alert to the fact that "some critics confer merit on music by taking it out of the realm of adolescent disrepute, to make it appear more socially significant. What other reason could there be for the proliferation of so many rock benefits, during the '70s and '80s, for a variety of social causes? Rarely did these bloated events ever aid the victims they sought to assist; it was a blanket attempt to legitimize music that the high-culture commissars had already dismissed" (270). If anything, caught between self-aggrandizing attempts at legitimation and increased commerce and a genuine attempt to help, these events gave some degree of focus to people seeking to express support for specific issues even as the dissenting nature of the events remained deeply troubled by the actual effect they had on the material realities of poverty, injustice, exploitation, military violence, sexism, racism, and so forth. This, in brief, is the dilemma of any discussion of musical resistance—if we only look to Western popular music as a source of political suasion.

Look beyond the West and its fascination with the starmaker machinery and other examples of the political force of resistant music quickly emerge. A sampling would include the massive singing festivals in the Baltic, which, as Andrew Cronshaw has pointed out, played a critical role in supporting the "national consciousness" that led to independence. Cronshaw cites the example of the "singing revolutions" that were initiated in 1988, "the year when…300,000 singers gathered at the *Eestima Laul* (Estonian Song) rally in Tallinn" (16) to musick for independence. Cronshaw also points to the irony that "Stalinist policy…had decreed Baltic folk music dead and ordered its replacement by mass song" (16), an observation that demonstrates how states have legislated against music for fear of its political effects even as people have subversively turned state-imposed music to other uses. David Lodge and Bill Badley further elaborate how the Islamic ban on music in the seventh century, in addition to being a response to the supposed decadence of the *mukhanathin*, transvestite slaves who provided the "majority of male musicians well into the early days of Islam" (324), expressed the profound allegiance between music and ideology, one reflected in the fact that "Still today in the practice of Islam there is no music" (324).[15] Lodge and Badley note that when Islam "arrived in the seventh century, the singing and playing of musical instruments were considered sins, and swiftly banned" (324). In 1994, the death of *raï* superstar Cheb Hasni, shot by commandos of the Armed Islamic Group near his home in Oran, Algeria, and then a few months later the death of Rachid Baba Ahmed, a producer of *raï* music, point to the dangers faced by musicians who articulate sentiments aligned with decadent street culture and the dispossessed in the context of struggles over fundamentalist and oppressive belief systems.[16]

In Zimbabwe, the career of Thomas Mapfumo, who provided the musical backbeat to the independence struggle then turned to vociferous critique (signaled in such songs as "Corruption" and "We are slaves in our own country") of post-independence government corruption under the leadership of Robert Mugabe, is instructive. As Judy Kenning and Banning Eyre point out, "electric mbira [thumb piano] music became a tool of the liberation war in the 1970s. Mapfumo's *chimurenga* songs (*chimurenga* means 'struggle' [and also resistance and revolution]) were used to good effect during the *pungwes*—all-night meetings of villagers with the liberation fighters. The irresistible beat provided an opportunity for community song and dance, an affirmation that was vitally necessary to a society split by secrecy, repression, guerilla warfare and counter-terrorist activities" (709). Mapfumo's importance in the history of how music has been used to fight off colonial and imperial cultures in a so-called postcolonial historical context is paramount. *Chimurenga* is indissociable from its cultural contexts in the Shona language. As Mapfumo points out, "This music, *chimurenga*, came about in 1972 when I started writing revolutionary songs. This music had no following at all because people thought it was ancient music of those who actually died a long time ago. They didn't know that was their own culture they were trying to throw away" (Nopper 271). "The first *chimurenga* of the Shona people," as Sheila Nopper notes, "was fought from 1890 to 1897—seven years of resistance against the invasion of the white settlers who then defeated the Africans and settled their land. The white supremacist government then began the systematic oppression of the indigenous people. The next uprising started to brew in the 1960s, and by 1972 the Freedom Fighters were organized and armed resistance began. This second *chimurenga* was also fought for seven years but this time the people won their liberation" (271). The irony that this liberation culminated in yet more bad governance necessitating yet more of the kind of critical and deeply revolutionary music that has been Mapfumo's trademark is a sad historical reality. And thus Mapfumo's music provides an unbroken succession of resistant critiques of political systems gone awry—and it provided (and continues to do so) an important locus for generating communities of resistance that have had their effect in shaping important discourses pertaining to civil liberties in oppressive state contexts.

Multiple examples of one form of exploitative government being replaced by yet another exist in the transition from colonial to post-independence rule in Africa—and elsewhere. The case of Guinea's independence (achieved in 1958) is instructive for how Sékou Touré used music and the arts to promote "the politics of establishing a revolutionary society" (Keïta 17): "With a high degree of perfection in execution and a modern style production, the ballet [Djoliba National

Ballet, *Les Ballets Africains*, and the National Ballet of the People's Army] reflects…African history and African life, in close coordination with the sociopolitical progress of the revolution in Guinea" (text from the National Festival cited in Keïta 40). Inevitably, as in post-revolutionary Cuba, Guinean musicians were demoted to being underpaid "cultural functionaries" (Keïta 18) as the revolutionary ideals of their political leaders mutated into tyranny and dictatorship. In Cuba, the 1960s and 70s movement known as *nueva trova* and *canción* "are often thought of as 'protest songs'—though they rarely have any direct message. However, by singing of everyday life and beliefs—and in Cuba that meant the shaping, everyday influence of the Revolution—the songs had an intrinsic political aspect" (Fairley 408). The huge influence of people like Pablo Milanés and Silvio Rodriguez was mitigated by the fact that "With their attitude, dress and music, these new trovadores were regarded as suspect at a time of dogmatic Communist cultural values. Milanés was actually sent for eighteen months on 'special military service'—a euphemism for the camps where bohemians and gays were sent for hard-labour, cutting cane in the fields" (Fairley 409). Again, musicians paid the price for their dissidence as revolution spun its wheels and musicians sang out.

Similarly, in post-revolutionary China restrictive changes in the political uses of music occurred. Stephen Jones recounts how "After the Communist victory of 1949, the whole ethos of traditional music was challenged. Anything 'feudal' or 'superstitious'—which included a lot of traditional folk customs and music—was severely restricted, while Chinese melodies were 'cleaned up' with the addition of rudimentary harmonies and bass lines…During the Cultural Revolution (1966-76) musical life was driven underground, with only eight model operas and ballets permitted on stage" (34). And in the Central Asian Republics attacks on traditional musical forms resulted from ideological struggle: "the most elevated tradition of Central Asia is Shashmaqam…As a courtly music of the upper classes, it earned disapproval from the communists and was forbidden for almost a decade (from 1948 until Kruschev's reforms in 1957) as it 'didn't represent the needs of the people.' In an attempt to make it more politically acceptable, texts by popular communist poets were used, and you can hear famous Shashmaqam-style songs in the archives with improvised paeans such as 'Oh, my dear Communist Party!,' 'I love you, my collective farm' and 'Oh, Great Lenin, undying glory'…" (Sultanova and Broughton 24). More recent developments in the political uses of music in China have involved the association of rock and punk with the democracy protest movements exemplified in the "protest-rock of guitarist-trumpeter Cui Jian" (Lee 51-52).

In Australia, the music of singer-songwriters Kev Carmody and Archie Roach, both aboriginals who directly experienced the Australian government policy of forced assimilation, has given voice to important critiques of state policies that destroy families and indigenous culture. Marcus Breen notes how, after a long history of being treated like animals dating back to 1778 when Australia was developed as a penal colony, the "recognition of Aboriginal rights [is] a relatively recent phenomenon. The sudden growth of modern Aboriginal music has been a consciousness-raising accompaniment to this political movement" (8). As Breen tells it, in the 1950s and 60s Australia's policy of taking children of "mixed race from their parents and raising them in white foster homes and institutions" (15) involved literally kidnapping the children and telling them their parents were dead—a despicable act carried out by the Orwellian-sounding Aborigenes Protection Board. Carmody was taken from his family when he was 10 and Roach when he was 3. In 1990 Carmody produced an album (*Pillars of Society*) based on his experience researching the treatment of indigenes in Australia for his doctorate, and in the song "Thou Shalt Not Steal" he attacks European culture for its contradictory use of Christianity to produce genocidal effects (Breen 15-16).

> *Hey black man thou shalt not steal*
> *We're gonna change your black barbaric lives*
> *And teach you how to kneel*
> *But your history couldn't hide the genocide,*
> *The hypocrisy was real*
> *'cause your Jesus said you're supposed to*
> *give the oppressed a better deal*
> *We say to you yes our land thou shalt not*
> *Steal, Oh our land you better heal.*

Similarly, Roach uses his music to address the political abuses that led to his own forcible assimilation and subsequent years of misery. And in both cases, music plays an important function in producing and disseminating alternative histories and resistant voicings to outrageous injustices.

In eighteenth- and nineteenth-century Brazil, constant pressure was placed on *batuques*, "a generic term…meaning any kind of black dance with drumming" (Fryer 96), and debates persisted about the threat that black music posed to society (with little grasp of how such debates themselves showed how far so-called civil society had failed in the project of encounter). Peter Fryer, in *Rhythms of Resistance: African Musical Heritage in Brazil*, details how African musickings were seen as barbarous disturbances that allowed for the possibility of dissidence. Citing one legislative example, Fryer tells how "The Count of Arcos (governor of Bahia, 1810-18) and his masters in Lisbon used the word [*batuque*] in the same sense when the latter ordered him in 1814 to put a stop to the *batuques de Negros*; to enforce his predecessor's ban on slaves' gathering in groups of more than four; and to stop their being in towns at night without their owners' written permission. The Count warned, however, that banning black dances would indirectly promote unity among the slaves…with potentially dreadful consequences" (96). Africadian poet George Elliott Clarke, in his essay in this book, reminds us that in a very different cultural context an ocean away, "in 1789, the white government of the Loyalist settlement of Shelburne (Nova Scotia) passed a by-law 'forbidding Negro dances and frolics.'" In both cases, and yet again, the threat of community formation occasioned by musical discourse is immanent. The rights to community and to assembly, let alone to freedom of expression, are directly targeted by restrictions on music in this historical instance. And assembly and community, in this paranoid form of statism, are symbolized in potentially dissident musical strategies.

In more recent Afro-Brazilian musics, particularly those grouped around Olodum (formed in 1979), a "Carnival club" and "a voice–and-drum ensemble [that] began to animate regular street festivities" (Armstrong 180) in the Afro-Brazilian community of Salvador, Bahia, the Count de Arcos's predictions have proved all too true. With its powerful combination of community involvement as a cultural organization with hundreds of members and its alignment with Afro-Brazilian concerns pertinent to the African diaspora (and including "Afro-Bahian civil dissidence" [180]), Olodum's music and its politics are explicitly connected. Olodum pushes beyond discourses of the diaspora by downplaying "race in its stress on societal reform and its acceptance of nonblacks as active participants. Olodum focuses on nonethnic moral issues and explicitly acknowledges the legitimacy of subalteries other than black (gays, prostitutes, the poor)" (186). Moreover, as Piers Armstrong explains, though "racism is the original cause of the black community's alterity…for Olodum this is an alert to the struggle against various other structural ills in society (eradicating oppressions and liberating creativity)" (186), a feat that Olodum's example places precisely in the making of music in relation to the making of community. Music focuses community. And that power is to be feared by those who are threatened by it, and celebrated by those who use it to resist oppression and liberate expression.

A recent example of the power of music to critique state tyranny is detailed in Matthew Collin's *Guerilla Radio: Rock 'n' Roll Radio and Serbia's Underground Resistance*. As the cover blurb exclaims, "Armed only with a stack of old punk records and a dream of freedom, one defiant Belgrade radio station waged a ten year war against Slobodan Milosevic's dictatorship—and won." Overstatement certainly. And yet Collin's book conclusively demonstrates the power of popular youth music when it is aligned with larger forces seeking global justice and equity. As he states, "Punk's anti-establishment slogans struck a deep chord with those young people who desired liberty from the rigid order of the Communist state, and gave them a medium to express their frustration and discontent" (12). The feat accomplished by the Belgrade pirate radio station B92—which provided a focus for opposition to Milosevic's régime and which used all sorts of innovative strategies to survive, including disseminating news bulletins on the Internet even after it had been shut down (114)—was profoundly linked to the music that the station played in conjunction with the news it was also broadcasting. The importance of technologies of musical dissemination, then, also plays its role in the struggle for rights, the resistant discourses with which music is associated. As Stephen Dunifer of Radio Free

Berkeley argues in conversation with Ron Sakolsky, autonomous community radio is vital to freedom of speech and democratic governance precisely because it ensures "against interference of content and analysis" (Sakolsky and Dunifer 175). Speaking of Haiti, Dunifer suggests that grassroots radio ensures democratic voicings of dissent and difference and is in Haiti effectively "a form of coup insurance...if you have dozens to hundreds of small radio stations operating throughout the entire country that are portable...then it'll be impossible for any sort of occupation forces to deal with them all" (175).

The use of radio to disseminate songs with information about political and even military resistance is exemplified in what happened in Nicaragua prior to the 1979 victory of the Sandinistas over the Somoza dictatorship: "brothers Carlos and Luis Enrique Mejia Godoy composed 'Carabina—M1' and other instructional songs. Broadcast on clandestine guerilla radio, they cheerfully gave instructions to a scattered population, many of them illiterate, on how to clean and assemble their weapons and participate in the armed uprising. Their songs were important as much for their direct advice on how to make Molotov cocktails, as for the feeling of contact and solidarity they gave to isolated groups of fighters" (Fairley 368). Jan Fairley describes in further detail how the Sandinistas used music as a crucial part of the struggle during (and after) the Nicaraguan revolution: "the 'Volcanto' (a fusion of 'volcano' and 'song') movement was launched to bring musicians together. Song was involved in much needed literacy campaigns and even in encouraging people to eat maize products when the North American embargo caused a wheat shortage" (Fairley 368). As Anthony Seeger points out in addressing the uses of music in a Latin American context, "Music must be considered a potent political tool. Over the centuries, governments have harassed, censored, banned, exiled, jailed, tortured, and killed composers and performers from widely different social classes. In addition to the religious repression of musical styles, political persecutions have occurred repeatedly" (60).

Yet another example of this sort of repression occurs with the tango, which as "an expression of the working classes...linked with social and political developments in Argentina" especially in relation to the "social classes [these developments] empowered" was "seen as a potentially subversive force" and suppressed by the army (Peiro and Fairley 307). And Dale A. Olsen notes how in Latin America "many native American musical forms...that do continue are often important components of revolutionary movements by native Americans (as in Mexico and Guatemala)" (81). The battle, then, in these diverse contexts to control *who* gets to disseminate *which* sounds is no trivial thing.[17] Nor is the impact of these sorts of struggles on the kinds of community formations that produce meaningful civil rights changes to be underestimated. The capacity to sustain independent voices of dissent, as the use of radio to broadcast specific forms of music in the cases of B92 and Nicaragua suggests, can play a vital role in activating and sustaining political resistance through musical discourses that come to be associated with that resistance.

Within the same spectrum of musical discourses we're calling rebel musics there's also room for Rage Against the Machine's scathing attack (in the rock 'n roll version of Noam Chomsky's *Manufacturing Consent*) on conventional radio and media as disseminators of distorted realities, especially in relation to war: "Yeah, we're gettin' ready to shut down the programs of Vietnow. Turn on the radio, nah, fuck it.—Turn it off…Fear is your only god on the radio…Terror is the products you push…shut down the devil sound" ("Vietnow," Rage Against the Machine). Rage Against the Machine links its music with responsible and critical practices of citizenship by providing a wealth of links to organizations, texts, and thinkers that resist structures of oppression and social injustice in the materials that accompany its CDs, DVDs, videos, website, and band promotional literature. For instance, the band's DVD *Rage Against the Machine*, lists for its audience numerous contacts in sync with the band's political agenda, including, in the case of its critique of corrupt media in "Vietnow," the contact for Fairness & Accuracy in Reporting (FAIR), which is the "national media watch group offering well documented criticism in an effort to correct bias and imbalance. FAIR focuses public awareness on the narrow corporate ownership of the press, the media's allegiance to official agendas and their insensitivity to women, labor, minorities, and other public interest constituencies. FAIR seeks to invigorate the First Amendment by advocating for greater pluralism and the inclusion of public interest voices in national debates." On the same DVD, contacts are included for organizations supportive of prisoners' rights, support groups for children and women living with HIV/AIDS, women's health groups like Rock For Choice, which fights for women's reproductive rights, support groups for high risk, homeless, and street youth, the National Commission for Democracy in Mexico, and so forth. Though it would be naïve to suggest that either the music or the listing of such contacts necessarily get consumed in the way the band might desire, the political consciousness and attempt to educate its listeners extends far beyond the political commitment shown by the rock industry generally, especially in its cynical reliance on dinosaur bands endlessly touring their worn goods in the name of corporate and self-interest.

The struggle to censor music and the dissemination of resistant sounds is an integral part of the relationship between rights and music that this book addresses. Again, Frank Zappa's critical voice is pertinent. In his landmark concept album *Joe's Garage* (1979), Zappa provides a trenchant critique of the reactionary forces working to limit musical expression in the consolidation of state power. Courrier provides the context that "As the decade was coming to an end in 1979, the American economy continued to slump, and the forces of right-wing reaction were building, especially after Americans were taken hostage in their embassy in Iran on November 4, by radical fundamentalist Muslims led by the Ayatollah Khomeini" (330). This backdrop set the scene for *Joe's Garage,* which presciently (and a bit too uncannily) prefigured Zappa's very public battle in the mid-80s with the Parents' Music Resource Center (PMRC), a group of wives of American senators seeking to set limits on musical expression and First Amendment rights. Zappa, it must be remembered, was no political dilettante but rather someone who throughout his life spoke and involved himself politically—whether, among others, in the anti-censorship battles he fought (he appeared before the Maryland State Senate Judiciary when it was seeking to revise its pornography laws); his struggles to combat voter apathy in the United States ("The United States is the least registered industrial country on Earth…Something like a mere 15 per cent of the eligible voters between eighteen and twenty-four cast ballots in the 1984 elections…I don't believe an American has a right to complain about the system if he can vote and doesn't" [Courrier 434]); his cynicism regarding 60s student radicalism in its oversimplification of complex political realities; and his involvement with the October 1989 Velvet Revolution in the former Czechoslovakia that saw the installation of playwright (and Zappa fan) Vaclav Havel as president. Upon arriving in Prague:

> Almost a quarter century after Zappa had asked the question Who Are the Brain Police?, [Zappa] finally confronted the real fruit of totalitarianism. Americans took their democracy for granted, flirting with rock-music censorship and allowing Christian fundamentalism to stage a 20th century witchhunt. While America denounced Zappa as a perverted freak, here were people who had literally taken beatings to hear what Zappa recorded. He suddenly encountered a hideous irony, something that always lurked somewhere in his compositions—those deprived of freedom learn to understand it and value it; those who have it, as in America, fail to embrace it. (Courrier 465-66)

Joe's Garage is an extended musical comment on the right to freedom that is framed by Zappa's sarcastic and self-deprecating album notes on the subject of state interference and control of music:

> All governments perpetuate themselves through the daily commission of acts which a rational person might find to be stupid or dangerous (or both). Naturally, our government is no exception…for instance, if the President (any one of them) went on TV and sat there with the flag in the background (or maybe a rustic scene on a little backdrop, plus the flag) and stared sincerely into the camera and told everybody that all energy problems and all inflationary problems *had been traced to* and *could be solved by the abolition of* MUSIC, the chances are that most people would believe him and think that the illegalization of this obnoxious form of noise pollution would be a small price to pay for the chance to buy gas like the good ol' days…*Joe's Garage* is a stupid story about how the government is going to try to do away with music (a prime cause of unwanted mass behavior)…if the idea of The Central Scrutinizer enforcing laws that haven't been passed yet makes you giggle, just be glad you don't live in one of the cheerful little countries, where, at this very moment, music is either severely restricted…or, as it is in Iran, totally illegal. (liner notes 5)

Music, as a "prime cause of unwanted mass behavior," is precisely the issue for Zappa. This power, necessarily, links expressive freedom and the freedom of association. The latter are rights guaranteed in the American Convention on Human Rights, signed in 1969 and entered into force of law by the Organization of American States Treaty in 1978. Articles 13 and 16 in that Convention give clear instructions on both freedom of thought and expression and freedom of association that interestingly enough provide legislative loopholes, one specifically limited to "entertainment": Article 13, paragraph 4, which addresses freedom of thought and expression, states that "public entertainments may be subject by law to prior censorship for the sole purpose of regulating access to them for the moral protection of childhood and adolescence" (Ishay 446). Article 16, paragraph 2 similarly states that "The exercise of this right [to associate freely for ideological, religious, political, economic, labor, social, cultural, sports, or other purposes] shall be subject only to such restrictions established by law as may be necessary in a democratic society, in the interest of national security, public safety or public order, or to protect public health and morals or the rights and freedoms of others" (Ishay 447). In both cases what appear to be important freedoms established in treaty conventions are in fact qualified in such a way as to allow for the possibility of severe restrictions on those rights, a form of what might be called judicial or legislative intervention into rights, which become equivocal as a function of such loopholes.

Interestingly, "public entertainments," which would obviously include displays of musical dissension, are singled out for mention as possible targets for "prior censorship." In the context of *Joe's Garage*, Zappa's premonitory insights about the expressive powers of music and the threat to state self-interest they might pose culminates in the crude comment made by The Central Scrutinizer, an Orwellian (or Foucauldian) Big Brother/panopticon character whose voice (Zappa's ironic own) narrates the non-linear narrative of the album: "This is the CENTRAL SCRUTINIZER…As you can see, MUSIC can get you pretty fucked up…Take a tip from Joe, do like he did, hock your imaginary guitar and get a good job…Joe did, and he's a happy guy now, on the day shift at the Utility Muffin Research Kitchen, arrogantly twisting the sterile canvas snoot of a fully-charged icing anointment utensil" (liner notes 21). Even as the Central Scrutinizer disses music as a threat to normalcy, Zappa hilariously spoofs the deadened world of the Utility Muffin Research Kitchen in which his archetypal hero Joe ends up as an indentured slave, arrogantly "anointing" muffins with icing. The line presents a cutting attack on the delusional world of normalcy where a good job is equated with mindless labour, the technological overkill of the muffin factory, and the linkage between religious fundamentalism and lives devoid of meaning. In the context of American popular music, with its brilliant parodic attack on censorship and its startling deployment of music and words, Zappa's album sounded an articulate call to resist any kind of state intervention into restrictions on assembly and freedom of speech embodied in dissenting, radical music like his own. And remember: this album was released at virtually the same time that the American Convention on Human Rights gained the force of law.

At virtually the same moment in history, the Chilean group Ortiga, at some considerable personal risk, "performed the 'Cantata de los derechos humanos' [Cantata of Human Rights], written by the Chilean priest Esteban Gumicio and Alejandro Guarello. The cantata, presented on November 22, 1978, in the Catedral de Santiago under the protective umbrella of the Catholic Church, touched on central themes of human rights without alluding to specific rights violations in Chile" (Mattern 59). The performance and the oppressive political pressures that necessitated its being protected are indicative of the kinds of tensions between the musical expression of rights discourses and repressive state policies seeking to eliminate or curb such discourses. And in 1979, El Funoun (The Arts), a Palestinian ensemble dedicated to preserving traditional Palestinian music, was formed in the face of efforts to squelch any such enterprise on the grounds it consolidated Palestinian nationalist sentiment. Daniel Rosenberg observes that members of El Funoun "faced repeated border closings, the arrest of many of its members, travel restrictions, and even bans on public performances" (388). Omar Barghouti, a member of the group, acknowledges that "according to the Israelis, we [Palestinians] were supposed to be a people without a culture. Over the years, we have faced numerous attempts to suppress it" (Rosenberg 388). This suppression extended into the Intifada ("a youth-led, stone-throwing revolt initiated in the Gaza strip in December 1987" [Morgan and Adileh 387]) during which covert rehearsals were the norm for the group and the constant threat of being a participant in banned musical activities was present—frequently resulting in the arrest of many of the group's members.

Again, state oppression of music had a singular purpose: the eradication of important sites of cultural memory (like traditional music) in which the combination of community formation and/or affirmation and freedom of speech were perceived as threatening to state self-interest and a justification for censorship. Suhail Khoury, a major musical figure in the Intifada, gives a telling account of what Palestinian musicians faced as a result of the perceived threat they represented.

> "It was a very powerful time, a very revolutionary time. People were in the streets every day. Ordinary people were fighting the occupation. And music was a part of this. I did a tape called *Sharrar* (Spark). The lyrics were very powerful, talking about things that had happened just a few days before. How they'd kicked the Israelis out of Nablus and so on. It was describing the daily life of the Intifada and it was a very powerful tool." After making the tape Khoury was stopped at a checkpoint in his car and arrested. The car and the tapes were confiscated. "Somehow one tape leaked out into the community and it was copied in tens of thousands, one to another. We estimated that at least 100,000 were made. A big number in a small state. And the Israelis did quite a good marketing service for me because they announced on the radio and TV that I was arrested for making music and could be imprisoned for ten years. So everybody wanted to know what kind of tape that was. Of course, I'm laughing now, *but I was tortured for twelve days*. They wanted to know who composed, who sang, who played. I didn't tell them anything and I was sentenced to six months imprisonment." (cited in Morgan and Adileh 387; our emphasis)

Israel had signed on to the 1984 Convention Against Torture and Other Cruel, Inhuman or Degrading Treatment or Punishment, but lamentably, as is so often the case with international rights treaties, had failed to observe or implement its articles in any meaningful way.[18] Khoury's story, like so many others, reinforces the power of musical expression to coalesce resistance and public opinion in the face of suppression that contravenes rights instruments that are supposed to have the legal force of law. Sometimes things coalesce across borders that seem impassable as is the case with Chava Alberstein, an Israeli singer-songwriter whose music has been likened to the protest music of Pete Seeger and Joan Baez and who has said "From a distance, I was involved with all kinds of rights movements in America" (Broughton 364). A song "Chad Gadya" (One Goat) that was written during the Intifada and that faced an attempted ban by Israeli authorities talks about cycles of violence as "Israeli soldiers in the occupied territories were behaving very brutally towards Palestinian women and children which was something new and shocking in Israel. This wasn't necessarily the soldiers' fault—it was the fault of the situation. To stop these people behaving like animals the occupation needed to be stopped" (Broughton 364). Alberstein explicitly ties this cross-border political insight with the material conditions that gave rise to the song and her experience in conjunction with that of Khoury's points to the creative allegiances that rebel musics can develop across intercultural sites of resistance.

The politics of music making, then, necessarily entail the politics of the uses to which music is put as it is made. But as Lawrence Kramer has insightfully argued, "the effort (for instance by Theodor Adorno) to understand musical form as a reflection or 'mediation' of context necessarily chokes off the symbolizing impetus" (14) in music—another way of arguing that there always remains a supplement to any context into which music is placed and through which it is attributed with meaning. Rebel musics occur in specific contexts, to be sure. Yet we are arguing that the meaning of rebel musics is not confined to their contexts. Kramer's insight that "acts of interpretation" mediate "a symbolic object [like music] and its context" (14) needs to be pushed further in the case of rebel musics. There is no such thing as music without context, after all. But is it possible that rebel musics call upon us through their symbolic power? Is it possible that rebel musics generate that supplement that resists any and all forms of reductive thinking? Is it possible that rebel musics ask us to think through the relation between contexts and the interpretative acts they necessitate? If so, then rebel musics also ask that we gather our forces of critique in the name of a critical politics without which meaningful human rights discourses would be unimaginable.

NOTES

1. For useful discussions of how activist musical politics are implicated in political change see Greil Marcus's salutary critiques of the MUSE (Musicians United for Safe Energy) project (which took place in New York in 1979), 141-45, and the "We Are the World" project under the rubric of the dubiously titled umbrella group United Support of Artists for Africa (USA for AFRICA), 280-84. Also see Robin Denselow's essential work on the politics of pop music. Like Marcus, Denselow recognizes how "The civil rights years produced some of the finest political music of the century, but they were hardly an unqualified triumph for rock 'n' roll" (30), which as Marcus and others have recognized is historically rooted in black music while at the same time generally ghettoizing blacks (with the rare Hendrix-like exception) not to mention, until recently, excluding women—hardly the most politically progressive legacy from which to build an activist politics. The importance of black musicians (of both genders) to civil rights battles is absolutely critical. Denselow, for instance, quotes Bernice Johnson Reagon, leader of Sweet Honey in the Rock, "the best black women's harmony group in the USA," as saying "'How important were the musicians during the civil rights years?…They were crucial. You couldn't call black people together in any committed way without a ritual that involved an enormous amount of singing. The singing was used to create the climate, to get people ready to address the issues. So any statement from lawyers, or a testimony from someone who'd been arrested, was always presented on a bed of song. And the song-leaders were absolutely essential'" (31).

2. Our juxtaposition of Dylan with Stravinsky and Varèse is not accidental. Though this book is about forms of musicking that are not "classical," we would argue that there is a significant history to be written of how classical music has been aligned with the politics of resistance. Anthony Arblaster's useful book *Viva la Libertà: Politics in Opera*, examines the politics of opera in relation to "revolution" and cites numerous examples: from Mozart's depiction of pre-revolutionary class struggle and privilege, *Le nozze di Figaro* (1786) through to Beethoven's *Fidelio* (1805-14), which addresses issues of freedom and the French Revolution, and John Adams's *The Death of Klinghoffer* (1991), which deals with terrorism in the context of

the Palestinian and Israeli conflict. Music that represents oppositional politics or that critiques injustice is, in short, not limited by genre or period.

3. Zappa talks about a style of improvisation he and the Mothers of Invention evolved called "meltdown," in which nightly musical improvisations that changed all the time were overlaid on a set of unchanging lyrics: "The accompaniment was designed to *provide rhythm, texture and sound effects*, not necessarily *chords, melody and a 'good beat'*—a sort of rock *Sprechstimme* setting, combining a parody of the 'poetry and jazz' aroma of *beatnikism* with an abstraction of the type of onomatopoeia found in those Beethoven meadowland movements—with the cuckoos and wind, etc." (184).

4. Tellingly used by Kevin Courrier as an epigraph to the opening chapter of his book on Frank Zappa, *Dangerous Kitchen: The Subversive World of Zappa* (1).

5. In Cuba in the early months of 2003, Lennon's "Imagine" was played regularly in anti-terrorist and anti-war television commercials (against the invasion of Iraq), even as the Cuban state was carrying out a massive roundup of dissidents ("counter-revolutionaries"), who were jailed after one-day trials, as well as summary executions of people whose desperate attempts to escape the country were constructed as "terrorist hijackings." In this case, the concepts of world peace and harmony (laudable aspects of the Cuban revolution's stated goals) were clearly co-opted in the service of preserving a repressive state ideology, as Cuba has increasingly and distressingly succumbed to the cult of leadership focussed on Castro in which virtually no dissidence is tolerated. In a complicated political situation such as this the uses of Lennon's "Imagine" is a not-so-subtle reminder of the divergent propaganda uses to which so-called rebel musics may be adapted.

6. We are alert to how systematic discussion on these topics has barely begun and warrants further work. Attilio Favorini and Gillette Elvegren's research on musical documentary theatre, for example, examines the power of "nostalgia-laden conventions of music hall to stage a confrontation of memory with history" and connects labour history in Canada, the United States, and England with how musical documentary enables the "imperative of giving voice to the voiceless, of reclaiming for history the forgotten past of an unheeded community" (183). Our point is that there is a formidable array of cultural sites in which music is used to produce resistant meaning and alternative strategies of memory and community formation, all key elements in rights thinking generally.

7. For a sustained discussion of rap in relation to political resistance see Rose's *Black Noise: Rap Music and Black Culture in Contemporary America*, especially 99-145.

8. The Human Development Report 2002, *Deepening Democracy in a Fragmented World,* produced by the United Nations, states unequivocally that "The level of inequality worldwide is grotesque" noting that: "The world's richest 1% of people receive as much income as the poorest 57%. The richest 10% of the U.S. population has an income equal to that of the poorest 43% of the world. Put differently, the income of the richest 25 million Americans is equal to that of almost 2 billion people. The income of the world's richest 5% is 114 times that of the poorest 5%" (19).

9. This is not to diminish the agency of the Sex Pistols in anti-censorship and freedom of speech battles. Greil Marcus remarks on how "Punk was a new music, a new social critique, but most of all it was a new kind of free speech…There was an absolute denial of censorship in the Sex Pistols' songs that gave people who heard them permission to speak freely" (2-3). And in comparing the two bands Marcus notes how "if the Sex Pistols were frankly nihilistic, asking for destruction and not caring what came of it, The Clash are out for community, the self-discovery of individuals as a means to solidarity, a new 'I' as the means to a discovery of an old 'we'" (29). The Clash's *London Calling* album ends with a tune called "Revolution Rock," which suggests that "while revolution made by music is a joke, rebellion sustained by music might not be" (Marcus 91-92), further evidence of the critical consciousness that made the band so important.

10. These sorts of contradictions are not limited to rebel musics. Anthropologist June Nash, in her brilliant study of Mayan community, asks: "Now that indigenous people compete with global enterprises for the forest, oil and hydraulic energy sources, and the biodiversity once in their custodianship, in what new geopolitical spaces will indigenous peoples revitalize their culture?" (31). An analogous question is worth asking in relation to rebel musics as they are produced and integrated into the very geopolitical spaces they critique.

11. Gonczy addresses the "connection between folk music and what would become the anti-war ferment" in his discussion of Bob Dylan's hugely important *Freewheelin'* album (1963): "It included scathing and unequivocal denunciations of the psychology and mechanics of militarism…With Dylan's emergence, the spirit of activism and protest began to take on some coherence and a sense of unity develop…[and] Dylan's music had, by 1964, become inseparable from the growing radicalism" (10-11). Recently, a spate of releases in the country, folk, rock genres have suggested a renewed sense of musical radicalism from musicians not normally associated with sustained critical thinking in relation to rights issues. Steve Earle's *Jerusalem* has been seen as a musical and highly critical anti-State of the Union address post September 11th. Earle admits in newspaper interviews that he reads Marx and sardonically affirms that "Marx talked in analogies, the way Texans do" (a dig at George W. Bush). His song "Amerika V 6.0 (The Best We Can Do)" was pulled from the film *John Q.* because the "film's distributors had decided it was too critical of the [George W.] Bush administration" (Harris). Similarly, Neil Young's most recent album *Greendale* takes on the Bush administration in relation to issues of "media intrusion, ecological conservation and illegal surveillance by government agencies" (Sweeting). In an interview Young observes that "A lot of the people's civil rights have been compromised [post-September 11]…Music is being banned, and we have people in control of the radio stations who are the same people in control of the concert halls. They're also tied into the [United States] administration and are sponsoring pro-war rallies. It's not good" (Sweeting).

12. A compilation double album entitled *Rebel Music* and a film biography of Bob Marley both bear the name. The film project *Musiques rebelles*, developed by Productions Multi-Monde and discussed at length elsewhere in this book is also obviously indebted to this phrase as are two chapters in Denselow's book, which address rebel music in Ireland and in Trinidad, Jamaica, Zimbabwe, and Britain.

13. "On stage Los Illegals would show slides, Willie [Herron] would wear a mask—modeled after Zorro—while performing a set dominated by hard rhythms and loud guitars. They moved easily between rock 'n' roll and Chicano politics. One minute they would be playing a speeded-up version of "Wooly Bully," or the Dave Clark Five's "Bits and Pieces," and the next they would be singing about broken homes, gangs, or the long arm of the Immigration and Naturalization Service" (Reyes and Waldman 137).

14. Robert Everett-Green comments on how rock music has evacuated itself of political content by "mutat[ing] into rebellion without a cause, infinitely marketable (as the…Rolling Stones' Licks tour demonstrates) and constantly searching for a new leader to keep the whole enterprise from becoming ridiculous" (R4). Everett-Green points to how rock "carries a gene from a culture of protest that was born in the Depression and went global during the Vietnam War. To be a true rocker was to be in permanent opposition, to The Man, the sell-out, and the whole nine-to-five suburban nightmare" (R4). The forces that have transformed this historical heritage into empty-headed fluff that sells millions of copies are decried by Everett-Green in his assertion that "Rock needs all the enemies it can get" (R4). This kind of assertion is a long way from English cultural critic Simon Frith's acknowledgement in 1981 (in reaction to English Thatcherism and rampant attacks by right wing groups and skinheads on gays and lesbians, people of colour, leftists, feminists, and so forth) that "Rock…is the only medium that makes any sense of life—aesthetically or politically—at all" (cited in Marcus 188). Greil Marcus notes how by "Raising unemployment and inflation with her right hand, while slashing social services and pressing if-you're

white-you're-right immigration policies with her other right hand, [Prime Minister Margaret Thatcher] fostered an upsurge of music made in a critical spirit" (175).

15. From 1994 on, Afghanistan under the Islamist fundamentalist movement known as the Taliban, began to "[enforce] further bans on public music-making. To show they meant business, the Taliban authorities destroyed musical instruments and videotapes, and occasionally imprisoned musicians caught in the act of playing" (Doubleday 3).

16. "Raï—the word means 'opinion'—originated in the Western Algerian port of Oran. It has traditional roots in Bedouin music, with its distinctive refrain (ha-ya-rai), but as a modern phenomenon has more in common with Western music…Its lyrics reflect highly contemporary concerns—cars, sex, sometimes alcohol—which have created some friction with the authorities" (Muddyman 575).

17. Canadian composer R. Murray Schafer has argued that "When radio was invented…two models of broadcasting grew up: the political model, born of the rage for power; and the 'enlightenment model', born in opposition to it" (207-08). The crucial point for rebel musics lies in how a particular music is disseminated and contextualized in relation to oppositional discourses. The question remains as to whether rebel musics actually produce critical listeners with the capacity for understanding the ways in which a given music is used to address larger social and political issues.

18. The 2000 World Report produced by Human Rights Watch states that in Israel, torture by the "General Security Service (GSS) was widespread and systematic, with one Jerusalem-based organization, the Public Committee Against Torture in Israel (PCATI), reporting that by mid-September it had filed fifty-five petitions for injunctions against torture" (366).

WORKS CITED

Adorno, Theodor W. Introduction to the Sociology of Music. Trans. E. B. Ashton. New York: Continuum, 1989.

Arblaster, Anthony. Viva la Libertà! Politics in Opera. London: Verso, 1992.

Armstrong, Piers. "Songs of Olodum: Ethnicity, Activism, and Art in a Globalized Carnival Community." Brazilian Popular Music & Globalization. Eds. Charles A. Perrone and Christopher Dunn. New York: Routledge, 2002. 177-191.

Barrow, Steve and Peter Dalton. The Rough Guide to Reggae: The Definitive Guide to Jamaican Music, from Ska through Roots to Ragga. London: Rough Guides, 2001.

Billmeier, Uschi. Mamady Keïta: A Life for the Djembé—Traditional Rhythms of the Malinke. Freiburg: Arun-Verlag, 1999.

Bradley, Lloyd. Bass Culture: When Reggae Was King. London: Penguin, 2001.

Breen, Marcus. "Australia: Aboriginal Music." World Music. Volume 2: Latin and North America, Caribbean, India, Asia and Pacific. Eds. Simon Brought and Mark Ellingham. With James McConnachie and Orla Duane. London: Rough Guides, 2000. 8-19.

Broughton, Simon. "Chava Alberstein: Israel's Joan Baez." World Music. Volume 1: Africa, Europe and the Middle-East. Eds. Simon Brought, Mark Ellingham and Richard Trillo. With Orla Duane and Vanessa Dowell. London: Rough Guides, 2000. 364.

Chuck D. Fight the Power: Rap, Race, and Reality. With Yusuf Jah. New York: Delta, 1997.

Collin, Matthew. Guerrilla Radio: Rock 'n' Roll Radio and Serbia's Underground Resistance. New York: Thunder's Mouth, 2001.

Courrier, Kevin. Dangerous Kitchen: The Subversive World of Zappa. Toronto: ECW Press, 2002.

Cronshaw, Andrew. "The Baltic States: Singing revolutions." *World Music. Volume 1: Africa, Europe and the Middle-East*. Eds. Simon Brought, Mark Ellingham and Richard Trillo. With Orla Duane and Vanessa Dowell. London: Rough Guides, 2000. 16.

Denselow, Robin. *When the Music's Over: The Story of Political Pop*. London: Faber and Faber, 1989.

Doubleday, Veronica. "Afghanistan." *World Music. Volume 2: Latin and North America, Caribbean, India, Asia and Pacific*. Eds. Simon Brought and Mark Ellingham. With James Mc Connachie and Orla Duane. London: Rough Guides, 2000. 3-7.

Everett-Green, Robert. "Wanted: enemies of rock." *The Globe and Mail* 9 Nov. 2002: R4.

Fairley, Jan. "Cuba: Trova and Nueva Trova." *World Music. Volume 2: Latin and North America, Caribbean, India, Asia and Pacific*. Eds. Simon Brought and Mark Ellingham. With James McConnachie and Orla Duane. London: Rough Guides, 2000. 408-13.

——. "Chile/Latin America. Nueva canción." *World Music. Volume 2: Latin and North America, Caribbean, India, Asia and Pacific*. Eds. Simon Brought and Mark Ellingham. With James McConnachie and Orla Duane. London: Rough Guides, 2000. 362-71.

Favorini, Attilio and Gillette Elvgren. "I Sing of Cities: The Musical Documentary." *Performing Democracy: International Perspectives on Urban Community-Based Performances*. Eds. Susan C. Haedicke and Tobin Nellhaus. Ann Arbor: U of Michigan P, 2001. 181-196.

Fryer, Peter. *Rhythms of Resistance: African Musical Heritage in Brazil*. Hanover: Wesleyan UP, 2000.

Galeano, Eduardo. "I'd Like to Know." *New Internationalist* 356 (May 2003): 34-35.

Garr, Gillian G. *She's a Rebel: The History of Women in Rock & Roll*. Expanded second edition. New York: Seal, 2002.

Gonczy, Daniel J. "The Folk Music of the 1960s: Its Rise and Fall." *The Dylan Companion*. Eds. Elizabeth Thomson and David Gutman. New York: Da Capo, 2001. 4-17.

Harris, John. "Good Ol' Bad Boy." *The Globe and Mail* 30 Sept. 2002: R6.

Howard, Rhoda E. *Human Rights and the Search for Community*. Colorado: Westview, 1995.

Human Development Report 2002. *Deepening Democracy in a Fragmented World*. New York: Oxford UP, 2002.

Human Rights Watch. *World Report 2000: Events of 1999 (November 1998-October 1999)*. New York: Human Rights Watch, 1999.

Ishay, Micheline R., ed. *The Human Rights Reader: Major Political Essays, Speeches, and Documents from the Bible to the Present*. New York: Routledge, 1997.

Johnson, Scott. "The Counter Point of Species." *Arcana: Musicians on Music*. Ed. John Zorn. New York: Granary Books, 2000. 18-58.

Jones, Stephen. "China: Han Traditional." *World Music. Volume 2: Latin and North America, Caribbean, India, Asia and Pacific*. Eds. Simon Brought and Mark Ellingham. With James McConnachie and Orla Duane. London: Rough Guides, 2000. 33-43.

Kramer, Lawrence. *Musical Meaning: Toward a Critical History*. Berkeley: U of California P, 2002.

Lee, Joanna. "China/Hong Kong. Pop and Rock." *World Music. Volume 2: Latin and North America, Caribbean, India, Asia and Pacific*. Eds. Simon Brought and Mark Ellingham. With James McConnachie and Orla Duane. London: Rough Guides, 2000. 49-55.

Lipsitz, George. *Dangerous Crossroads: Popular Music, Postmodernism and the Poetics of Place*. London: Verso, 1994.

Lodge, David and Bill Badley. "Arab World/Egypt: Classical." *World Music. Volume 1: Africa, Europe and the Middle-East*. Eds. Simon Brought, Mark Ellingham and Richard Trillo. With Orla Duane and Vanessa Dowell. London: Rough Guides, 2000. 323-331.

Marcus, Greil. *Ranters & Crowd Pleasers: Punk in Pop Music, 1977-92*. Doubleday, 1993.

Mattern, Mark. *Acting in Concert: Music, Community, and Political Action*. New Brunswick: Rutgers UP, 1998.

Morgan, Andy. "Algeria: Rai: Music Under Fire." *World Music. Volume 1: Africa, Europe and the Middle-East*. Eds. Simon Brought, Mark Ellingham and Richard Trillo. With Orla Duane and Vanessa Dowell. London: Rough Guides, 2000. 413-24.

Morgan, Andy and Mu'tasem Adileh. "Palestinian Music: "The Sounds of Struggle." *World Music. Volume 1: Africa, Europe and the Middle-East*. Eds. Simon Brought, Mark Ellingham and Richard Trillo. With Orla Duane and Vanessa Dowell. London: Rough Guides, 2000. 385-90.

Muddyman, David. "Morocco: A Basic Expression of Life." *World Music. Volume 1: Africa, Europe and the Middle-East*. Eds. Simon Brought, Mark Ellingham and Richard Trillo. With Orla Duane and Vanessa Dowell. London: Rough Guides, 2000. 567-78.

Musiques Rebelles Quebec. Dir. Marie Boti. Prod. Malcolm Guy. With Acalanto, Landriault, Loco Locass, and Norman Nawrocki. Cinéma libre, 2002.

Nash, June C. *Mayan Visions: The Quest for Autonomy in an Age of Globalization*. New York: Routledge, 2001.

Nawrocki, Norman. *The Anarchist and the Devil*. Montréal: Black Rose Books, 2003.

Negus, Keith. *Music Genres and Corporate Cultures*. London: Routledge, 1999.

Nopper, Sheila. "Thomas Mapfumo: The Lion of Zimbabwe." *Sounding Off! Music As Subversion/Resistance/Revolution*. Eds. Ron Sakolsky and Fred Wei-han Ho. Brooklyn: Autonomedia, 1995. 271-276.

Olsen, Dale A. "Native American Musical Cultures." *The Garland Handbook of Latin American Music*. Eds. Dale A. Olsen and Daniel E. Sheehy. New York and London: Garland, 2000. 78-82.

Olsen, Dale A. and Daniel E. Sheehy. Eds. *The Garland Handbook of Latin American Music*. New York and London: Garland, 2000.

Pareles, Jon. "Joe Strummer Is Dead at 50; Political Rebel of Punk Era." *The New York Times* 24 Dec. 2002, late ed.: C12.

Parker, William and the Little Huey Creative Music Orchestra. *Sunrise in the Tone World*. AUM Fidelity, 1997.

Peiro, Teddy and Jan Fairley. "Argentina. Tango." *World Music. Volume 2: Latin and North America, Caribbean, India, Asia and Pacific*. Eds. Simon Brought and Mark Ellingham. With James McConnachie and Orla Duane. London: Rough Guides, 2000. 304-14.

Pratt, Ray. *Rhythm and Resistance: The Political Uses of American Popular Music*. Washington: Smithsonian, 1994.

Rage Against the Machine (DVD). Dir. Rage Against the Machine and Aimee Macauley. Epic Music Video, 1997.

Rebel Music: The Bob Marley Story. Prod. And Dir. Jeremy Marr. Antelope Productions, 2001.

Reyes, David and Tom Waldman. *Land of a Thousand Dances: Chicano Rock 'n' Roll from Southern California*. Albuquerque: U of New Mexico P, 1998.

Robertson, Geoffrey. *Crimes Against Humanity: The Struggle for Global Justice*. New York: New Press, 1999.

Rose, Tricia. *Black Noise: Rap Music and Black Culture in Contemporary America*. Hanover: Wesleyan UP, 1994.

Rosenberg, Daniel. "El Funoun—Palestinian Art-Music." *World Music. Volume 1: Africa, Europe and the Middle-East*. Eds. Simon Brought, Mark Ellingham and Richard Trillo. With Orla Duane and Vanessa Dowell. London: Rough Guides, 2000. 388.

Rosenberg, Matthew. "'Who can Bwogo me?': The song behind the campaign." *The Ottawa Citizen* 27 Dec. 2002: A10.

Rhythm Activism. *Blood & Mud*. Les Pages Noires. Montréal, Québec, 1994.

—. *More Kick! Live in Europe*. Les Pages Noires. Montréal, Québec, 1995.

Sakolsky, Ron and Stephen Dunifer, eds. *Seizing the Airwaves: A Free Radio Handbook*. San Francisco: AK Press, 1998.

Schafer, R. Murray. "Radical Radio." *Sound by Artists*. Eds. Dan Lander and Micah Lexier. Toronto: Art Metropole, 1990. 207-216.

Seeger, Anthony. "Social Structure, Musicians, and Behavior." *The Garland Handbook of Latin American Music*. Eds. Dale A. Olsen and Daniel E. Sheehy. New York and London: Garland, 2000. 54-65.

Simone, Nina. "Mississippi Goddamn." *Nina Simone*. PolyGram Records, 1993.

Sinker, Daniel, Ed. *we owe you nothing: punk planet: the interviews*. New York: Akashic Books, 2001.

Sultanova, Razia and Simon Broughton. "Central Asian Republics." *World Music. Volume 2: Latin and North America, Caribbean, India, Asia and Pacific*. Eds. Simon Brought and Mark Ellingham. With James McConnachie and Orla Duane. London: Rough Guides, 2000. 24-32.

Sweeting, Adam. "U.S. is like a baby with a bomb." *The Globe and Mail* 24 May 2003: R6.

Tenaille, Frank. *Music is the Weapon of the Future: Fifty Years of African Popular Music*. Trans. Stephen Toussaint and Hope Sandrine. Chicago: Lawrence Hill Books, 2002.

White, Timothy. *Catch a Fire: The Life of Bob Marley*. Revised and enlarged. New York: Henry Holt and Company, 2000.

World Music. Volume 1: Africa, Europe and the Middle-East. Eds. Simon Brought, Mark Ellingham and Richard Trillo. With Orla Duane and Vanessa Dowell. London: Rough Guides, 2000.

World Music. Volume 2: Latin and North America, Caribbean, India, Asia and Pacific. Eds. Simon Brought and Mark Ellingham. With James McConnachie and Orla Duane. London: Rough Guides, 2000.

Zappa, Frank. *Joe's Garage: Acts I, II & III*. Rykodisc, 1987.

—. *The Real Frank Zappa Book*. With Peter Occhiogrosso. New York: Poseidon, 1989.

Ron Sakolsky

1 / Hangin' Out on the Corner of Music and Resistance

When I reflect upon my nearly six decades on the planet, it seems clear to me that the corner of Music and Resistance has always been one of my favorite hangouts.

RON SAKOLSKY is the editor of *Surrealist Subversions* (Autonomedia, 2002), and the co-editor of *Seizing The Airwaves: A Free Radio Handbook* (with Stephen Dunifer, AK Press, 1998), *Sounding Off!: Music as Subversion/Resistance/Revolution* (with Fred Ho, Autonomedia, 1995), and *Gone to Croatan: Origins of Drop-Out Culture in North America* (with James Koehnline, Autonomedia, 1993). He continues to write regular music reviews and features for *The Beat* magazine and is a dancehall selector for the *Fools Paradise Sound System.*

It is the unmapped intersection where Jayne Cortez dubs a spitfire blues poem at the revolutionary tea party thrown by Lillian Allen; where the ghost of Johnny Dyani kicks out an anti-apartheid bass line for a Dead Prez throw down; where Fela Kuti explodes like a time bomb set off by the imprisonment of people's poet Mzwakhe Mbuli, and where Brother Resistance steps out from a Carnival mas band to stop traffic for Michael Franti as he blows up a television set causing Boots Riley of The Coup to detonate a wicked laugh that shatters the illusions of global capitalism as his musical partner in thought crime Pam the Funkstress scratches its shitstemic epitaph in vinyl.

Speaking as a writer, while such rebel musics have not been my exclusive focus, they have been my constant companion. They have nurtured my critical consciousness, sparked fresh intellectual insights, uplifted my spirits, reinforced my anger at injustice, and fueled my utopian dreams of a better world. Politically engaged music has often been the soundtrack that has aided and abetted the process of breaking free from the chains of oppression and emerging from the shadows of alienation. It has sustained me in hard political times when I might otherwise have fallen victim to a disempowering isolation. In the streets, it has buoyed my energy level like an in-your-face batucada adrenaline rush from the Infernal Noise Brigade or a blast of hot wind cut from Bakunin's Bum directly into the face of the corporate state.

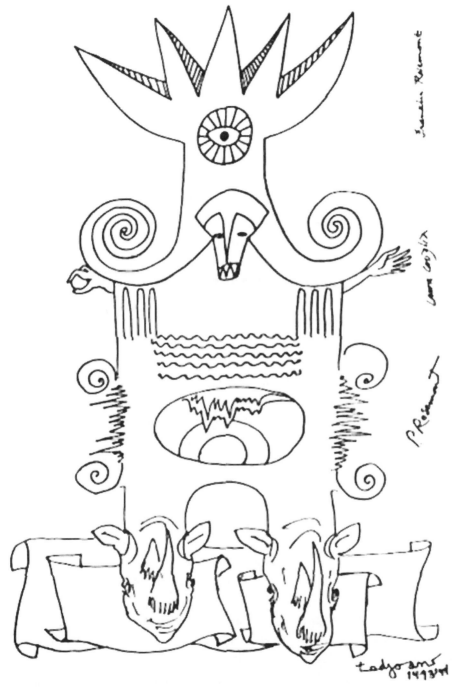

*"Thank You, Thelonious Monk": Exquisite Corpse by Franklin Rosemont, Laura Corsiglia,
Penelope Rosemont and Ted Joans (ink drawing, 1993)*

Though the above artists were/are often self-consciously political in their music, that is not where the story begins for me. People often ask me who my biggest influences were in forming a radical political consciousness in Sixties America, expecting me to rattle off a list of authors and books. My immediate response, John Coltrane, has typically confounded these expectations. Yet, it was precisely Trane's expansive diasporic consciousness and his improvisational flights of exploration that encouraged me to see beyond the chord changes of consensus reality. Long before that, however, the first 45 rpm record that I ever laid my hands on was "Get A Job" by the Silhouettes on the tiny Ember label.

While known in oldies circles these days mostly for its shananana refrain, it is a much more complex record than your average doowop love song of the period, and I think that even with a preteen consciousness, I realized its complexity way back then. After all, though I was raised in a working-class neighborhood in Brooklyn, it was the first song that I'd ever heard about anything that was even remotely about working people's lives. The fact that it was not about romantic love or teenage dating was in itself a revelation. It was a tune not about work, but the humiliations of having to look for a job and not finding one. Clearly, this was not a lefty folk hymn to the dignity of labor or a poem to full employment. As was often the case with earlier blues records, written boldly between the lines was an implicit understanding that having to get a job was about succumbing to participation in an economic system that kept black men at the lowest rungs of the employment ladder.

Though in the song it is the stereotypically nagging wife who sends our working class hero out of bed crying to pound the pavement looking for a gig that he knows he'll never find, in a larger context it is the pressures of the capitalist system and institutionalized racism that composes the subtext of the Want Ads that issue the "Get A Job" ultimatum. Moreover, the stereotype of the lazy black male cannot be separated from the black street slang of the period, which referred to a job as a "slave." That this song treats the wage slavery problems it encounters by making a mockery of the job search and the likelihood of finding self-affirming employment is its strength. Foregoing the directness of the "protest song," it offers a humorous sendup of the racism imbedded in the work ethic sung from the bottom up point of view of the reluctant wage slave himself. By 2001, The Coup's "Lazymuthafucka" would take the critique of the economics of racism that was latent in "Get A Job," and make it blatant by turning the tables on "laziness" to indict the parasitical rich.

Though my Brooklyn neighborhood was solidly working class, it was racially segregated. The only diaspora I knew of was the Jewish one. Through what miracle then did this pivotal Silhouettes song come to my attention as a youth? The answer is radio, where black rhythm and blues records were being played for the first time in the Fifties on AM stations that had a predominantly white listenership. It was here/hear that my love affair with radio began. Back then, radio opened the door into the world of black music for me, and once that door opened there was no turning back. It was not long before I was learning the history of jazz and getting a taste for free jazz improvisation and experimental music by listening to college and community radio stations. By the time I started paying attention to African diasporic musics beyond the U.S., I was myself a veteran radio programmer on WSSU, located at the state university in Springfield, Illinois where I taught, doing at first a free jazz show, then a reggae show, and lastly an African show which returned me to the roots of the music I had been immersed in for, by that time, 30 years. Even today, as the U.S. radio spectrum has become increasingly colonized by the National Association of Broadcasters (corporate) and National Public Radio (public) media moguls, college, community and pirate radio stations continue, in varying degrees, to keep aflame the torch of radio as an emancipatory practice. It is only on such stations that you can hear The Coup, who must sacrifice mainstream airplay for the kind of in-your-face rap honesty about race and class that characterizes "Lazymuthafucka."

Of course, my musical evolution did not occur in a vacuum. All around me as a youth were the street sounds of the civil rights, black power, third world liberation and anti-war movements. In reference to jazz alone, I heard the call and response of political ferment in Charles Mingus' "Fables of Faubus," Max Roach's "Freedom Now Suite," John Coltrane's "Alabama," Archie Shepp's "Malcolm, Malcolm, Semper Malcolm," the Art Ensemble of Chicago's "People In Sorrow," the Revolutionary Ensemble's "Vietnam," Freddie Hubbard's "Sing Me A Song of Songmy," Sun Ra's "Nuclear War" and the entire output of the Last Poets and Charlie Haden's Liberation Music Orchestra, just to name a few. As a jazz radio disc jockey on WSSU, I played these politically-motivated compositions along with music from the larger spectrum of avant garde jazz, and then the African diaspora, until the station became a subsidiary of National Public Radio (NPR) and such shows were cancelled in favor of the exclusively mainstream jazz programming that, along with light European classical music, better suited the upscale market demographics that now determined programming decisions.

Not coincidentally, the college itself, Sangamon State University, became the victim of a hostile takeover by the University of Illinois at the behest of the conservative state legislature which was aimed at busting the faculty union and eliminating the more radical academic programs that still existed. The Studies in Social Change Program, of which I had been a founding faculty member, had already been eradicated by the governing Board of Regents around the same time that jazz programming was being trimmed of any radical substance in either form or content. In recent years, this insidious trend toward absorption of once adventurous college radio stations under the more conservative aegis of campus-based National Public Radio affiliates has been on the increase in the States. Lately, as even college and community outlets become increasingly market driven, radical radio activists are increasingly turning to free radio.

The story of the free radio movement in the United States is one with which my own evolution as a radio activist, programmer and writer has been closely intertwined, culminating in the publication of *Seizing The Airwaves* with Stephen Dunifer of Free Radio Berkeley as co-editor. In the Fall of 2002, because of that book and my long-term involvement with Black Liberation Radio (now Human Rights Radio) in Springfield, Illinois, the station that set off the micropower radio tremors that rocked the airwaves in the late Eighties, I was invited by the Cascadia Media Alliance to the "Reclaim The Media" convergence in Seattle, Washington. One of the main issues on the agenda in Seattle was the Federal Communications Commission (FCC) restriction of licensed Low Power FM (LPFM) options to a legally-mandated separation of three bandwidths between stations rather than the two bandwidth distance that they originally proposed for such stations.

Since LPFM had itself been fronted by the FCC at the turn of the twenty-first century as a way of co-opting the explosion of pirate radio stations in the Nineties, this new increase in restrictions was a further dilution of an already compromised project. Enacted at the behest of the National Association of Broadcasters (NAB) and National Public Radio (NPR), this more conservative approach to LPFM effectively downsized the number of licensed stations that would be legally permissible on the dial, not to mention the already-outlawed pirate stations that were retroactively rendered unqualified for licensing or were themselves unwilling to be licensed. Clearly, the "right to communicate"—which had been the original factor that motivated early micropower radio activist Mbanna Kantako to go on the air with what was eventually to become Human Rights Radio—has, over time, become increasingly circumscribed in an LPFM context.

With this in mind, the "Reclaim The Media" events were scheduled to be held during the week of the annual National Association of Broadcasters convention in order to protest NAB-driven media policies and to let us gather for our own grassroots shadow convention as community media activists from all over North America descended upon Seattle to hear speakers, attend workshops, and bounce off of each other's creative energy. By the end of the convergence, 10 free radio stations had been "illegally" set up just two bandwidths apart on the FM dial in open defiance of the official three bandwidth LPFM requirement. In effect, the three bandwidth rule has created a situation in the States in which LPFM stations are not legally feasible in urban areas like Seattle. As a free radio advocate and activist, I was invited (along with several other prominent media critics) to do a recorded three-minute rant on the subject of "media and democracy," which would then be made available to download for airplay not only to the ten stations just put up in Seattle, but to interested community and pirate radio stations anywhere in the world. In addition, I was slated to kick off the week of convergence events with a talk that would mix my anarchist take on media activism with my long term interest in surrealism which, in the case of the latter, had just culminated in the publication of my book *Surrealist Subversions*.

Ron Sakolsky pictured with another media activist jointly hold up a placard denouncing the unholy alliance between the National Association of Broadcasters, Clear Channel, Telecom, and the Federal Communications Commission

Since my talk that evening at the Seattle Independent Media Center was essentially an elaboration on the ideas originally broached in my three-minute radio piece, let's start with the text of that diatribe.

As an anarchist, my affinity with democracy is not about voting for someone to better represent us, but rather taking action to directly represent ourselves. Just as I don't consent to being ruled by some politician, no matter how Green, Left or Libertarian, I don't trust some professional media talking head to frame my reality for me. My conception of how media and democracy are related involves a radical critique of both.

I know a surrealist poet named Jayne Cortez, who says in one of her poems:

> *'Find Your own voice & use it*
> *Use your own voice & find it.'*

So if we are to take the science that Jayne is droppin' on us seriously, we've got to lift our collective voices against injustice and on behalf of our dreams for a world of freedom. And when we do this together, we are each stronger for it because we find our own voices in the process of passionately using them in our own chosen ways to resist oppression and to insist on liberation.

Now when we compare this radical vision of democracy to the miserabilism of our currently mediated lives, we must inevitably confront the gap between the fatally compromised illusions that comprise what is called political reality and our own brightly burning desires for personal and social autonomy and an end to hierarchy and domination.

It is then that we begin to question our socially assigned roles as passive citizen/spectators, and to demand control over the means of cultural production, representation and distribution which today are largely the domain of the corporate and public media giants.

In so doing, we emerge from the velvet prison of consumerism and market demographics and become alive to revolutionary possibilities outside the one world of global capitalism. As we awaken from our media-induced trance, we unleash the insurgent power of the creative imagination, shake off the shackles of the reality police, and break the silence of cynicism and despair.

> *'Find your own voice & use it.*
> *Use your own voice & find it.'*

For the Cascadia Media Alliance,

this is Ron Sakolsky.

In my subsequent talk, I tried to raise thorny strategy questions for anarchists involved in the media democracy movement. Rather than a strategy built upon the nostalgic myth of once having been in the driver's seat in relation to broadcast media, what we are reclaiming is our very ability to imagine a radio soundscape that satisfies our deepest desires. Thriving on dreams of revolt, surrealism has been a part of the radical political imagination since the Twenties, though even many radicals do not recognize the role of imagination as pivotal to social transformation, and even dismiss its value by contemptuously labeling it as "unrealistic." Given the depth of what surrealists demand—the transformation of reality itself—their strategies tend to be, like those of anarchists, revolutionary rather than reformist. Surrealism is not populist, and its demand for an end to the artificial dichotomy between dream and reality cannot be subsumed in the rhetoric of social democracy or recuperated in the bureaucratic language of corporations or regulatory agencies. Like anarchists, surrealists demand the impossible, pushing beyond the already-existing boundaries of the possible into the uncharted terrain of the Marvelous. Instead of confining themselves to the pragmatic politics of the possible, which are rooted in a miserablist acceptance of so-called "realistic" limitations, surrealists seek to create fault lines in our consciousness about what might indeed be "possible" in a world of unfettered imagination.

How then might a radical media politics that recognizes the worth of both surrealism and anarchism be formulated? Instead of expanding upon a foundation of populism, we would be seeking out those elements of refusal that connect with both anarchism and surrealism, building upon them, and seeking insights that might inspire us in exciting new directions while simultaneously raising the stakes of what is desirable. Though historically an inaccurate metaphor for even the limited populism of the early days of the broadcast media, I believe that we can poetically use the metaphor of "the commons" to spark our resistance to what is increasingly being seen as a new form of enclosure, not on the land, but in relation to the airwaves that surround it. The pirate radio strategy of "squatting" the airwaves differs from the LPFM approach in that the latter is an institutionalization strategy that lends itself to recuperation; to quote Steve Englander, a chronicler of the interconnected Dutch squatter and free radio movements of the Eighties, it risks being "officially conquered by state administered tolerance" (Adilkno 9). As media activists, we must ask ourselves if our goal is institutionalization or deinstitutionalization. Do we want to merely achieve the institutionalization of our radical demands vis-à-vis radio in particular and media in general OR, alternatively, to demand the radical transformation of that which has been appropriated, institutionalized, legally sanctioned and regulated "in the public interest"?

In our strategizing, perhaps we should take a lesson from jazz improvisation. As African American surrealist poet Ted Joans sees it, jazz as an improvisational music is about "surrealizing a song" (quoted in Sakolsky 138)—that is, using the transformative powers of our imagination as the basis for reclaiming our creativity in a world of miserabilist compromises. Even popular culture at its most banal is "reclaimable" in this sense. Radical music scholar and percussionist Chris Cutler once remarked that it seemed odd to him that given John Coltrane's brilliant improvisation on "My Favorite Things," the composer credits are still given to Rodgers and Hammerstein (Sakolsky and Ho 70). Instead, if we could imagine a more radical and non-Eurocentric approach to rewarding creativity, Trane would be acknowledged as the author of that tune. And by going further in the direction of free improvisation, as Trane did, we can even leave the song form itself behind.

Ornette Coleman, according to A.B. Spellman, prized the "beautiful accidents" by which the psychic automatism of spontaneous improvisation reveals what surrealists call the Marvelous (83). Further exploring the ideas of Ornette Coleman and Albert Ayler in a Black Bohemian context, the Art Ensemble of Chicago, as Robin D.G. Kelley has pointed out, "re-invented modernism through meditations and reflections on the meanings of freedom. In addition, they have moved Africa and its sprawling Diaspora from being the 'counter' modern (the primitive/the folk) to the very center of modernity. They claimed modernism for Black people, without apology" (quoted in Sakolsky 644). Similarly, hip hop turntablists who cut up, remix and creatively sample a song are "surrealizing" that tune through a technological process of layered improvisation, even though intellectual property laws still do not recognize this approach as artistically valid in its own right and require copyright fees that can cripple independent record label budgets. Surrealism has a natural affinity for collage. Not only turntablists and experimental sound artists, but on-air audio collagists like Mannlicher Carcano , who engage in collaborative improvisation using radio as their vehicle, can produce the kind of "convulsive beauty" that exists beyond the song form.

In my own personal history, it was the free jazz and sound experiments of the aforementioned Association for the Advancement of Creative Musicians (AACM), and its formative relationship to the Art Ensemble of Chicago, that alerted me to the improvisational connection between surrealism and music. When I first moved from New York to the Chicago area in 1972, I kept writing to my former homies about the AACM underground. As typical New Yorkers, who think NYC is the center of the universe, they kindly but condescendingly humored me and reminded me of how much I was missing in relation to the burgeoning "loft jazz" scene that I now only got to sample during my occasional visits out East. I would report back on the marvels of going to see Muhal Richard Abrams' Experimental Big Band in Monday night rehearsals at Transitions East, an unassuming storefront which was located at 79th and Cottage Grove on Chicago's Southside. Later, at the 1976 World Surrealist Exhibition in Chicago, which had as its theme "Marvelous Freedom/Vigilance of Desire," the AACM was given an exalted place in the surrealist firmament. Amidst the 600 surrealist works by 150 visual artists from 31 countries all over the world was featured the AACM's "Great Black Music: Ancient To The Future."

As a touchstone part of the Exhibition, a much anticipated performance was mounted by the Sun Song Ensemble, featuring such AACM stalwarts as consummate reed player/composer Douglas Ewart, master drummer Hamid (then Hank) Drake, experimental composer George Lewis on trombone and percussion, and free form vocalists Gloria Brooks and Rrata Christine Jones. Jones danced in her self-designed costume made of newspaper, while Brooks emitted lyrical screams from the depths of her being. Piano giant Cecil Taylor flew in from New York especially for the Exhibition. His surrealist poem, "The Musician," had just been published in *Arsenal* 3, the magazine of the Chicago Surrealist Group, along with AACM saxophonist/composer Joseph Jarman's mythopoetic piece, "Odawalla." Jarman also composed an original piece inspired by the Exhibition that as yet remains unrecorded. In that same issue of *Arsenal*, Franklin Rosemont had praised another of Jarman's compositions, "Non-Cognitive Aspects of the City," as an "expedition into the heart of a dark becoming, into the secret of freedom itself, lighting an infinite match in some hidden doorway between hope and despair—an expedition so inspiring, so total, that he has inevitably drawn on the emergency fuel of every poetic advance: chance, fear, humor and surprise. In the oneiric transformation of the city's grillwork and grimaces into the very nerves of revolutionary anticipation, Jarman seeks and finds living elements of the new mythology gathering momentum on the other side of all the stopped clocks in the world" (110).

That the magic of the AACM's improvisational music should find a linkage to surrealism's emphasis on the realization of poetry in everyday life, along with the AACM's longstanding association with the international movement for Black Liberation—from Négritude to Black Power—should come as no surprise. One of the factors distinguishing surrealism from all other "avant garde" cultural movements of European origin is its multiracial character. Quite naturally then, Chicago surrealists saw the collective manifestation of AACM musical projects as a "complimentary adventure." The music championed by the AACM was not meant to be decorative, but as urgent as the heated struggle against colonialism that had originally been addressed in the Fifties by surrealist poet Aimé Cesaire in his *Discourse on Colonialism*, issued like a hurricane warning from the French imperial outpost of his native Martinique. In the Sixties, as the defeated French pulled up their stakes in another colonial outpost, Vietnam, the U.S. sought to pick up the pieces of empire.

At about this time, in the midst of my own efforts in opposition to the war in Vietnam as a college student, my consciousness of the imperial presence of the United States in the world was growing in leaps and bounds. In those days, the term "American Empire" was not the open secret it is now, and to use it in mainstream discourse was to be labeled as delusionary. At that time, in terms of conventional logic, the U.S. was, though imperfect, the world's greatest democracy, and it was the Soviet Union that was what Ronald Reagan would later call the Evil Empire. Both Marxists and anarchists were in agreement in labeling the Vietnam War as an imperialist venture, but as long as the Soviet state existed, the use of the word imperialism seemed tarred with the brush of authoritarian state socialism. Anarchism was often simplistically lumped in with Marxism as part of the international communist conspiracy. Even today, though acknowledging that the thrust of global capitalism is clearly linked to the might of the U.S. Empire, there is still a reluctance by some radicals to use the term *cultural* imperialism on the grounds that it has too much Old Left baggage to be an effective tool of communication given the complexities of the post-Cold War era.

However, while cultural imperialism is indeed complexly nuanced and is not as narrowly monolithic as vulgar cause-and-effect economistic interpretations allow, it nevertheless seems to me to still be a useful concept. For example, in Africa, where African American music is typically prized above all other American music, there is a selective choice being made that is a product both of U.S. cultural imperialism's control of media and marketing *and* a diasporic consciousness of the music's African derivation. In recognizing this complexity, our analyses have to discern the balance between the imperial and the diasporic. Moreover, while the diasporic connection is obvious for something like, say, rap, what about country music and rock? What do we make of the fact that there was once a vogue in West Africa for a country singer named Gentleman Jim Reeves or that U.S.-based country music continues to be a big seller in Jamaica? In trying to explain these seeming anomalies, it is helpful to be aware of the fact that country music is not simplistically "white" in origin and even bluegrass has African roots.

Where are you Arnold Shultz? Though he never recorded, his spirit hovers over American folk music, whispering his hidden secret to all those with ears to listen to the interraciality of what is typically portrayed as racially separate. Topical folksinger and amateur ethno-musicologist Dave Lippman recounts Shultz's story in his excellent but sadly neglected self-published book *Bleaching Our Roots: Race and Culture In American Popular Music*. Receiving his slave name from Revolutionary War veteran and slavemaster Mathias Shultz of the Green River region of western Kentucky, Arnold was the child of the last of his ancestors to have once lived in slavery. He began as a songster playing guitar around the turn of the century at a time when, in isolated mountain communities, those of African American and European American descent made music together at square dances, picnics and other occasions, calling for string bands.

Though standards of "racial etiquette" were certainly in effect at these gatherings, one of Shultz's playing partners was a fiddler by the name of Pendleton Venderver, later to be known to bluegrass audiences as Bill Monroe's "Uncle Pen" as a result of the song of the same name. As Monroe himself once put it in an interview with James Rooney:

> There's things in my music, you know, that come from Arnold Shultz—runs that I use in
> a lot of my music I don't say that I make them the same way that he could make them
> 'cause he was powerful with it. In following a fiddle piece or a breakdown, he used a

pick and he could just run from one chord to another the prettiest you've ever heard. There's no guitar picker today that could do that. I tried to keep in mind a little of it—what I could salvage to use in my music. Then he could play blues and I wanted some blues in my music too, you see. (Rooney 23-24)

The music industry has created a popular assumption that bluegrass music, and much of the country music that followed in its wake, carries an unquestionable originary "whiteness." Yet, as Harry Smith so slyly revealed in his Anthology of *American Folk Music* (and as the revisionist film *O Brother Where Art Thou?* hints), the widely acknowledged "father" of bluegrass was in fact "inventing" a music deeply biracial in its origins.

Taking this one step further, the music of Elvis Presley is sometimes acknowledged as being an ingenious or insidious (take your pick) combination of the blues and country music into what came to be known as rock 'n roll, a plateau in the long tradition of American minstrelsy that has now moved beyond the blues to swallow rap and spit up Eminem. In relation to Elvis, the example usually cited in this regard is his first Sun single, with one side a note-for-note cover of bluesman Arnold "Big Boy" Cruddup's "That's All Right Mama" and the other an updating of "Blue Moon of Kentucky," originally a bluegrass tune by none other than Bill Monroe. What is now revealed by the previous discussion is that the style of music on that pivotal recording was in fact a combination, not of "white" music on one side and "black" music on the other as we have been led to believe, but of music that was even more decidedly African American than was originally imagined by many of the most astute scholarly observers, for the side assumed to be exclusively "white" was itself the product of interracial cross-pollination via Arnold Schultz.

Rock and roll in its very origins, not to mention recent efforts by the Black Rock Coalition to reevaluate the continuing contributions of African Americans to rock music, is quite simply unthinkable without the presence of African elements within American musical expression, whether those elements were freely offered or callously appropriated by the dominant Euro-American culture. In this sense, when those on the African continent find an affinity with certain types of rock music, they are not simply being manipulated by the ploys of global marketing conglomerates since their choices are based at least in part upon taking pleasure in what has been borrowed or recognizing what has been stolen. However, even where the music in question has more obvious African American roots than a genre like bluegrass or rock, the pull to that music is still problematic because it is complicated by cultural imperialism.

In this context, what are we to make of African American bluesman Johnny Copeland's 1982 tour of Africa (Burkina Faso, Cameroun, Guinea, Ivory Coast, Liberia, Senegal, Sierra Leone, Republic of Congo, and what was then Zaire) sponsored by the United States Information Agency (USIA)? While it produced an illuminating roots album, *Bringin' It All Back Home*, which featured a mix of American and African musicians recorded in the Motherland, does its USIA association add a layer of State Department propaganda that clouds what was otherwise a bright diasporic project? When compared to the U.S.-based collaboration, *From Senegal to Senatobia* which features Otha Turner and the Afrossippi Allstars in an exhilarating down-home mix of Mississippi fife and drums, and blues combined with African percussion and kora played by Mori Keba Koyate, Mussa Sutton and Manu Walton—the dilemma of U.S. government sponsorship is sidestepped, but the question of "To whose home do we bring it all back?" is raised.

Beyond the African continent and the Caribbean with its majority black culture, other issues of cultural affinity come into play. As African Canadian author George Elliott Clarke has put it in relation to the written word, "Given the gravitational attractiveness of Black America and the re-pellent force of frequently racist, Anglo-Canadian (and Québécois de *souche*) nationalism, Afri-can-Canadian writers feel themselves caught between the Scylla of an essentially U.S.-tincted cultural nationalism and the Charybdis of their marginalization within Canadian cultural dis-courses that perceive them as 'alien'." With this cultural tension in mind, let's look at dub poetry where "word soun ave power" and its manifestation at the First International Dub Poetry Festival held in Toronto in 1993, which I originally covered as a journalist for *The Beat*.

Certainly being a dub poet in Toronto or London, England is a very different diasporic experi-ence than being based in Kingston, and even if gender is added to the equation, then dub poets whose diasporic context is as diverse as ahdri zhina mandiela (Canada), Jean "Binta" Breeze (UK) and Cherry Natural (Jamaica) produce their own variations on the dub poetry theme. Amidst the positive vibes of diasporic unity couched in what Jamaican dub poet Mutabaruka termed "the African oral tradition" and the creation of a space free of U.S. cultural domination and what he called its "hip hop Americanization of Jamaican lyrics over American rhythms" (quoted in Sakolsky and Ho 258-9), differences of approach at and within the global, national and local lev-els did not go unacknowledged among those present at the Dub Poetry Festival.

Unity does not necessarily imply a facile unanimity on issues of politics, poetics, perfor-mance, and aesthetics. Moreover, in evaluating the shifting balance between American imposi-tion and African affinity as it relates to specific musical instances, one must question the degree to which even affinity itself is imposed by the hegemonic position of African American music in the diasporic marketplace. Within and beyond that market, a related issue is the predominant worldwide distribution of what are typically the most commercial kinds of African American mu-sic. Certainly, other African diasporic musics have had an impact on musical developments on the African continent. Cuban rumba, Trinidadian calypso and Jamaican reggae/dancehall are the best known examples. However, a chicken and egg complexity still remains since these diasporic musics in turn have been influenced in *their* origins by African American jazz, soul, funk and hip hop.

Adding to these complications, when we focus on the history of rap and examine the hidden Caribbean roots of such Bronx hip hop originators as Kool Herc and Grandmaster Flash, we can see emergent trends toward more of a two-way diasporic flow. Similarly, as it developed in the crucible of the United States, that African American music called jazz has had its own major contributors of "West Indian" descent, such as saxophone colossus Sonny Rollins. In England, a younger jazz tenor man of Jamaican descent, Courtney Pine, has embraced elements of hip hop turntablism in his music. On the South American side of the Atlantic, Brazilian "tropicalistas" faced with the onslaught of American culture in the late Sixties, including jazz appropriation and rock proliferation, consciously devised a creatively subversive response to cultural imperialism and its essentialist racial constructions of Brazilian music by embracing carnivalesque cosmopolitanism, with a decidedly creole sensibility, a witty tongue in cheek playfulness, and a characteristically irreverent "cultural cannibalism" à la Brazilian modernist poet Oswald de Andrade (Veloso 153-6).

In terms of African influences, hard bop/soul funk pianist Horace Silver's creole heritage was celebrated in his seminal 1963 Blue Note recording "Song For My Father" (Cantiga Para Meu Pai), which I first heard on a Latin radio show hosted by Symphony Sid in New York. This song was composed of an African and Portuguese ancestral mix characteristic of the Cape Verde home of his father, whom he remembers fondly playing violin and guitar at informal family musical parties. It expresses the musical connections between Silver's Cape Verde heritage and its Black Atlantic relative, Brazilian bossa nova, combined with a touch of African American blues. By way of comparison, in South Africa, jazz was viewed by the African National Congress as progressive in its ability to transcend ethnic divisions among blacks. Often thought of as apolitical in the cultural context of the States, jazz has long been identified with freedom, racial dignity, and interracial harmony in South Africa, where it was re-Africanized and politicized as part of the anti-imperialist struggle to end apartheid. The real question being raised in all of these examples then is not about the validity of musical sharing, which is inevitable and can, in whole or in part, be liberating or debilitating in its effects, but about the nature and degree of reciprocity involved in cultural exchange.

Diasporic thinking becomes a more valuable tool of analysis when African American music is put in perspective as but one form of creolized African-based music. As in Canada, black music is considered minority music in the USA only because those of African descent are a minority of the population, but on a global scale, African American music has had a major impact because of a combination of diasporic consciousness and the inequalities of the global music industry which give any American music a privileged position in the world market. Theoretically, if the playing field were more level, African American music would be more likely to appear on the world stage as an integral part of, rather than the dominant force in, Black Atlantic musical production. Such an egalitarian vision involves a strategy of hastening the breakdown of the overwhelmingly one way flow emanating from the U.S. to the world metropoles, in the interests of creating a "yard to yard" diasporic network capable of reconfiguring distribution or even bypassing transnational corporate media conglomerates entirely. Like any cross-cultural musical exchange, diasporic or otherwise, it is the dynamics of the cultural contact, rather than the contact itself, which are ultimately important. In this sense, a more nuanced approach to cultural imperialism allows us to see the process of diasporic musical sharing as occasionally two way or even multivalent and, in political terms, as contested terrain.

Given its relative post-revolutionary isolation from the onslaughts of U.S. cultural imperialism, I decided to visit Cuba in the early Nineties to study Afro-Cuban music. During the Seventies and Eighties, I had luckily been able to receive Cuban records in the mail from a friend in Poland in exchange for Chicago blues sides. Because of the Cold War, Cuban music was as unavailable in Illinois as the blues was in East Bloc cities like Warsaw or New York City salsa was in Cuba. I now live in British Columbia in a state of voluntary exile from the United Snakes of America. Here in Canada it is quite normal to visit Cuba, but, when I lived in the States, it was decidedly abnormal, even suspect, for a U.S. citizen to fly to Havana. My visit as a journalist for *The Beat* magazine was prior to the sonic tourism generated by Ry Cooder's "discovery" of Cuban music and the subsequent *Buena Vista Social Club* phenomenon. Upon visiting, what I found in Cuba was, as one might expect, a more direct connection to African culture than is the case in the States. The Motherland spiritual traditions and practices of Santería were widely dispersed among Cubans of African descent, drawing heavily on African ritual music and using the Yoruba language rather than Spanish to invoke the African divinities renamed "santos" or "orishas" in the colonial context.

What's more, even non-Africans in the Cuban population were familiar with these traditions. As the late African American cultural democracy activist Larry Abrams once explained this situation, in relation to his own visit to Cuba in 1989:

> I was returning late one night from a gig at a high-rise beach resort outside Havana where my friends in a band called Afro-Jazz played two sets a night for the mostly Latin American tourists. At that time of morning, the bus was loaded with hotel workers returning home to the city, along with the musicians. As I have seen happen in the U.S. at such times, when weary and bored from the long trip, people began to sing puerile folk songs of the kind that everyone knows from grade school, like our "Oh! Suzanna." Only these were from the folk tradition of Spain. The bus was about half-and-half, whites and blacks, and I had already become accustomed to seeing this kind of spontaneous unity between the races that I have rarely seen in the U.S., especially among the working class, so I was not too surprised at this strategy to lighten the ennui of the long trip back to the city. But then someone, perhaps one of the band members, began to tap a syncopated rhythm on the back of a seat, and soon others had joined in the drumming, and to my utter astonishment, there arose from the very same throats that had been indoctrinated with the Spanish folk songs, the haunting and qualitatively different chanting of Yoruba songs to the *Orishas*. And everyone, whites and blacks, seemed to know the words!

> There is no cultural equivalent to that in the U.S. (68-69)

However, in the time between Abrams' visit and mine, some significant changes were beginning to occur in Cuba. It was possible to receive American music television from Miami, and the "dollar stores" flaunted brand name clothing and shiny new consumer technology from the USA. The commodities displayed were in stark contrast to the threadbare state of the economy during the lean years of the "special period" after the collapse of Cuba's major trading partner, the Soviet Union, and, during my visit, a poor sugarcane harvest exacerbated the ongoing stranglehold of the U.S. economic embargo. These cultural and economic tensions in Cuba had mounted even further by the time of Ry Cooder's decision to explore the "forbidden island" with director

Wim Wenders, which then led to the lionizing of Cuban music in the States as a result of the 1997 film, *Buena Vista Social Club*. By focusing on the musical old timers, Cooder was providing long overdue international recognition to the deserving artists who were recommended to him by veteran Cuban musician Juan de Marcos González, but what of the younger generation of Cuban "timba" musicians and "rappers" who were excluded from the nostalgia-bathed film? Contemporary timba songs often comment upon the seamy side of the return of capitalism to the island, involving rampant consumerism and open prostitution. Charanga Habanera's "El Temba" ("The Rich Guy") and "La Turística" ("The Tourist-Minded Girl") from their 1996 album, *Para Que Se Entere La Habana*, predictably received no airplay in Miami, but in a case of strange bedfellows, the record was interpreted by the Cuban government as an accusation that Cuba was "selling out" to the forces of the market, and so it was actually banned on the island for a time (quoted in Waxer 68).

On the other hand, what are we to make of the trend by younger Cuban musicians to go back to the earlier syncretic roots music of "son"? Is this a welcome return to Cuban tradition that rejects televised American influences from Miami, or does it represent a reactionary stifling of the island's musical development to appeal to the tastes of relatively affluent middle-aged re-cord buyers in the U.S. who were entranced by the film? Does it matter that some of these "problematic" Miami influences are from TV stations that program to the Latino community in Spanish? What if Cooder's project had included the musicians from Mali who were originally supposed to be in the film, but whose visas were denied and so they were unable to make it from Africa to Cuba?

What about African American saxophonist Steve Coleman's largely unnoticed visit to Cuba in 1996, documented in his major label recording, *The Sign and The Seal: Transmissions of the Metaphysics of A Culture*, which featured the traditional musicians of de Mantanzas and was steeped in African spiritual exploration? In 1997, the same year as the Buena Vista release, Afri-can American trumpeter Roy Hargrove visited Cuba, along with saxman Gary Bartz. Using top notch Cuban musicians to form his "Cristol" band, he made the recording *Habana* which, though on the long-established Verve jazz label, still remains obscure in comparison to the megasuccess of the Ry Cooder project.

Could the racialized trope of the white "discovery" of Latin music be part of the explanation for this difference in reception? Canadian soprano saxophonist/flautist, Jane Bunnett (lately billed as "Habana Juana"), though a woman, has had great critical success with her recorded collaborations with Cuban artists. On *Alma De Santiago*, a 2001 release, the liner notes describe these collaborations as a project that involves her "desire to explore the uncharted musical terri-tories of her adopted island." By pointing out this contextual framework of "discovery," I do not mean to denigrate either her musicianship or her intentions, only to comment on the ever pres-ent issue of white skin privilege, which seemingly can transcend male privilege or even American nationality when it comes to marketability. When taken together, these questions raise the larger question of how diasporically connected musics interact within the racist marketing practices of the global economy.

Yet, as the veil is increasingly lifted and Cuban culture becomes more visibly African in nature, African Americans are more and more realizing that, while their governments might not like each other much, there is a connection between Cuba and the U.S. that cannot be denied. After all, some of the eager record consumers mentioned above were African Americans who were seeking to connect with their African roots by way of Cuba. Many years earlier, during the AfroCuban phase of the bebop era, African American jazz bassist Al McKibbon explained his fascination with the music of the Cuban drummer Chano Pozo, featured with the Dizzy Gillespie band. He succinctly remarked to his fellow band members, who had teasingly referred to McKibbon as a Cuban wannabe, "No, man, I don't want to become Cuban, this is black" (43). How this renewed diasporic awareness will play itself out in the future is anybody's guess, but it seems that the tide is beginning to turn on the cultural isolation originally imposed on Cuba by the Cold War log jam.

With the growth of a diasporic consciousness, just as Americans are hearing a sprinkling of Jamaican patois on the airwaves by way of raggamuffin dancehall artists ranging from Beanie Man in Jamaica to Shaggy in the USA, Latino rappers are once again occasionally heard singing in Spanish or bilingually on "urban" formatted radio stations. It is as if the Latin Boogaloo (Latin/SoulFunk) flower had never died, but had, instead, been growing deeper roots since the seed was originally planted alongside the Harlem River Drive in the Sixties. That seed has been nurtured in more recent years by (just to name a few, not all of whom receive airplay) such Nuyorican hip hoppers as deejay Charlie Chase, rappers Hurricane G, Big Pun, Angie Martinez and old schoolers Latin Empire on the East Coast; while Chicano rappers Aztlan Underground (who dedicated their 1995 recording, *Decolonize*, to the Zapatistas), A Lighter Shade of Brown, Proper Dos, A.L.T. and the Lost Civilization, Kid Frost, and Cuban-American, Mellow Man Ace have held forth on the West Coast. Both Ace and Frost were teamed with the politically conscious pan-Latin studio band Latin Alliance, and the torch of Latino political consciousness has been taken up more recently by the California-based Latin rap crossover band Ozomatli. Rappers originating outside the U.S., but not unknown among North American Latinos, include Mexico's El Gran Silencio, Puerto Rico's Lisa M, the Orishas, a Cuban-French aggregation, and, from Panama, El General, who kicks it in a reggaespañol vein.

Moreover, African American and Latino artists in the United States seem to be engaging in more partnerships in recent years with not only expatriate Cuban jazz musicians who live part-time in the States, like Omar , or younger generation Cuban Americans, like rapper Mellow Man Ace (who himself has jammed on record with Cuban-based timba artists Bamboleo), but even more strikingly, in the last decade, U.S.-based Latinos are going to the African source of the diaspora to seek out artists with whom to collaborate, not as exotic guests as so often happens in "world music" circles, but as equals and sometimes leaders in their own right. In this latter regard, Zairean-born vocalist Ricardo Lemvo has formed his own band, Makina Loca, with Latino musicians in Los Angeles, and brought along African rumba vocalists like Sam Mangwana and Nyboma, as well as soukous guitarists like Syran Mbenza and Bopol Mansiamina to sit in on recording sessions..

Further, recalling the golden epoch of "rumba congolaise" and anticipating its present resurgence in what is now called "salsa africaine," producer Ibrahim Sylla of Senegal (whose Latin record collection reputedly includes 6,000 Cuban albums) started working together with Malian flautist/arranger Boncana Maiga in 1993 to put together a series of Africando recordings that make creative links between stellar African pop musicians and their Latino and Caribbean counterparts. In the Africando context, African vocalists Salif Keita, Sekouba "Bambino" Diabate, Thione Seck, Pape Seck, Gnonnas Pedro, Laba Sosseh, Medoune Diallo, Tabu Ley Rochereau and Koffi Olomide (often singing in indigenous African languages rather than the colonial ones) are teamed with such diasporic collaborators as vocalist Roger "Shoubou" Eugéne of Haiti's Tabou Combo and Hector Casanova of Puerto Rico's El Gran Combo, along with such New York City-based salseros as vocalists Adalberto Santiago and Ronnie Baro and saxophonists José "Chombo" Silva and Mario Rivera.

Talking about saxophonists, expatriate African American jazzman David Murray traveled to Africa in 1996 to collaborate with Senegalese master drummer Doudou N'Daiye Rose, vocalist Tidianne Gaye and rappers Positive Black Soul on the recording Fo deuk Revue, for which he acknowledges Malcolm X as his inspiration in the liner notes. Not surprisingly, it features some hard-hitting diasporic poetry by African American artist Amiri Baraka. A few years later, as newly appointed "Poet Laureate of New Jersey," Baraka was publicly attacked in the media for his controversial post-9/11 poem, "Somebody Blew Up America." Coming to his defense was the Surrealist Movement of the United States, which issued the 2002 proclamation, "Poetry Matters!" on his behalf, co-signed by, among many others, jazz artists Joseph Jarman, Archie Shepp, and Ted Joans. Interestingly, the latter two had made a similar "homecoming" trip to North Africa in the late Sixties that was a precursor to Murray's West African sojourn. In regard to the Murray recording, it should be noted that "Fo deuk" means "where do you come from" in Wolof.

On a later recording date, Murray even took a back seat to Tidiane and appeared as a guest artist himself on the former's debut recording, Salimata. As a charter member of the World Saxophone Quartet, Murray, along with the other members, was not content with only playing advanced horn charts. The WSQ has always reached out to Africa, featuring a host of Senegalese and Nigerian master drummers (Mor Thiam, Mar Gueye and Chief Bey) on Metamorphosis in 1991 and even more prominently on the later 1996 excursion, Four Now. Still on the diaspora trail, Murray also traveled to Guadeloupe in 1998 to record on Creole with such masters of the

African-based Gwo-Ka tradition as vocalist Guy Konket and drummer Klod Kiavue, and brought them to New York City to record *Yonn-Dé* in 2000.

In between the Guadeloupe record dates, Murray joined with South African artists in 1999 for a posthumous tribute to cultural freedom fighter and jazz Johnny "Mbizo" Dyani, on the recording which bears his name. It is a tribute not only to Mbizo, who had himself appeared and recorded with such African American musicians as Don Cherry, Archie Shepp, Billy Hart and Joseph Jarman, as well as Murray himself, but to Mongezi Feza, Dudu Pukwana, Chris McGregor and Louis Moholo, the latter being the last living member of the legendary South African band The Blue Notes, with which the others were affiliated as well. Included in the proceedings are Xhosa, Tswana, Swazi and Zulu musicians, along with Konket and Kiavue from Guadeloupe. In 1991, the Art Ensemble of Chicago had, similarly, thrown in their lot with the South African male chorus Amabotho to transform themselves into a new band, billing themselves as The Art Ensemble of Soweto on the recording *America-South Africa*. A decade earlier, René McClean, who had his saxophone passed on to him by his father, Jackie, made his "return" to Africa as a longterm result of originally meeting South African trumpeter Hugh Masekela back in 1962. He joined the latter's band in 1978, traveled to Botswana and Lesotho, and eventually settled in South Africa himself, recording an album in 1993, *In African Eyes*, with Masekela as a featured guest artist.

Similarly, in 1995, veteran African American jazz pianist Hank Jones sought out organist/percussionist Seck of Mali to be the musical director of his *Sarala* project, a fruitful excursion into the Mandingo musical roots of jazz and blues, which featured a West African all-star band dubbed the Mandinkas, including such luminaries as guitarists Manfila Kanté, Sékou Diabate, Ousmane Kouyaté and Djely-Moussa Kouyaté, as well as a number of other more traditional African instrumentalists, such as Djely-Moussa Condé on kora, Lansine Kouyaté on balafon, Moriba Koita on n'goni, Moussa Sissokho on djembe/tama and Maré Sanoso on doun doun, along with vocalists like Kass-Mady Diabaté, Fatoumata "Mama" Kouyaté and Amina Annabi. In this same return-to-Africa mode, but tapping into a more mystical root, Randy Weston, who lived in Morroco for many years, has fronted several recordings featuring the drumming and vocals of gnawa trance musicians, a concept most fully realized in *Spirit!: The Power of Music*, released in 2000. Also in that year, African American free jazz trumpeter Wadada Leo Smith returned to the African zion of his earlier "world music" roots by uniting his band, N'Da Kulture with the mbira-based guitar sound of the Lion of Zimbabwe, Thomas Mapfumo, and his band, The Blacks Unlimited, on a recording entitled *Dreams and Secrets* during the latter's U.S. residency.

No longer is Africa just a symbolic or imagined place for African American jazz musicians, as when Miles Davis recorded Sonny Rollins' "Airegin" (Nigeria backwards) in 1954; rather, the Motherland is fast becoming a focal point for more direct collaborations. Before his death, Miles acknowledged the influence of the Afrobeat style of Nigerian Fela Kuti on his later music, just as Fela had himself reported being influenced by Miles during his brief stay (1969-70) in the United States as a young man (Veal 70-71, 256). Miles' former sideman, John Coltrane, recorded the tune "Tunji" with his own quartet in 1962, in honor of his friend, Nigerian master drummer Olatunji with whom he had hoped to visit Africa one day. Though he did incorporate African musical elements into his own jazz compositions on occasion, he never made it to Africa himself due to his untimely death.

Yet, as alluded to previously, as far back as 1969 tenor saxophonist Archie Shepp, along with Clifford Thornton (cornet), Grachan Moncur III (trombone), Dave Burrell (piano), Alan Silva (bass), Sonny Murray (drums) and surrealist poet Ted Joans recorded a live album at the Pan African Festival in Algiers, improvising freely with a host of Algerian and Touareg musicians. Joans' poem for the occasion was appropriately entitled, "We Have Come Back." A couple of years later, in 1971, the Sun Ra Arkestra jammed in Egypt with such members of the Cairo Jazz Band and the Cairo Free Jazz Ensemble as Egyptian drummer Salah Ragab and German percussionist Hartmut Geerken. Geerken later organized a tour of Guinea, Sierra Leone and Liberia in 1985 as part of a free jazz trio which also included Art Ensemble of Chicago drummer Famadou Don Moye (who got to meet his chosen namesake, Guinean master drummer Famadou Konaté) and tenor saxophonist John Tchicai, who is himself partly of Congolese heritage. During their journey they exchanged musical energies with local musicians, not only in Conakry, Freetown and Monrovia, but in scattered bush villages along the way, with the results eventually compiled on a recording dubbed *The African Tapes*. And the diasporic wheel is still in spin as the younger generation enters the picture via rap.

With the ascendance of conscious rap on the world stage, musical relationships with African musicians are increasingly based on mutual respect, and in some cases American-based artists are not the leaders but rather the guests within an "outernational" context that is not strictly confined to the narrow boundaries of nation state or lowest common denominator transnational corporate marketing strategies. In recent years, U.S.-based rappers like The Roots and Common have collaborated with Femi Kuti. Femi's controversial father, the late Fela Kuti, was an uncompromising opponent of cultural imperialism and its "colonial mentality." While his own music was heavily influenced by James Brown, whose polyrhythmic approach struck a diasporic chord, he remained very much his own man, refusing to collaborate unless he retained control of both the recording process and the aesthetic outcome. Since his death, his son, Femi, has sought to situate the terms of the diasporic cultural exchange process between himself and his African American collaborators in a setting that increases the possibilities for collaboration while maintaining the cultural integrity of his music's "Africaness." Rather than Femi simply appearing as a sideman on a The Roots or Common record date, it is Afrobeat music with which they all in-

teract by implicitly recognizing the Africaness of funk, the funk roots of Afrobeat and their confluence in a hip hop context.

While such collaborations are not too far removed from Fela's earlier jams with Art Ensemble of Chicago trumpeter Lester Bowie (who was a touring member and featured soloist with
Fela's Afrika 70 for three months) or jazz vibraphonist Roy Ayers (who together with Fela released a recording entitled *Music of Many Colours*), the fact that many of the more recent collaborations are with rappers rather than jazz musicians is significant in that they enable Femi to
reach a wider and a younger audience, while still remaining the artist receiving credit for the music. In contrast to George Clinton's release of "Nubian Hut" which incorporated chorus lines
from Fela's "Mr. Follow Follow" or Masters at Work's (Kenny "Dope" Gonzalez and "Little Louis"
Vega) dancefloor-filling remix of Fela's "Expensive Shit," entitled "MAW Expensive (A Tribute to
Fela)" which were released under their respective names as recording artists, the remix of Femi's
"Black Man Know Yourself" by The Roots (from his *Shoki Shoki* CD) was released under Femi's
name. While the latter record has achieved predictable success with an African American audience by painting a positive Afrocentric image of Africa as the "cradle of civilization," the more re-
cent Common collaboration "Missing Link" from his *Fight to Win* recording problematizes
Afrocentrism in that it is very clear about the oppressive nature of African dictatorship, as is King
Britt's Oba Funke remix of Femi's "Traitors of Africa" taken from that same CD and also listed under Femi's name. And the beat goes on…

Though Fela was to die of AIDS-related complications, during his lifetime he had publicly
scoffed at the very existence of an African AIDS epidemic by labeling it a "whiteman's disease,"
calling the use of condoms "un-African," denying that he could get a sexually transmitted illness, and refusing to the end to be tested. Femi, on the other hand, seems to be following in the
footsteps of his uncle, Olikoye Kuti, who, as Minister of Health under the Babangida government in the late Eighties, had repeatedly warned Nigerians of the scourge of AIDS (Veal 236-7).
In 2002, Femi and his band, Positive Force, agreed to collaborate on the recording, *Red, Hot &
Riot: The Music and Spirit of Fela Kuti*, which is simultaneously a tribute to Fela and a fundraiser
for AIDS awareness activities and other AIDS prevention and relief efforts in Africa and around
the world.

Other Afrobeat artists who were part of this project include Tony Allen, former drummer
and arranger for Fela, and Antibalas from the USA. It features samples of Fela himself, along
with recordings of his songs by such hip hop heavies as Dead Prez, Common, Talib Kweli, Gift of
Gab and Lateef of Blackalicious (who had previously sampled Fela in "Smithzonian Institute of
Rhyme"), and Senegalese rappers Positive Black Soul. Beyond rap, musicians included are as far
apart on the African American music spectrum as folkbluesmaster Taj Mahal (who had earlier in
1999 gone to Africa to record with West African musicians like Toumani Diabate on *Kulanjan*)
and soulfunkmaster D'Angelo. Participating diasporic artists include pop vocalists Kellis, Sade,

Macy Gray, and Me Shell Ndegeocello, guitarist Nile Rodgers, jazzmen like veteran Archie Shepp and younger generation trumpeter Roy Hargrove, bassist Melvin Gibbs and tenor saxman Ron Blake. On the pan-Latin tip, such artists as Jorge Ben, Lenine and Arto Lindsay of Brazil, Yerba Buena, Nuyoricans like Andy Gonzalez and expatriate Cubans like Orlando "Puntilla" Rios make an appearance. Back to Africa, such internationally-recognized African pop figures as Baaba Maal, Manu Dibango, Ray Lema, Cheik Lo, Djelimady Tounkara, Kaouding Cissoko, Les Nubians and Wunmi (late of Soul II Soul by way of Nigeria) are featured as well. What Fela himself would have thought of such a project either musically or politically is pure conjecture, though his iconic status as the quintessential diasporic rebel musician is insured as a result of it.

So, welcome to the Rebel Corner, where Femi Kuti duets with Bob Marley on "Africa Unite;" where the MC5 morphs into Tribe 8 and holds down Theodor Adorno as Kathleen Hanna strips him of all his high culture pretensions so he can appreciate the difference between Le Tigre and Bikini Kill; where Phil Ochs is cut down from his gold lame cross by Chris Cutler and returned to Dar Es Salaam to sit in on a session with Robert Wyatt on talking drums as Peetie Wheatstraw, the High Sheriff From Hell, poetically ignites a piano, while Ruben Blades fans the flames by clapping his hands in clave; where Pat Andrade and Chuck D lay down a ballistic bassline for a raging Black Indian war dance on John Wayne's Head; where Utah Phillips laughs uproariously as Negativland teaches Mr. Block "The ABCs of Anarchism," Chumbawamba-style, and where William Parker still searches for the "raincoat in the river."

Denman Island, 2003

WORKS CONSULTED

Abrams, Larry. "How I Couldn't Learn To Do The Rooster Dance." *Griot* (Winter 93/94): 65-72.

Adilkno. *Cracking the Movement* Brooklyn: Autonomedia, 1990.

Carpentier, Alejo. *Music in Cuba*. Minneapolis: U of Minnesota P, 2001.

Cesaire, Aimé. *Discourse on Colonialism*. New York: Monthly Review Press, 2000.

Clarke, George Elliott. "Must All Blackness Be American: Locating Canada in Borden's "Tightrope Time," or Nationalizing Gilroy's *The Black Atlantic*." <www.athabascau.ca/writers/geclarke_essay.html>.

Cooper, Carolyn. *Noises in the Blood: Orality, Gender and the Vulgar Body of Jamaican Culture*. Durham, NC: Duke UP, 1993.

Cutler, Chris. *File Under Popular*. London: November Books, 1985.

Fernandez, Raul. *Latin Jazz: The Perfect Combination*. San Francisco: Chronicle Books, 2002.

Ferrell, Jeff. *Tearing Down the Streets: Adventures in Urban Anarchy*. New York: Palgrave, 2001.

Flores, Juan. *From Bomba to Hip Hop: Puerto Rican Culture and Latino Identity*. New York: Columbia UP, 2000.

Gilroy, Paul. *The Black Atlantic: Modernity and Double Consciousness*. Cambridge: Harvard UP, 1993.

Jarman, Joseph. "Odawalla'." *Arsenal #3* (1976): 33.

Lippman, Dave. *Bleaching Our Roots: Race and Culture in American Popular Music.* Self-Published, 1996.

Lipsitz, George. *Dangerous Crossroads: Popular Music, Postmodernism and the Poetics of Place.* London: Verso, 1994.

Manuel, Peter. *Caribbean Currents: Caribbean Music From Rumba to Reggae.* Philadelphia: Temple UP, 1995.

McKibbon, Al. "Afterword." *Latin Jazz: The Perfect Combination.* By Raul Fernandez. San Francisco: Chronicle Books, 2002.

Moore, Carlos. *Fela Fela: This Bitch of a Life.* London: Allison and Busby, 1982.

Moore, Robin. "'Cha-cha with a backbeat':Songs and Stories of Latin Boogaloo." *Situating Salsa: Global Markets and Local Meaning in Latin Popular Music.* Ed. Lise Waxer. New York: Routledge, 2002.

Rooney, James. *Bossmen: Bill Monroe and Muddy Waters.* New York: Dial, 1971.

Rosemont, Franklin. "Joseph Jarman." *Arsenal #3* (1976): 110.

Sakolsky, Ron and Fred Ho, eds. *Sounding Off!: Music as Subversion/Resistance/Revolution.* Brooklyn: Autonomedia, 1995.

Sakolsky, Ron and Stephen Dunifer, eds. *Seizing The Airwaves: A Free Radio Handbook.* San Francisco: AK Press, 1998.

Sakolsky, Ron, ed. *Surrealist Subversions: Rants, Writings and Images by the Surrealist Movement in the United States.* Brooklyn: Autonomedia, 2002.

Spellman, A.B. *Black Music: Four Lives in the Bebop Business.* New York: Pantheon Books, 1966.

Taylor, Cecil. "The Musician," *Arsenal #3* (1976): 12-15.

Taylor, Timothy. *Global Pop: World Music, World Markets.* New York: Routledge, 1997.

Veal, Michael. *Fela: The Life and Times of an African Musical Icon.* Philadelphia: Temple UP, 2000.

Veloso, Caetano. *Tropical Truth: A Story of Music and Revolution in Brazil.* New York: Alfred A. Knopf, 2002.

Waterman, Ellen. "Making No Noise: The Mannlicher Carcano Radio Hour." *Musicworks* (Fall, 2001), 36-43.

Waxer, Lise, ed. *Situating Salsa: Global Markets and Local Meaning in Latin Popular Music.* New York: Routledge, 2002.

Weinstein, Norman. *A Night In Tunisia: Imaginings of Africa in Jazz.* New York: Limelight, 1992.

Marie Boti and Malcolm Guy, with Elysée Nouvet and Hind Benchekroun

2 / Making Rebel Musics: The Films[1]

"In the world today all culture, all literature and art belong to definite classes and are geared to definite political lines. There is in fact no such thing as art for art's sake, art that stands above classes, art that is detached from or independent of politics. Proletarian literature and art are part of the whole proletarian revolutionary cause." —Mao Zedong

"Watch music; it is an important art form. Rulers should be careful about what songs they allow to be sung." —Plato

MARIE BOTI and MALCOLM GUY are filmmakers from Montreal whose work reflects over 25 years of globalized political activism. They are currently working on a collection of documentary films entitled *Rebel Music*, produced by Productions Multi-Monde,[2] a company they founded in 1987. *Musiques Rebelles Québec* was released in 2002, *Rebel Music Américas* is in production, and they are developing further films with Hind Benchekroun in Africa and Asia.

Rulers know the power of songs; they know that music and politics are a potent mix. All countries have a national anthem; it stirs patriotic sentiment, summons defense for the homeland, or calls troops to battle. Political movements of all stripes use music to reinforce their appeal and their message. Even when music seems apolitical, it still carries values—if only to reinforce the status quo by lulling minds and preventing critical thought. Cultural products are the number one export of the United States and a crucial element contributing to American military, political, and economic hegemony.

Musicians the world over have been censored, imprisoned and even assassinated because they were seen as representing a threat to the powers-that-be. In Chile, the Pinochet dictatorship tortured and murdered singer/guitarist Victor Jara (discussed in detail by Martha Nandorfy elsewhere in this book); in Nigeria, singer Fela Kuti spent years in jail because of his open criticism of the corrupt ruling system; in Algeria, in the midst of religious tension, the Kabil singer Lounes was killed by unknown assassins; in 1972, Uruguayan *cancionista* Daniel Viglietti, famous for his pro-indigene *Canción para mi América* was imprisoned by the military dictatorship—and all around the world, wherever protest occurs, sound and its repression are in constant tension.

Some musicians pay for their convictions and stance for justice and the people with their lives; others make sacrifices in their careers and lifestyle. In *Musiques Rebelles*, we set out to paint a documentary portrait of political music today—*"la musique engagée"*—through the artists that perform it, the public that is inspired by it, and the movements that nourish it. We wanted a sociopolitical musical project of documentary films that would sway, swing, and sing along to rhythms of reggae, afro-beat, samba, hip-hop, rap, folk music, and more. We wanted to look around the world at the fighting spirit of people and the creative and talented artists that give them a voice. We wanted to look at the social and political realities in each country through these musicians' eyes.

A Long History of "Engagement"

Liberation movements the world over have their troubadours and artists. In Morocco, the mixture of traditional and modern Arabic strains of Nass El Ghiwane influenced an entire generation of young dissidents to the regime; in Jamaica, it was the Rastafarians who sang about the evils of big finance, Babylon, and their yearning for Africa; in the Philippines, artists like Joey Ayala, Asin and Buklod risked their lives under martial law to sing against the Marcos dictatorship; closer to home, artists like Pauline Julien and Gilles Vigneault were harassed and jailed under the War Measures Act for voicing the aspirations of the Québécois people.

An important tradition of cause-oriented artists also marks the history of the United States. Woody Guthrie and Leadbelly set the stage for the sixties, when baby boomers in the West came of age to the songs of Pete Seeger and Joan Baez, whose lyrics symbolized opposition to the Vietnam War. There was a lull during the 80s and 90s, as social movements took a back seat to the idolatry of business and the stock market.

It is generally political movements that give rebel music inspiration and, especially, an impact. A couple of decades of political disarray on the left in Canada in the 80s and 90s put rebel music in the closet. As participants in the emergent worldwide resistance to imperialist globalization, we have observed that music with content, art with a cause, is back in style—not on the pop charts, mind you, but with growing audiences at home and around the world. The time was clearly ripe for a documentary film or films about them.

For the past fifteen years we have been making documentary films at Productions Multi-Monde about people's resistance to the ills of capitalism and imperialism. Many have focussed on the South, or the "Third World" as Mao Zedong called it, inspired by organizations leading powerful movements for social and revolutionary change, particularly in the Philippines. Music has always played an important role in our films, to convey mood, emotion, memory, and determination. We have long recognized and used its power to move and capture the imagination—to supplement and complete the image. What sweeter experience than to hear a wonderful melody or a beat with words that stir your faith in humankind.

The rebel music documentaries we set out to make were not intended as a survey of socially and politically involved musicians, and we had no pretensions of being able to encompass all forms of music and resistance. Documentaries form a personal vision, shaped by the contacts, musical tastes, and political and social involvement of the creative team behind each film. They do aim, however, to provide a vision of the diversity, strength, and creativity of the singers and musicians we have chosen as well as the social and political movements that inspire them and, in turn, are inspired by them.

Evolution of the Concept

At first, we thought we would make one film about the phenomenon of rebel music internationally. We were all grooving to world music beats, Manu Chao was playing over the loudspeakers in local restaurants in Montréal, and Tiken Ja Fakoly of Ivory Coast, Gilberto Gil from Brazil, and Femi Kuti from Nigeria were headliners at the Montréal International Jazz Festival. We, like many others, saw this as a sign of openness to new influences, to the new wave of political music, and of resistance to the American cultural steamroller.

At our production company, Productions Multi-Monde, Hind Benchekroun and Marie Boti formulated the original idea for the film and drafted project proposals. As research progressed, however, we realized it was an impossible task for a single documentary—there were too many diverse realities, contexts, and artists to choose from. We also saw that world music itself was being commercialized and mainstreamed. We wanted to show the music in the context that gave rise to it, the people and the local movements that inspired it, rather than as a disembodied sound that was becoming homogenized for mass audiences in the name of powerful forces of commercialization.

We decided it would take a series of films even to begin to do the subject justice. We envisaged it being organized broadly by continent—the Americas, Africa, Asia, Europe. Getting the financing for such a thing, though, was far from easy. In 1999-2000 the film community was under a rigid régime of "Canadian-content" regulations that virtually blocked funding for any documentary films shot abroad. Canadian filmmakers had to make films only about Canada or Canadians, or be cut off from the principal public funding sources. The absurdity of the policy and campaigning by the independent film and artistic community finally encouraged the Canadian Television Fund and Telefilm Canada recently to revise the policy.

Another obstacle was the music/political documentary concept. When our associate Lucie Pageau approached arts channels for a broadcast license,[3] they told her the artists were not high-profile enough and, at any rate, they did documentaries on art, *not* politics. They sent us to documentary programmers, who in turn insisted this musical concept was fare for the arts or music channels. MusiquePlus (MuchMusic), while keen about the concept, had no money to put into it (in fact they do not pay for virtually anything they broadcast). Generally when we have spent a couple of years trying to get a project going unsuccessfully, we either set it aside, try to modify the concept, or go ahead and do it anyway, guerilla-style. We didn't want to drop the concept, but couldn't really shoot around the world without a budget, so we decided to look closer to home.

With the anti-globalization movement converging in Québec City for the Summit of the Americas, we saw a unique opportunity to look at what political artists were doing in Québec. We quickly wrote up a concept for that film, *Musiques Rebelles Québec,* and Télé-Québec, the Québec public broadcaster with a good track record for supporting documentary work, decided to give us a license. This meant we could approach other funding institutions to complete the (modest) budget. The delays being what they are, we only got Télé-Québec's answer at the end of February 2001; even if we were successful in every other stage of applications, no funding would be in place until the fall. And meanwhile, the summit, a key event in our project proposal, was happening in April 2001.

We had no choice but to go the guerilla route, and hope the money would come in later. The script was written by Hind Benchekroun and Marie Boti. Marie assumed the role of director and Lucie Pageau took on the responsibilities of producer. We were lucky to enlist the collaboration of a great team of cinematographers, sound recordists, assistants, editors, and numerous trainees (see film end credits). The shoots were often action-packed, in the middle of protests, occupations, or benefit shows. We spent hours backstage with crowds pumped up on music and politics. We even managed to go on a weekend tour to the Gaspé with one group, and followed another on their first trip together to Paris—a definite high point of the filming.

Musiques Rebelles Québec was completed, launched, and broadcast in September 2002. It had been funded as a one-off, not as part of a series. So we had to start new proposals and funding applications to continue the project. The second film, *Musiques Rebelles Americas,* which we developed while producing the first film, was again supported by Télé-Québec, and is currently (2003) in production. We will be filming in Mexico, Colombia, Argentina, and Brazil. *Musiques Rebelles Afrique* is in development, with the others, we hope, to follow.

Choice of Artists

Celebrating a resurgence of rebel music and movements within a set documentary film format meant making choices in terms of artists and the issues with which their music engaged. The criteria for choosing the musicians we would feature were discussed at length by all members of our creative team. There were tough choices. For the first documentary, we had a 52-minute length to respect. Moreover, we wanted to avoid a voice-over and didactic approach, and bank on the real strength of a documentary, the emotional, affective impact.

We chose artists with different musical styles, from diverse political, social, and musical traditions. Their ideologies did not necessarily coincide with ours (some of us at Multi-Monde are from the communist tradition), but there was mutual respect between us and the artists. Consistent with our initial intention, we considered artists first and foremost for their resonance with the growing social discontent we were witnessing *vis-à-vis* the processes and consequences of imperialist-capitalist-driven globalization. As documentary filmmakers involved in anti-capitalist and anti-imperialist struggles ourselves, we wanted artists who were cause-oriented in word, but also in practice, artists who were not afraid to call themselves "rebel" and who were identified with a cause.

Musiques Rebelles Québec

Musiques Rebelles Québec features Loco Locass, Norman Nawrocki, Acalanto and Landriault. These musicians are not the classic troubadours with a guitar—they push musical barriers from the rap ska of Loco Locass, the intense black-flag rock of Landriault, the Latin American experimental folk of Acalanto, and the multilingual-cabaret and Slovakian klezmer beat of Nawrocki's Rhythm Activism. Besides providing our film with musically—and cinematographically—rich performances, these were all artists who shared a vision of rebel music being at the heart of today's global movements for change.

Significant in our decision-making process was the fact that these individuals also shared a commitment to denouncing the anti-democratic and poverty-increasing effects of capitalist globalization. The planning of *Musiques Rebelles Québec* was inspired and organized, as we've already indicated, around what was an upcoming major anti-globalization action: the April 2001 Summit of the Americas protests in Québec City. The Summit was historic in its mobilization of tens of thousands of globalization's opponents, and it provided the perfect opportunity to show what being "rebel" means and looks like in Québec today. Seeking to document the connection between rebel music and rebel action for social change, we wanted artists who would be on the front lines of this confrontation.[4]

Musiques Rebelles Québec documents a shift away from the culture of protest 25 years ago, inspired predominantly by Québécois national aspirations. For many years, the "chansonniers" had carried the vision of a brighter future where the people of Québec could stand proud. Today, the flag of rebel music in *la Belle Province* is no longer just white and blue—it is more multi-hued. No longer motivated solely by the national question, the musicians constituting the rebel scene in Québec, while opposing national oppression, hold varied views on the question of Québec independence; they work with social and political movements that oppose globalization, racism, homophobia, and the capitalist system itself.

Landriault

L'anarchie c'est un cri
Un poids dans la poitrine
Un combat contre la guillotine

Et ce combat perdure

Comme un ciel qui flamboie

Dans l'espoir que l'anarchie vaincra

(Excerpt from Landriault's "La liberté ou la mort")

Anarchy is a shout

A weight in the gut

A battle against the guillotine

And this battle endures

Like a sky that blazes

In the hope that anarchy will triumph.

(Our translation)

Wrapped in his black flag, with his raw and provocative hard-rock sound, Landriault calls himself Québec's Number 1 rebel artist. And with reason: he can be found at most radical demonstrations and actions, be it alongside the students and youth surrounding the Québec Parliament during the Youth Summit, or with punks and squeegees denouncing police brutality, poverty, and racism. He blares out "La liberté ou la mort," and all the demonstrators chant the refrains, not surprising since the CD by that name was fifth on the pop charts in Quebéc City and was displayed in record stores beside, astonishingly, Celine Dion's!

When we went to meet Landriault for the first time, he did not fit our preconceived image. He is an imposing man in his fifties with a mane of long gray hair, larger than life. Articulate and provocative, Landriault makes full use of his verbal skills in his songs and on his weekly community radio program. He calls himself an anarchist, as do many of the youth activists in Québec today. Their visible presence in the anti-globalization movement made Landriault and his politics an obvious choice.

Loco Locass

La monarchie des marchands

Je ne marche plus là-dedans

Je refuse obstinément que le globe me gobe globalement

Fuck le périmètre de sécurité

Je ne suis pas d'accord avec l'Accord Multilatéral d'Investissement

Qui traite l'art comme du lard

Et la culture comme l'agriculture

Avec un pareil AMI pas besoin d'ennemi

Toutes les Nations Unies lui déroulent le tapis

(Excerpt from Loco Locass' "L'empire du Pire en Pire")

The monarchy of merchants
I no longer walk within
I refuse obstinately that the globe swallow me globally
Fuck the Security Perimeter
I do not agree with the Multilateral Agreement on Investment
Which treats art like lard
And culture like agriculture
With the likes of these MAI friends no need for enemies
As the United Nations unfolds the red carpet for it.
(Our translation)

Amongst Québec's rap groups, Loco Locass is one of the most popular and socially engaged. Composed of three young rappers, Biz, Batlam and Chafiik, Loco Locass invaded the Montréal scene in the mid 1990s. Since that time they have won numerous awards and a reputation for their loquacious word games and sharp political commentaries. Loco Locass takes great pleasure in drowning their public in an orgy of word-plays, some historic and academic, and others just crazy, attacking everything from the silliness of the mass media to the rioters of Saint-Jean-Baptiste[5] to American imperialism.

The first time Marie Boti and Hind Bechekroun went to meet the group, Batlam greeted Hind like a long-lost sister. It turned out that Batlam, who is also a stage actor, stayed with Hind's family during a trip to Morocco with a theatre group in the early 1990s. The bond was immediate.

Loco Locass' Chaf during shooting of Musiques Rebelles Québec 2001

While Loco Locass engages politically with issues that are global, the group situates itself within the Québec tradition of nationalist and rebel poets like Gaston Miron and Claude Gavrau. Their festive French compositions, as they explained to us, aim at providing audiences with a bridge to collective memory.

> *Nerfs d'une guerre langagière*
> *Que l'on mène avec front et fiers*
> *Aux frontières d'hier et d'aujourd'hui en pensant a demain*
> (Excerpt from Loco Locass' "Langages-toi")

> *With nerves from a linguistic war*
> *That we lead head-on and proud*
> *To the frontiers of yesterday and today while thinking about tomorrow*
> (Our translation)

We were very happy Loco Locass agreed to take part, because while their cause is very much about Québécois independence and the defense of the French language, these young musicians use rap as a tool for consciousness-raising: "Today, no one would listen to us if we recited poetry—that's why we chose rap," says Biz.

Acalanto

Marie Boti first heard Carmen Pavez at a solidarity evening for the Dominican people. Alone on the stage, Carmen had spontaneously agreed to sing, and Marie was unprepared for the emotions she provoked: "My throat tightened, tears rolled down my cheeks as I listened to this deep voice, words sung with such conviction and intelligence. I looked over at my Ecuadorian friend: she too was crying. We exchanged broad smiles of complicity and pleasure," remembers Marie.

Acalanto's Carmen Pavez at the April 2001 Québec Summit of the Americas

Acalanto consists of four members of a Chilean family and a Québécois friend: Carmen Pavez, Dominique Azocar, Renato Pavez, Rafael Azocar, and Norman Raymond. Carmen, Renato, and Rafael grew up in Chile during a tumultuous political era. Their family was involved in the social movement that brought Salvador Allende to power and they preserve the socialist ideals he stood for. The group is committed to preserving the spirit and contributing to the development of Latin American music in Québec. They sing in Spanish as part of their struggle to resist the cultural hegemonies of North America. Aside from their own compositions, Acalanto draws on the repertoire of Latin American music and poetry of resistance, including Victor Jara, Violeta Parra, and Pablo Neruda. With reference to Neruda's *Canto General*, an epic work of poetry in the mode of populist history, Carmen explains: "For us, the *Canto General* is the 'obstinate' voice in the liberatory project of all the peoples of the Americas for 500 years. Enveloping Neruda's verse with our music is our way of combating indifference and sweeping away the obstacles to our long-awaited freedom." Latin American rebel music, in the context of Acalanto's performance practices, is an integral part of the 500-year-old resistance to colonialism, capitalism, and imperialism. Furthermore, the Latin community is one of the most vibrant cultural communities in Québec, and many of its members, like Carmen, Renato, and Rafael, came to Canada as political refugees. We felt it was important to acknowledge this influence in Québec's rebel music movement.

Acalanto regularly lends its voice to social causes, from performing at fundraising events for struggles in Latin America to supporting immigrant workers or progressive movements in Québec. Through their cross-cultural music, Acalanto has found a way to contribute to the weaving of solidarities between causes and continents.

Norman Nawrocki and Rhythm Activism

Why am I an anarchist?
Parce que...
Parce que old age pensioners eat dogfood,
Because single moms on welfare cry,
Because politicians steal our future,
Cuz women can`t walk the street safely,
Cuz I wanna breathe fresh clean air,
Because hope, freedom & dignity are never on special at Wal-Mart,
Because one day—me, all of us—will dance on the grave of capitalism.
(Excerpt from Nawrocki's "Why am I an anarchist?")

We first met Norman Nawrocki at an evening we organized to welcome visiting Filipino popular theatre artists. Norman recited a poem that transported us to the steps of Manila's presidential palace, a spot called Mendiola, where a plastic sandal lay. On that day, peasant farmers had traveled to the capital to ask the government to respect its promise of land reform. The army answered them with bullets and twelve unarmed farmers were shot. Although Norman had never been to the Philippines, he had written his monologue from a scattering of newspaper articles, seizing upon the fundamental injustices at the heart of this massacre.

Our first collaboration with Norman was in 1991, when he composed the title track for "Brown Woman, Blond Babies," a documentary about Filipino domestic workers (1992, directors: Marie Boti and Florchita Bautista). Rhythm Activism, the group he formed with Sylvain Côté, has sung about a wide range of political and social issues, including the Zapatista struggle in Mexico, police brutality, native demands, and abortion rights, among others–like their borderless music which moves in and out of punk, rock, Eastern European klezmer, gospel, and jazz influences. Nawrocki is on the front lines at squat stand-offs and anti-globalization demos, but he also performs his cabaret act at poetry festivals, community centers, and night clubs.

At Multi-Monde, we were fans of Nawrocki's calls to 'rebel' action through cutting political satire. Rhythm Activism is unique because of its inspiration from burlesque cabaret. This political art form was developed before the Second World War as a means of resistance to growing fascism. Nawrocki and Rhythm Activism have performed their political participatory theatre in Montréal's low-income neighborhoods, where their shows have made them folk heroes. For Nawrocki, the burlesque, as provocation, is social action. Similarly, social criticism can be most effective when humour is present, and change promoted effectively through entertainment. Nawrocki explains:

> Of course, you have to take to the streets to change the world, but you have to do it with a smile. What can be more boring than endlessly chanting "solidarity forever"? We want to dance to the revolution.

In many ways these artists selected themselves because they represent the vibrant face of a new Québec—colorful, politically diverse, and open to the world. These articulate individuals were speaking and singing for a generation of Québécois, putting into words and music the concerns of a generation of young (and not so young) people tired of hearing about the benefits of the neoliberal agenda.

Musiques Rebelles Americas

For Musiques Rebelles Americas, we wanted a view from the south of the Americas—popular, rebellious, creative, and more often than not, "anti-American." We wanted to sketch a portrait of continental resistance that would spark reflection about North-South relations and about the populations in the South as key agents of change in a world that marginalizes most of humanity. In parallel, we sought to provoke dialogue on the role of the artist, so essential to these winds of change. This second film, then, was developed based on our experience gained in the first. And yet it differed in two important respects. For one, we had a whole continent to cover, and a multitude of rebel musicians with centuries-long traditions of singing resistance. Secondly, whereas in Québec we had largely selected musicians based on our overlapping solidarity networks with them, in Latin America we could not rely on our first-hand knowledge of the musicians' engagement. For these reasons, the challenge was considerable and the process longer.

The sociopolitical situation of Latin America is complex and its resistance movements multiple. After much discussion and research, we narrowed down our options by deciding to focus on major social and political realities shaping the Americas today. Among these were the issues of land ownership, forced displacement and the impact of war, the economic crisis, and the border between the North and the South. Following this initial decision, we selected countries we thought would be key in contextualizing resistance to these Latin American realities. In Brazil, the MST (Movimento dos Trabalhadores Rurais Sim Terras or Landless Peasants' Movement) was a legendary force for agricultural reform in a country where land ownership was at its most blatantly unequal—less than one per cent of the Brazilian population controls almost half of cultivatable land. Combined with its harboring of the largest population in the Americas and a fascinating musical history informed by various diasporic influences, Brazil became a certain choice.

Meanwhile, Argentina, once the poster child of the World Bank and International Monetary Fund policies, had just collapsed after one of the most severe economic crises in the history of the Americas. The country has emerged as the site of a powerful mass movement that managed to topple four governments in one month (December 2001), and seemed an obvious choice to address disillusion with neoliberal agendas and policies widespread in the region.

In Colombia, almost 2 million people are internal refugees. Following decades of internal strife that has just intensified due to the most expensive foreign-controlled military operation in the Americas—the so-called Plan Colombia—peasants' displacement was reaching new crisis levels. While peasant displacement is unfortunately pervasive in many Latin American nations, we chose Colombia because of the strong revolutionary movement there and the huge U.S. offensive underway to crush it, including the persistent threat of a U.S. invasion.

Finally, Mexico, physical neighbor to the United States, yet weaker and dependent, seemed to symbolize the enormous contradictions between North and South. With Mexico, we saw the opportunity to underline this inequality through the tangible Mexico-U.S. borderlands. Here, thousands of individuals risk their lives in the hopes of building a Disneyfied future for themselves and their families, more often than not getting stuck instead in the capitalist present. Further, the rich and varied musical traditions in Mexico—in which, for example, *corrido* form comments on local culture, and indigenous musical practices are interwoven with social critique—struck us as important aspects of the kinds of rebel and regional traditions we wanted to represent in the film.

Having made a preliminary decision as to themes and national contexts that would most effectively articulate some key motives for resistance throughout the Americas, we then considered artists whose lyrics and lives were engaged in these four realities.

Anibal, Santa Revuelta: Argentina on the Edge

Piquetero, piquetero
Asi me dicen yo soy
Si no hay pan y no hay trabajo
De la ruta no me voy
Piqueteras, piqueteros
Hemos venido a pelear
Patria te han tira'o al basurero
Y te tenemos que sacar
(Excerpt from Santa Revuelta's "Soy Piquetero")

Picketer, picketer
That's what they tell me I am
If there is no food and no work
I will not leave this road
Picketers, picketers
We came to fight
Country, they've thrown you in the garbage
And we have to get you out
(Our translation)

Anibal, from the group Santa Revuelta (literaly, Holy Revolt!), met us at the airport on our first research trip to Buenos Aires, and we knew immediately we had hit paydirt. He was a bundle of energy, knew everybody worth knowing in the left political movement in town, had studied to be an economist, loved the camera, and even spoke a little French. Anibal, and his guitarist friend Charly, proceeded to take us on a two-week whirlwind tour of picket lines, strikes, demonstrations, and meetings. At virtually every site they would pull out their rudimentary equipment, often asking someone to clamber up the nearest lamp post to provide electricity, and soon have the crowd of tired picketers up dancing, laughing, and cheering.

On other occasions they would arrive at the demonstration early in Anibal's beaten up car (borrowed from his father), help set up the stage, loudspeakers, and microphones for the day's events, pass the hat to help pay for their work, and before the day was out, perform for the crowd with an energy that defies description. In the context of a continental economic crisis that has been particularly brutal in Argentina, the songs of Santa Revuelta have become slogans—almost hymns—embraced in the mobilization of workers and the recently unemployed alike.

Blending hope, humour, and scathing political critique, the songs of Santa Revuelta and the daily struggles for subsistence of its members invite a personal understanding of what it is to live in a country where the economy has collapsed following decades of neoliberal policies and dependence on international monetary bodies.

Oyeme Chocó and the Struggle of the Displaced

Unidos como hermanos

Retornaremos

A esa tierra querida

A esa tierra natal

La tierra en que nuestros padres nos enseñaron a jugar

(Excerpt from "Oyeme Chocó" on the Oyeme Chocó CD)

United as brothers

We will return

To that loved land

To that native land

The land in which our parents taught us to play

(Our translation)

On the edge of the Cacarica river, at the heart of the Colombian jungle, the CAVIDA (Communities for Auto-determination, Life, and Dignity) occupy what they call "a territory of life." This is Chocó, one of the poorest regions of Colombia. Here, between the 24th and 28th of February 1997, the 500 families inhabiting the 23 hamlets of the region were forced to flee the murders and terror caused by paramilitary groups in the region. Leaving their homes, they thus contributed to the two million internal refugees displaced in Colombia. In 1998, with the help of fellow Colombians and the international community, these Afro-Colombians had defied death and dared to return to their homes and their land. To recount their story in song, they wrote and recorded a CD, *Oyeme Chocó*.

Le vengo a contar una historia

De nuestro desplazamiento

Como se sucedió, Es tanto en El Chocó

Es una cosa muy dura

Para qu'el mundo lo acepte

Nos sacaron a fuerza

Con bombas y metralletas

I'm coming to tell you a story

about our displacement

the way it happened, so often in El Chocó

It's a very hard thing

for the world to accept

they threw us out by force ·

with bombs and machine guns

(Our translation)

We heard about the CAVIDA in Montréal through Colombian friends. Listening to the CD dedicated to their land, we knew we wanted to visit this community where music was a tool of resistance that emerged from the constant threat to a way of life. This was rebel music at its most fundamental: peasants singing for their brothers and sisters and thus recording a history counter to "official" narratives, providing strength and courage, channeling sadness and anger, offering hope.

To reach the village we would have to travel by plane, taxi, boat, canoe, and foot through mosquito-infested jungle, with the paramilitary forces liable to turn up at any moment. But it was worth it: despite the obvious difficulties and fears of further attacks and possible displacements, music saturated the entire community, from the youngest child to the village elders. And everyone knew the lyrics, whether they were the *vallenato* songs of the elders, or the rap of the youth, because they told the story of their lives.

Music at the heart of the Cacarica, Columbia
Some of our friends from CAVIDA

Yo tengo una tierra
Una tierra allá
¿Cuál es esa tierra?
Es la tierra natal
¿Y dónde está esa tierra?
Está en El Chocó
¿Y dónde está El Chocó?
Donde estamos desplazados

I have a land
A country over there
And what is this land?
It is the native land
And where is this land?
It is in El Chocó
And where is El Chocó?
Whence we have been displaced
(Our translation)

The songs we heard in El Chocó bear witness to over 70 assassinations within the community, denounce the illegal exploitation of their lands, and demand that the guilty be punished in the name of justice, fraternity, life, and dignity. They are not afraid to name and expose the ploy of the government using the war on the guerillas to drive them off their land:

En el gobierno la gente
no deja trabajar
Al pueblo campesino

Nos sacan de nuestra tierra
Porque hay una guerilla
Eso todo hacen
Para quedarse con ella
Esta bonita tierra

The people in the government
Don`t let the peasants work
They kick us off our land
Because there is a guerilla
This they do
To take possession of her,
This beautiful land.
(Our translation)

Chico and the MST

We met Afro-Brazilian pop star Chico César in Montréal when he came to perform in 2001. We remember our friends, Gavin Andrews and Luciana Capiberibe, had gotten married that same day. Chico knew Luciana's family since her father was Governor of the state of Amapá in the northern tip of Brazil and her mother was also an active member of the state government—among the most forward-thinking administrations in Brazil at the time. They had implemented a far-reaching program of sustainable development in the Amazon, giving land titles to the indigenous groups there and transferring funds to them for health and education.

Chico put on a great show at the wonderful Montréal club, Kola Note, and we were all up dancing and sweating up a storm to "Mama Africa" and other songs. Chico then asked the band members to leave him alone on stage, picked up his acoustic guitar, and called Gavin and Luciana up to join him. As they shared a celebratory wedding dance behind him, Chico sang his heart out, tears streaming down his face.

Quando me chamou eu vim
Quando dei por mim tava aqui
Quando lhe achei me perdi
Quando vi você me apaixonei
(Extract from "Primera Vista")

When she called, I came
When I came to myself, I was here
When I found you, I lost myself
When I saw you, I fell in love.
(Translation of excerpt from "On First Sight")

It was a magical moment, and if we had had any doubts before, our choice was made for us. Besides, Chico was known as a supporter of the huge Brazilian peasant movement, the MST (Movimento dos Trabalhadores Rurais Sim Terras or Landless Peasants' Movement), and the chance to combine such a great musician with a crucial theme in the Americas—landlessness and the control of land—made the decision obvious.

The MST is the largest social movement in the Americas. Denouncing hunger, homelessness, and massive discrepancies in wealth, their mandate resonates with the experience of an entire continent. Since its establishment in 1984, the MST (affiliated with the international peasants' solidarity network Via Campesina) has won land titles for 250 thousand families and inspired resistance amongst thousands more.

Mama Africa
Mama Africa (a minha mae)
E mae solteira
E tem de fazer mamadiera todo dia
Alem de travalhar como empacotadeira

Mama Africa (my mother)
Is a single mother
And she has to prepare
Baby's bottles every day
Besides working
As a packer in Casas Bahia[6]
(Excerpt from Chico César's "Mama Africa")

Chico César is the symbol of success over huge odds, the son of a poor black family in the country's poorest area, the Nordeste—a land where slavery is not uncommon and half the population migrates to urban areas to work as cheap labourers. César takes pride in his roots and his songs are peppered with references to the Nordeste, his home state of Paraiba and to the *retirantes* or migrants. His two hugely popular video clips were both filmed in the Nordeste, one in his parents' village, and another at a land occupation site of the MST.

In a country where hundreds of words exist to distinguish between shades of blackness and corresponding social status, Chico César sings for respect for Mama Africa and his own black curls. Whether referring to social, racial, or political inequalities, Chico stresses the importance of tolerance and respect for difference.

Respeitem meus cabelos, brancos
Se eu quero pixaim, deixa
Se eu quero enrolar, deixa
Se eu quero colorir, deixa

Se eu quero assanhar, deixa

Deixa, deixa a madeixa balançar

Respect My Hair, You Whites

If I want to have kinky hair, so what?

If I want to twist it, so what?

If I want to dye it, so what?

If I want to frizz it up, so what?

Just let my locks swing.

(Translation from web site. Extract from "Respeitem meus cabelos, brancos" from the album by the same name)

As we finished this essay, we attended Chico's performance at an outdoor concert in Sao Paolo, Brazil, organized by Lula's ruling workers' party and against the ongoing war in Iraq. Interrupting his funky mix of Afro-pop, reggae, jazz, forro (dance music from the Nordeste) and Caribbean rhythms, Chico made a strong declaration against the unjust Anglo-American invasion and U.S. imperialism. This was our rebel musician: lighthearted and extravagant in multi-colored clothes. At a moment's notice he could turn in all seriousness to an adoring crowd and rally enthusiasm for the transformation of national and global societies.

Chico is a pop star, as the swarm of fans after each concert testified, a key figure of Musica Popular Brazileira (MPB), the eclectic popular music movement indigenous to this country. It is the rhythms, wordplays, and poetry of his songs that seduce the listener, and when they are charmed by these, Chico introduces more explicit political content in between songs, and at the benefits where he sings. But interestingly, he is not known mainly as a political singer. This may be due to much of his songs' political content being linked to a valorization of blackness: for those who do not acknowledge racism as a problem in Brazil, the theme of negritude is not necessarily perceived as political.

Lila Downs at the Border

On a darkened stage, Lila Downs is on her knees, as in prayer. Only her black braids and red-lipped face are visible. She wears a *huipil*, the woven dress of the Mixtec Indians, her maternal ancestors. Her presence is hypnotizing, her voice rich with emotion: invoking aboriginal myths, she sings of the coyote (people smuggler), NAFTA, the *maquiladoras* in a song dedicated to all women workers:

Ay long black hair, sad little face, Rosa Maria

every day and every night you look for a way out

for your happiness, only Sundays liberate you from

this hell

the 'maquiladora' will someday be only a memory
and the crop will be your own fruit one day
and there will be justice for the 'desaparecida'
(Lila Down's "The Girl," dedicated to all women workers)

The Mexico-U.S. borderlands are a site of tension where despair and hope, massive profit and total destitution co-exist. The creative team at Multi-Monde wanted to address the boundary between the Americas because of its importance as a real and imagined destination for so many in the Americas. Lila Downs was an obvious choice for this section. Her latest CD *Border/La Línea* is dedicated to those who lost their lives trying to cross into the United States. Her songs are inspired by life around the border: its workers, their dreams, daily challenges, and also the brutal racism experienced by indigenous people as in "Smoke," her account of the Acteal massacre. On December 22, 1997, forty-five indigenous peoples were massacred in the municipality of Chenalho, Chiapas. These women, children, and men had been displaced from their homes by paramilitary violence and were taking refuge in the community of Acteal when the paramilitary group, Paz y Justicia (Peace and Justice), known for its links with wealthy landowners in the area and financing from the then-ruling PRI party of Chiapas, attacked. In the song, Lila's plaintive, child-like voice asks:

How dark is the smoke that falls from the sky
And soaked in our blood are the feathers of time
our women and children were killed on that night
More than they could count when they threw them in trucks.

In this song, exceptionally, she sings in English. And she uses the indigenous mythology that permeates her songs to give a voice to those demanding justice:

But the eagle and the snake will stand for the truth
When the mother of corn has spoken
Oh axe of our fire bring justice to life
For we know that power was once sacrifice
Was once sacrifice
Of our people.

The album *Border/La Línea* resulted from a translation a neighbour asked her to do from English into Mixtec. The letter from American immigration authorities informed this neighbour of his son's death while crossing the border, an experience Lila refers to as being an "oracle of death" and one that propelled her work on the CD as a testimony to the plight of migrants. Lila's own experience is one of line crossings: born of a Mixtec Indian mother and a father from Minnesota, Lila grew up straddling the border. This cross-cultural existence is reflected in her music. Blending pre-Colombian instrumentation with traditional Mexican sounds (such as those used by the *mariachis* or the *norteños*) and a touch of hip-hop, jazz and gospel, she sings in Spanish, English, Nahuatl, Zapotec,

Lila, mother, and crew

and Mixtec. With her dramatic voice, powerful stage presence, and unique compositions, Lila is on the edge of a major international career. She recently appeared on the Oscars, alongside Brazilian headliner Caetano Veloso, singing the title song from the feature film *Frida*.

We visited Lila for the first time at her home in Oaxaca in January 2003. Following Lila's invitation, on our second morning we headed out to visit nearby San Juan. The town we entered looked relatively prosperous, with brick houses and several paved roads. However, there was an eerie silence. Lila explained that the town had been emptied, like many in the state of Oaxaca, as indigenous Mexicans headed for El Norte, hoping to send back money to keep those that remained behind in relative comfort. "The border is right here in Oaxaca," Lila continued. "There is no need to travel to Tijuana or Juárez to see the impact of the massive migration of our people. Hanging on to our culture and heritage, especially as Indios, is a challenge. But that is why we say that our umbilical cord is buried in Mexico, and we all come back one way or another."

Closing Thoughts

The selection of artists in *Musiques Rebelles Americas* was based on quite a different process than in the case of its Québécois predecessor. Whereas for *Musiques Rebelles Québec*, we drew on our experience in Montréal solidarity actions to select politically engaged artists, for *Musiques Rebelles Americas* the selection of artists felt more deliberately political. While months remain before this film is released, our hope is that these musicians' empowering songs and commitment to change will paint a portrait that works against prevalent Western expectations of Latin America and the Southern hemisphere in general as *post*-revolutionary, victim, and voiceless.

The *Musiques Rebelles* series aims to attest to a new wave of awareness in the world, a collective knowledge that imperialism and the inequalities it engenders have to be fought at all levels in all countries. The potential for this series is that it will generate hope and discussion about possibilities for real social change, while celebrating artists and individuals who commit their careers to a popular dream of social justice. Of course, while our intention is for the series to be widely distributed and screened in a variety of venues ranging from CEGEPs (pre-university colleges in Québec) and high schools to festivals and community organizations, distribution remains a challenge in a context where distribution costs generally outweigh available resources.

Despite the expected challenges of making a film for broadcast about issues that are so close to our lives and hopes, there is no question that the process has been extremely rewarding for all at Multi-Monde. In fact, this has been so much the case that plans are currently underway for a rebel music film on the situation in the Middle East and Iraq, and are well advanced for *Musiques Rebelles Africa*, with singers already contacted in Senegal, Ivory Coast, and Zimbabwe. Meanwhile we are pursuing the Americas project. We will be returning to Argentina and Santa Revuelta in summer 2003 to learn more about the situation there, while we are anxiously alert to the potentially dangerous situation of our friends who dared return home to Chocó.

Working within the framework of a series about "rebel music," we are constantly faced with questioning what "rebel" means, whether our expectations of the term can encompass all cultural experiences, and how defining the actions associated with this label may change over the course of an artist's career. Making *Musiques Rebelles Americas*, we have been faced with some interesting contradictions: while Chico celebrates Brazil's black culture, all the musicians in his group are white, and in March 2003 Lila Downs sang at the Academy Awards at a time when the United States is waging what most of the world considers an unjust war. Even if you are the first Mexican to have been invited to sing at this event, can you still be a rebel and sing at the Academy Awards? As we continue the work of this series, these and other questions present themselves as reminders of the rebellious cultural power embedded in music making and its social contexts—and, as well, of those forces that seek to mediate, manage, and constrain the critical force of music as a means to achieving social justice.

NOTES

1. Our concept for a series of documentaries about political music and resistance movements around the world began in 1999. With filming of the second of the documentaries currently underway, this essay describes the premises we set out with, the artists we chose, and some of the anecdotes relating to our experiences as we filmed.

2. The Multi-Monde creative team includes: Marie Boti, Malcolm Guy, Lucie Pageau, Hind Benchekroun, Michelle Smith, Sophie Morisset, Roberto Nieto and Elysée Nouvet.

3. A license grants the television network the right to broadcast the film over a fixed period of time in exchange for a fee, which in turn triggers access to film financing from other institutions like Tele-film.

4. For another documentary on the Québec Summit see the National Film Board of Canada's *View from the Summit*, directed by Magnus Isacsson and Paul Lapointe.

5. The Québec national holiday, June 24th.

6. A popular department store in Brazil.

Jesse Stewart

3 / Freedom Music: Jazz and Human Rights

In his introduction to *Living With Music: Ralph Ellison's Jazz Writings*,
Robert O'Meally describes a 1973 encounter between himself and
Ellison who, in addition to penning the classic American novel
Invisible Man, wrote extensively (and astutely) on jazz. " 'Don't you
think the Harlem Renaissance failed because we failed to create
institutions to preserve our gains?' " asks O'Meally. " 'No,' " replies
Ellison. " 'We *do* have institutions...We have the Constitution and the
Bill of Rights. *And we have jazz*' " (xi, emphasis in original).

JESSE STEWART is a percussionist,
composer, instrument builder, and
writer. He has performed with many
internationally acclaimed musicians
including jazz legends Roswell Rudd
and George Lewis as well as Carlo
Actis Dato, Gerry Hemingway, and
many others. In addition to
performing regularly as a soloist, he
is currently a member of the David
Mott Quintet.

For me, this exchange raises a number of questions: How is
jazz an institution? How can jazz preserve civil liberties?
How does it relate to the Constitution and the Bill of Rights,
the foundational documents of American democracy, and
how is this relationship complicated when jazz is played
in—and across—cultural contexts that lie beyond the borders of the United States? These questions provide a resonant point of entry for the present essay in which I'd like to
explore the complex and changing historical relationship
between jazz and human rights. Specifically, I'd like to ask
where the qualifier "free" comes from in relation to jazz,
and to examine some of the ways in which the idea of freedom has been conceptualized and articulated through jazz
performance.

Most music scholars trace the beginnings of the music
that would come to be called jazz to the American South
in the decade prior to the turn of the twentieth century. I
would like to suggest that an earlier event in American history may have contributed significantly to the music's gen-
esis at that particular time and place in American history—

the Emancipation Proclamation. Effective January 1, 1863, two years into the American Civil War, the Emancipation Proclamation declared the freedom of all slaves living in the southern rebellious states. In response to the ensuing push by African Americans for the enactment of laws protecting this promise of freedom, the Thirteenth Amendment to the United States Constitution abolished "slavery and involuntary servitude" throughout the country on December 6, 1865. This means that the first generation of African Americans born outside of slavery reached adulthood around the time cornetist Buddy Bolden and others were reportedly combining blues and marching music in New Orleans, in what has generally come to be regarded as the initial manifestations of jazz. It seems reasonable to assume that there would be a different collective mindset amongst a generation of individuals who did not grow up with the knowledge that they were regarded, both legally and in the eyes of their oppressors, as property. Moreover, it seems likely that this new collective mindset may have played a crucial role in the proliferation of new cultural forms, including jazz, in the 1890s.[1]

The hardships endured by African Americans in the southern United States certainly didn't disappear in 1863 with the legal abolishment of slavery. Indeed, it has been amply documented that sharecropping, which quickly replaced slavery in the aftermath of the Emancipation was, in many ways, slavery under a new name. The period after the Emancipation also saw the implementation of repressive segregation measures in the American South, not to mention the rise of white supremacist groups such as the Ku Klux Klan. In short, human rights abuses continued to be the norm rather than the exception in the decades following the Emancipation. There were, however, some reasons for hope. In his groundbreaking book *Blues People,* LeRoi Jones (now Amiri Baraka) explains: "However ineffectual Emancipation might have proven in its entirety, it did have a great deal of positive effect on the Negro...[T]he Reconstruction did give the Negro a certain feeling of autonomy and self-reliance that could never be fully eradicated even after the repressive segregation measures that followed..." (52). Baraka makes the case that this new feeling of autonomy played a crucial role in the development of blues. He writes:

> The emancipation of the slaves proposed for them a normal human existence, a humanity impossible under slavery. Of course, even after slavery the average Negro's life in America was, using the more ebullient standards of the average American white man, a shabby, barren existence. But still this was the black man's first experience of time when he could be alone. The leisure that could be extracted from even the most desolate sharecropper's shack in Mississippi was a novelty, and it served as an important catalyst for the next form blues took. (61)

I would argue that the new feeling of autonomy and freedom described by Baraka (an emergent index of the civil rights battles to be fought over the next century) was an important catalyst for the development of jazz also, itself having developed to a significant extent out of blues and its various antecedents. I would further argue that in many of its most trenchant historical examples, jazz has continued to both reflect and articulate a search for freedom within changing sets of social and musical constraints.

Framing the history of jazz in this way is not a particularly original idea. Indeed, in the introductory chapter of *The Freedom Principle: Jazz After 1958*, John Litweiler writes:

> The quest for freedom…appears at the very beginning of jazz and reappears at every growing point in the music's history. The earliest jazz musicians asserted their independence of melody, structure, rhythm, and expression from the turn-of-the-century musics that surrounded them; Louis Armstrong symbolized the liberation of the late twenties jazz soloist; the Count Basie band offered liberation of jazz rhythm; and Parker and Gillespie offered yet more new freedoms to jazz. (13-14)

Soprano saxophonist Steve Lacy has made a similar suggestion:

> I think that jazz, from the time it first began, was always concerned with degrees of freedom. The way Louis Armstrong played was 'more free' than earlier players. Roy Eldridge was 'more free' than his predecessors, Dizzy Gillespie was another stage and [Don] Cherry was another. And you have to keep it going otherwise you lose that freedom. And then the music is finished. It's a matter of life and death. The only criterion is: 'Is this stuff alive or is it dead?' (quoted in Bailey 55-6)

A number of musicians and writers have drawn connections between jazz and broader struggles for freedom and social justice as well. As early as 1919, an editorial entitled "Jazzing Away Prejudice" appeared in the *Chicago Defender*, one of the most important African American newspapers of the time. In response to a jazz concert by James Reese Europe and his band, the anonymous writer remarks:

> The most prejudiced enemy of our Race could not sit through an evening with Europe without coming away with a changed viewpoint. For he is compelled in spite of himself to see us in a new light. It is a well-known fact that the white people view us largely from the standpoint of the cook, porter, and waiter, and his limited opportunities are responsible for much of the distorted opinion held concerning us. Europe and his band are worth more to our Race than a thousand speeches from so-called Race orators and up-lifters…He has the white man's ear because he is giving the white man something new. He is meeting a popular demand and in catering to this love of syncopated music he is jazzing away the barriers of prejudice. (15-16)

Although history has shown that an appreciation of jazz and of African American musical performance generally has never been a guarantee of racial tolerance among white audiences, this quote suggests that even in its earliest incarnations, jazz was recognized by some in the African American community as having the potential to be a powerful political force.

More recently, tenor saxophonist and free jazz pioneer Archie Shepp has been even more explicit about the politics of jazz: "This music is political by its very nature" he is quoted as saying in a recent article in the *Village Voice*. "The first music we [African Americans] created was a protest music that recanted slavery and spoke for liberation and freedom, and it always has" (quoted in King, par. 25). Ken Burns's recent multi-part documentary entitled *Jazz* also draws numerous links between jazz and liberty in America, and this is a favourite theme of the film's appointed jazz authority and spokesperson, Wynton Marsalis. In a 1996 interview, Marsalis explains:

> The principle of American democracy is that you have freedom. The question is "How will you use it?" which is also the central question in jazz. In democracy, as in jazz, you have freedom with restraint. It's not absolute freedom, it's freedom within a structure.
>
> The connection between jazz and the American experience is profound. Believe me, that's the heart and soul of what jazz is. That's why jazz is so important. (Scherman 35)

As a non-American musician and writer whose creative practice is considerably indebted to the jazz tradition, I must admit that I'm somewhat uncomfortable with Marsalis's equation of jazz and American nationalism (an equation that is made continually in Burns's documentary—"Jazz music objectifies America" are the documentary's opening words, spoken by Marsalis). I am even more uncomfortable, however, with the exclusionary nature of Marsalis's apparent version of musical democracy. Elsewhere in the same interview he states, "It was with the type of things that that late-period Coltrane did that jazz destroyed its relationship with the public. The avant-garde conception of music that's loud and self-absorbed—nobody's interested in hearing that on a regular basis. I don't care how much publicity it gets. The public is not going to want to hear people play like that" (Scherman 35).

Marsalis excludes a wide range of musical activity since the 1960s from his narrative concerning jazz history and democracy/freedom. Particularly ironic, I would suggest, is his refusal to acknowledge the social and musical impact of "free" jazz and other forms of music that make explicit reference to the idea of freedom.[2] The Burns documentary is similarly exclusionary in my view. Relatively little attention is given in the ten-part series to jazz trends since the 1960s that lie outside the musical mainstream. The comments made by Wynton's usually less puritanical brother, Branford Marsalis, in response to pioneering free jazz pianist Cecil Taylor's suggestion that he prepared for his concerts and expected his audiences to do likewise ("That's total self-indulgent bullshit as far as I'm concerned") are indicative, I think, of the film's attitude towards "free" playing on a whole.

In the present essay, I'd like to focus primarily on the musics that Marsalis and Burns tend to avoid in their seemingly shared view of jazz history, and to explore the notion of freedom in relation to free jazz and other improvisational forms stemming from the jazz tradition since the 1960s. In my view, these musical practices represent not only the most explicit but also some of the most provocative examples of jazz conceptualized as a resistant cultural and social practice, a practice that I will argue is intimately linked with struggles for freedom and for human rights. In thinking about this complex issue, it may be useful to begin by considering the idea of freedom itself.

In an influential 1958 lecture entitled "Two Concepts of Liberty," the political philosopher Isaiah Berlin made the now famous distinction between what he termed "negative" and "positive" liberty or freedom. Negative freedom refers to the relative absence of external constraints limiting an individual or group's behaviour (that is, *freedom from* various forms of oppression). In contrast, positive freedom refers to one's ability to act out of his or her own accord—the *freedom to*—including the freedom to participate in collective self-rule. Scott Saul has discussed the way in which the distinction between negative and positive freedom was quickly assimilated and recast in the official discourse of Cold War America as the "philosophical dividing line between the West and East" (391). "Positive liberty" he notes "was recategorized as a type of antiliberty: too many totalitarian states had forced a specious obedience onto their 'citizenry,' driven by such high-minded ideals of total civic participation" (391). In the official rhetoric of Cold War America, "freedom" increasingly came to mean "free enterprise," the freedom to choose (and purchase) one product over another. Saul acknowledges that jazz wasn't impervious to Cold War politics and discourse.[3] However, he persuasively argues that the music of certain hard bop groups, Charles Mingus's Jazz Workshop in particular, provided a potent challenge to dominant conceptions of freedom through their emphasis on musical collectivity and struggle. I will return to this idea, but first I'd like to explore the concepts of negative and positive freedom in greater detail, particularly the ways in which this distinction has informed human rights discourses.

In her introduction to Michael Ignatieff's book *Human Rights as Politics and Idolatry*, Amy Gutman writes:

> Human rights protect the core of negative freedom, freedom from abuse, oppression, and cruelty. This is a starting point for some complex thinking about what the purpose and content of the evolving international human rights regime should be. But even the starting point is more complex—and contestable—than appearances might suggest. Protecting human agencies, and protecting human agents against abuse and oppression, cannot be identified simply (or solely) with negative liberty, freedom *from* interference. Nor is the core of human rights constituted only by negative freedoms. The right to subsistence is not a negative freedom, as the right against cruel and unusual punishment is. (ix)

She goes on to suggest that certain positive freedoms, including the right to collective self-rule, must also be included in human rights regulations, but she adds an important cautionary note: "Collective self-determination is a human right exercised in groups, which is conditional—as are all such group rights—on the group's respecting the other rights of individuals" (xv). This statement, it seems to me, might well be applied to jazz, particularly free jazz and its derivatives, which involve constant negotiation between the freedoms accorded to the individual improviser and those of the group as a whole.

There's another connection to be drawn between human rights discourse and many "free" jazz practices of the past several decades as well. Human rights education has focused on the need not only for the prevention of human rights abuses, but also on the importance of promoting human rights, in effect the promotion of a better world, a world in which human rights violations will not take place. At many times throughout jazz history, musicians have sought to be free from various forms of oppression (musical and otherwise). This is one of the things that has led historically to innovations in jazz. In addition to these negative freedoms, however, many musicians including Sun Ra, Horace Tapscott, the Art Ensemble of Chicago, and William Parker, to name only a few, have promoted alternate visions of reality, creating new musical and social formations through their music. Although the dual stress on prevention and promotion in human rights discourse[4] and in some of the musical discourses associated with jazz may not coincide exactly with negative and positive freedom as theorized by Isaiah Berlin, I'd like to employ this expanded definition for the purposes of this essay. So defined, the concepts of negative and positive freedom might provide a useful framework for beginning to theorize the complex relationship between human rights and jazz, as well as some of the ways in which the idea of freedom has been manifested historically through music.

Negative freedom in jazz has always had both musical and cultural dimensions. In terms of the music itself, there is a discernible trend throughout jazz history of musicians searching for freedom in the face of dominant modes of music making. As baritone saxophonist Fred Wei-han Ho (formerly Houn) explains, "[e]very major innovation in the history of the music has been from the struggle of musicians to attain greater and greater levels of expressive freedom through liberating the two basic fundamentals of music: time (meter) and sound (pitch/temperment/harmony)" (136). For many African American musicians, jazz has also been an important means of resisting oppressive political, social, and economic pressures. In response to these types of oppression, the jazz world has produced its share of explicitly resistant political works. In the 1960s in particular, at the height of the Civil Rights movement, many musicians gave their works politically suggestive titles and wrote liner notes dealing with political issues.[5] Many musicians of the period also performed at benefit concerts for organizations such as the National Association for the Advancement of Colored People (NAACP), the Student Nonviolent Coordinating Committee (SNCC), the Congress of Racial Equity (CORE) and other groups connected to the push for Civil Rights in America.[6] Song titles frequently made reference to Africa and African themes at a time when struggles for freedom from colonial rule amongst African nations were an important point of solidarity for many people of African descent.[7] Other pieces honoured African American political leaders, such as Max Roach's homage to Marcus Garvey entitled "Garvey's Ghost" and Archie Shepp's 1965 composition for Malcolm X entitled "Malcolm, Malcolm—Semper Malcolm." Many African American musicians, including Roach and Shepp, Charles Mingus, Bill Dixon, Sun Ra, Abbey Lincoln, Milford Graves, and others, spoke openly about the exploitative economic conditions surrounding the music. "You [whites] own the music," wrote Archie Shepp in an article that appeared in a 1965 issue of *Downbeat* "and we [African Americans] make it" (11). Charles Mingus, Max Roach, and Eric Dolphy even organized an "anti-festival" in Newport in 1960 to protest the lack of representation of African American performers at the official Newport Jazz Festival and the relatively low wages paid by the festival to African American musicians.

This period also saw the formation of a number of musical collectives aimed at combating the economic and social inequalities experienced by African American musicians. These included the short-lived but historically important Jazz Composer's Guild in New York, Horace Tapscott's Union of God's Musicians and Artists Ascension (UGMAA) in Los Angeles, the Black Artists Group (BAG) in St. Louis, and the Association for the Advancement of Creative Musicians (AACM) in Chicago. Motivated largely by the efforts of pianist Muhal Richard Abrams and trumpeter Phil Cohran, the AACM developed in part as a response to the climate of social and political unrest in the 1960s. Early AACM member, saxophonist Joseph Jarman, remembers:

> There was a tremendous anxiety in the political climate at the time because there was protest against the Vietnamese war, there were protests against the political activities in the Southern United States, protests against the flower generation in the North, there were political protests against the government. So it was a very exciting, nervous period. Of course *within* each community it was very calm and relaxed. We had experienced a view of union…we were experiencing unity in the various communities. The intent of the whole idea was to allow us the opportunity to perform; but to perform with dignity, with pride, without humiliation, without limitation. (quoted in Shipton 808)

In addition to its commitment to foster a communal atmosphere of sustained artistic exploration and growth, the AACM has been committed throughout its history to benefiting the wider African American community on Chicago's South Side. The organization presented regular concerts in the community and provided free lessons in music theory, musical technique, and African American music history to young people who might not have otherwise had such opportunities. The Underground Musicians Union (later the Union of God's Musicians and Artists Ascension), founded in 1961 by pianist Horace Tapscott, was similarly dedicated to community education as well as to the preservation and promotion of African American music and culture. "One of the group's primary goals," writes Eric Porter, "was to channel the energies of Los Angeles youth into activities that would benefit the community, principally through playing music. The organization performed in local community venues as the Pan Afrikan People's

Arkestra. They attempted to bring peace to their neighborhood during the 1965 Watts riots, performing outdoor shows on a flatbed truck" (210).

Perhaps the single most important political work from the period was Max Roach's 1960 recording *We Insist! Freedom Now Suite*. With pieces titled "Driva' Man," "Freedom Day," "Triptych: Prayer/Protest/Peace," "All Africa," and "Tears for Johannesburg," as well as an album cover depicting a lunch counter sit-in, the recording was a powerful cultural expression of the Civil Rights movement and it remains one of the most important documents of social protest from the period. "Driva' man," "Freedom Day," and "All Africa" feature poignant lyrics—written by Oscar Brown Jr. and passionately delivered by Abbey Lincoln—related to the themes of slavery, emancipation, and pan-African solidarity, respectively. In the middle passage of "All Africa," Lincoln chants the names of African tribes while, in response, Nigerian percussionist Olatunji "... relates a saying of each tribe concerning freedom—generally in his own Yoruba dialect..." (Hentoff, liner notes).

In some ways, the musical content of *We Insist!* might be considered an even more powerful statement than the recording's politically charged titles and lyrics. As Max Roach himself would later state: " 'The sound,' I tell them, that's the final answer to any question in music—the sound" (quoted in Rose 62). This is particularly evident in "Triptych: Prayer/Protest/Peace" which is, in many ways, the centerpiece of the recording. "Triptych" features Abbey Lincoln in a voice/drum dialogue with Roach. Although there are no words in this piece, the vocals are intensely affective, particularly in "Protest," which features Lincoln's piercing screams set against a flurry of percussive activity from Roach. In this context, Lincoln's vocals and Roach's drumming are powerful signifiers of what Nat Hentoff describes in the recording's liner notes as "a final, uncontrollable unleashing of rage and anger" in the face of the continued oppression and discrimination experienced by African Americans. "It is all forms of protest," writes Hentoff, "certainly including violence."

Contrary to many accounts of jazz history, there have continued to be a considerable number of explicitly political musical activities in jazz since the 1960s. In the days leading up to the recent invasion of Iraq by the United States, for example, a series of concerts advertised as "Jazz Against War" were held in New York City. On March 18, 2003, on the eve of the U.S. attack, guitarist Marc Ribot performed a piece entitled "Kaddish for American Democracy" at one such concert. Asian American musicians Fred Ho and Jon Jang have also written and recorded numerous pieces that deal with human rights issues, including Ho's suite entitled *Turn Pain Into Power!* and Jang's *Concerto for Jazz Ensemble and Taiko*, the third movement of which, "Reparations Now!," demands reparations to be paid to Japanese Americans interned during World War II. Another of Jang's extended compositions, a suite entitled *Tiananmen!*, commemorates the pro-democracy movement in China that was violently quashed by the Chinese military in Beijing's Tiananmen Square on June 4, 1989. Of *Tiananmen!*, Jang says the work "is a continuation of the language [he's] trying to develop for Asian and American (or African-American) music traditions together. Part of this is to acknowledge the struggle for freedom and democracy which is something common to Asian and African peoples" (quoted in Kelp). In each of these cases, as in earlier political works by Roach, Shepp, and others, jazz has been a powerful vehicle to assert the right to negative freedom—freedom from oppression—not only musically, but also in the cultural, political, and economic spheres surrounding the music.

As for the 'freedom to,' or positive side of the equation, writers have tended to focus on the freedoms afforded by jazz improvisation outside of the social and institutional constraints in which they take place. This has often led to the mistaken portrayal of jazz improvisation as merely the expression of individual freedom, something that musicians do "off the top of their heads" without preparation prior to musical performance. However, as ethnomusicologist Paul Berliner explains in his monumental *Thinking in Jazz*, "the popular conception of improvisation as 'performance without previous preparation' is fundamentally misleading. There is, in fact, a lifetime of preparation and knowledge behind every idea that an improviser performs" (17). The acclaimed trombonist, scholar, and educator George Lewis has similarly noted that improvisers working in what he terms "Afrological" forms[8] including jazz "seem to agree that freedom…is perceived as being possible only through discipline, defined as technical knowledge of music theory and of one's instrument as well as thorough attention to the background, history, and culture of one's music" ("Improvised,"114). In other words, a musician's freedom to organize sound in the jazz context (and I think this applies equally to "free" modes of playing as it does to earlier jazz styles) is highly contingent on a range of factors including not only technical competency, but also what might be termed *cultural competency* with respect to the music. When evaluating the "rebel" qualities of jazz, particularly in relation to human rights struggles and ideas about freedom, the cultural context(s) surrounding the music are clearly of vital importance.

In the 1980s and early 1990s, the emphasis on tradition (or, more correctly, certain aspects of tradition) in some jazz circles helped precipitate the spread of a conservative neoclassicism that had a limiting effect on positive musical freedom in jazz.[9] This tendency was compounded, I think, by the increased institutionalization of jazz education in recent decades and by a corporate world eager for music that is easily labeled, marketed, and sold. Despite these trends, however, a number of improvisers have continued to recognize musical innovation itself as being very much a part of the jazz tradition. The music of the Art Ensemble of Chicago, Anthony Braxton, George Lewis, Joe McPhee, and William Parker, to name only a few, demonstrates not only a thorough knowledge of the jazz tradition, but also a willingness and desire to extend that tradition. Consider, for example, George Lewis's 1979 recording, *Homage to Charles Parker*. In its original LP format, each of the two 17 minute-plus pieces, "Blues" and the title track, occupies one side of the record (a reminder that musical freedom is always framed by technological constraints, particularly in the recording studio). Of the first piece, Lewis has written the following in the record's liner notes:

> Blues (1977) has four basically diatonic "choruses", each of which uses the essential harmonic sequence of the classic blues form as a starting point. The temporal, timbral, and dynamic movements are controlled by the performers' creative interpretation of the guidelines given in the score. The resulting 'collective orchestration' allows each of the four soloists (Douglas Ewart, Anthony Davis, George Lewis, Richard Teitelbaum), as well as the ensemble, to retain blues feeling (magic), free from strict rhythmic/harmonic sequence. The occasional bi-tonality which results from the overlapping of 'choruses' in differing keys provides an ensemble multi-directionality which can facilitate either gradual change (as in the transition from the piano solo to the open improvisation) or quick, dramatic reversal, as in the opening of the trombone solo. (1979)

The piece sounds and feels remarkably bluesy; it clearly honours the blues tradition, acknowledging its profound influence not only on the performers of "Blues," but also on the musical and cultural landscape of the past 100 years generally. At the same time, its formal complexities expand significantly on the blues tradition, testing its limits and reinvigorating its strictures through melodic, harmonic, and timbral innovations. In a similar way, the recording's title track pays homage to Charlie Parker not through imitative reproduction of Parker's soloing technique or improvisational approach but rather through an innovative two-part extended composition that incorporates synthesizers (as does "Blues") and electronically manipulated sounds as well as "the traditional improvised solo with chordal accompaniment, a form which Charles Parker and other composer-performers before and since have brought to a rare level of perfection" (liner notes). I would argue that pushing the musical boundaries of a particular form in this way has been an important expression of positive musical freedom in jazz over the past several decades and, in fact, throughout its history.[10]

If working within a particular musical form while at the same time manipulating and extending that form can be viewed as one expression of positive freedom in the jazz context, the movement between forms has, in recent decades, become another. The music of the Art Ensemble of Chicago is particularly exemplary in this regard. Formed in the late 1960s, at the dawn of the post-modern era, the Art Ensemble of Chicago has, for more than thirty years, created music that references and juxtaposes a wide variety of musical traditions and histories. The late Art Ensemble trumpeter Lester Bowie summarized the group's approach in a 1997 interview: "We didn't have any mental encumbrance on what we wanted to do. We weren't restricted to bebop, free jazz, Dixieland, theater, or poetry. We could put it all together. We could sequence it any way we felt like it. It was entirely up to us. We didn't have any preset standards. We were open to try anything. Everything didn't work, but we were free to try it" (Beauchamp 46). Musical

Hamid Drake performing at the
2001 Guelph Jazz Festival

freedom in this context refers to the improvising musician's ability to draw on and articulate an intercultural network of musical styles, techniques, and histories. The fact that Art Ensemble members have historically rejected the label "jazz," referring to their work instead as "Great Black Music," is telling in itself. Unlike the term jazz, which is frequently used to denote a rather singular, linear conception of North American musical history (largely by commercial interests surrounding the music), the term "Great Black Music" encompasses a far wider range of pan-African musical practices that play a part in Art Ensemble performances.

Fellow Chicagoan, Hamid Drake (whose own performance practice also encompasses a remarkably broad range of musical traditions) expresses a similar view: "A free player to me" he has said, "is someone who's not limited by style. Style is not an entrapment for them." He continues:

> It's a player who is willing and able to check out every genre of what we might call the Great Tradition in music, meaning for lack of a better term jazz. And all of the things that stem from that and all of the things that contributed to that. And all of the things that are related to that on any level whether it be funk, R&B, blues, reggae, hip hop. Whatever it might be. Some people might call it the Great Tradition; they might call it Great Black Music. But to me a free player is a person who is really free and they have the ability to move through various forms. Form is not a hindrance to them...So I shouldn't have a problem with R&B. I shouldn't have a problem with swing. I shouldn't have a problem with reggae. I shouldn't have a problem with funk. At least not conceptually. Now playing those things is a different thing. You have to discipline yourself. You have to take time and practice those forms. But conceptually, there shouldn't be any difficulty in seeing the relationships even if you can't necessarily do it in playing fashion. But just seeing the relationships. Once we can see the relationships, that should alleviate all forms of prejudice that we might have towards any type of musical idiom...*You know, if we can understand humanity from that perspective, I mean deeply understand it, that could be a remedy even for race relations.* (emphasis added)

With this last remark, Drake touches on an important aspect of positive musical freedom in the jazz context—the potential to envision a better world through music making, a "Blutopia" as Graham Lock puts it.[11] Lester Bowie expresses a similar view about the music of the Art Ensemble: "One of the immediate goals of our music is to stimulate thought. *The main thing is to make the world a better place to live in, to make people able to function better together and really elevate their whole existence*" (Beauchamp 32, emphasis added).

The idea of envisioning and, in effect, *creating* a better world through music has been central to the work of New York bassist and improviser William Parker as well. In the liner notes to *Sunrise in the Tone World* he explains:

One of my dreams is for the music to eventually evolve to the point of limitless possibility. Where each player would have complete freedom to go wherever he or she wanted to in the music. Freedom to use any sound or color to create something beautiful. I am asked many times is the music we play composed or improvised. I am not really concerned with this question, for me improvisation is a form of composition. Everytime we improvise we are spontaneously composing. *I am more concerned with restoring life, with keeping the fire of human compassion burning.* (emphasis added)

I asked William Parker to elaborate on his views of musical freedom, to which he responded:

When I say free music it simply means that one is free to play anything in the universe of music that will work within the healing process. I'm free to play Mayan rhythms, Cherokee rhythms, Chinese, Korean, African, or Brazilian melodies, harmonies, rhythms, or ritual systems. I can play blues/gospel/cosmic/spiritual/Celestial systems. I'm free to use the entire language of sound and silence in the music. The main thing about freedom is that I'm free to let the flow of music move through me without trying to be something, without worrying about a style. *The style is life, is about saving lives. This is the concept of freedom.* ("Freedom," emphasis added)

For me, this highly provocative statement foregrounds the importance of subject position with respect to discourses about musical freedom. It occurs to me that referencing the musical traditions of historically aggrieved populations in the manner described by Parker might carry a different set of meanings for an African American performer than it would for a Euro-American musician (or Euro-Canadian, as in my case) whose cultural ancestry includes a legacy of slave ownership, colonialism, and oppression. In other words, for me to play Mayan or Cherokee rhythms or Chinese melodies in the course of a musical performance may very well *not* function within the healing process, as it does for Parker, or be a musical expression of freedom. It may, in fact, be seen as quite the opposite—a form of musical colonialism. If musical freedom is to be truly meaningful, I would suggest that performers need to be attentive to the social positionings and contexts (not only in terms of race but also in terms of gender, class, ethnicity, sexuality, and various other sorts of power relations) that are always involved in the music's creation.

Parker's statement about musical freedom raises another question: how can jazz—or any music for that matter—save lives? My sense is that this idea derives, at least in part, from a conception of the musician's role in society not as entertainer, but as healer. Hamid Drake explains:

To me the enlightened role of a musician is that of a healer. That's the enlightened role. The opposite of that would be the distorted role [which can] mean a lot of things, but it means essentially that there's an imbalance, a lack of illumination. William Parker uses the term "illuminated music" and I think that's the enlightened role of music. The greatest distortion would be egoism—the musician or artist thinking that they are better than others or that simply because they're an artist, they have the freedom to do whatever they want, when they want, to whom they want.

I have experienced this side of both Parker's and Drake's music myself. I am reminded in particular of a morning solo bass concert by William Parker at the 1999 edition of the Guelph Jazz Festival. Parker prefaced an arco piece entitled "Cathedral of Light" with the following words: "One day I was practicing long tones on the bass and I had a vision that each string that I played was a band of light and that the bow was a prism. When you send light through a prism, you get colours. And that's what I was interested in because I felt that these colours could be the thing that really heals people when they listen to music and that was more important than the notes—the colours underneath the notes, not the notes. So I started working on this concept of harmonics and colours." As he played, I remember noticing that many people in the audience were moved to tears.

For me, the question remains: how do we get from musical freedom to tangible *social change*? In my view, "freedom how" is more important in many ways than questions of "freedom from" and "freedom to." Christopher Small's arguments in *Music of the Common Tongue* might be usefully brought to bear on these questions. Small identifies two types of relationships that are created during a musical performance: "...*those which are created between sounds* (this is a matter of the forms and the techniques used by the performers—the ways in which they go about the making of music) *and, secondly, those which are created among the participants*" (62, emphasis in original). In both cases, Small argues, these musical relationships reflect and *produce* social formations that are brought into existence for the duration of a musical performance (what he calls the act of "musicking"). "We are moved by music" he writes, "because musicking creates the public image of our most inwardly desired relationships, not just *showing them to us* as they might be but actually *bringing them into existence* for the duration of the performance" (69-70, emphasis in original).

One of the salient features of free jazz and creative improvised music of the past forty years has been the move away from traditional Western harmonic structures that rely on prescriptive cadential formulas in which all dissonances and all movements away from the harmonic status quo are ultimately resolved. Accepting Small's argument, we might regard this system of tonality as embodying and affirming a social order from which there is no escape: dissonance (or dissidence) only exists as a temporary aberration that ultimately reaffirms dominant ideology through the symbolic return to the tonic.[12] In this light, the move away from tonality, which began with the work of free players like Ornette Coleman and Cecil Taylor and has continued in the work of subsequent generations of improvisers, can be seen as representing a huge shift not only musically but also ideologically. The following comments made by bassist Ron Carter in a 1969 interview suggest that this shift had important social ramifications as well:

William Parker performing an arco solo

whenever there has been a major change in jazz, there's been a major change in everything else afterward. It's incredible how it happens. Freedom music to me represents the
younger musicians getting tired of the establishment. The establishment to me is chord
progressions and a thirty-two bar form. The student radicals are like the freedom jazz
players who want to bypass most of the preset standards for playing a tune…In 1959,
when Ornette Coleman hit New York, he predicted this social change musically. You can
relate the Charlie Parker era to this, also. And you can relate the Dixieland-Louis
Armstrong style to the emergence of the black man trying to get free from the slavery he
was under. (quoted in Taylor 63)

Carter's comments seem to support the arguments that political economist Jacques Attali
makes in *Noise: The Political Economy of Music.* Attali suggests that music can have a premonitory function in society, anticipating and, in effect, precipitating changes in the social and economic order. For Attali, free jazz ultimately failed because it was unable to construct a new
mode of production outside of dominant capitalist frameworks (138-140). I would argue, however, that the success of free jazz (or any music for that matter) cannot be evaluated in economic
terms alone. For me, this is clear when one considers the second type of relationship identified
by Christopher Small, the relationship between participants in the musical experience.

Unlike earlier dissonant musical practices in the world of European concert music (the
twelve-tone works of Arnold Schoenberg, Alban Berg, and Anton Webern, for example) that
preserved stringent hierarchies in the relationships established between composer, conductor,
performers, and audience members, the relationships between participants in improvisational
musics of the past several decades have tended to be considerably more fluid. "Free" modes of
music making offer the potential for non-hierarchical patterns of musical and social interaction.
Recall Scott Saul's arguments about Charles Mingus's Jazz Workshop and its emphasis on freedom through collective musical action and struggle between musical participants. "Marked by
its volatility," he writes, "Mingus's music suggested that freedom had to be seized through
struggle—a struggle that engaged African Americans with one another and posed them against
their audience…Disciplined and liberating, it broke down the presumed antithesis between individual freedom and social order" (388).

Jazz has also been an important site for the restaging of contact between and across various
types of cultural difference including racial, gender, and cultural boundaries. In my view, the enabling of intercultural contact based on dialogue and mutual respect (rather than cultural appropriation and oppression) has been one of the key rights consequences of free jazz and
improvised music over the past several decades. "That's why I've been running around the
planet, going out of my way to meet European musicians, to learn their music, to play with
them" explains Anthony Braxton in a 1977 interview. "Because it's time to knock down these

barriers and come together to play music. It's past time actually but we may as well start now" (qtd. in Porter 282). Braxton, George Lewis, William Parker, and Hamid Drake have all worked extensively on both sides of the Atlantic, frequently collaborating with European improvisers in a variety of settings. Ongoing collaborations between improvisers from diverse cultural locations have led George Lewis to suggest that improvisation ought to be regarded as a "transcultural practice" ("Improvised" 113). "For example," writes Lewis, "California's large and vibrant Asian-American improvisers' community…has made a point of exploring and researching the musical, cultural, and political links between Afro-American, Euro-American, and Asian-American musical forms" ("Improvised" 113). Along with Fred Ho's Asian American Art Ensemble and Jon Jang's Pan Asian Arkestra, the music of Japanese American Miya Masaoka might be considered an exemplary model of improvisation as transcultural practice. Her repertoire includes traditional Japanese folk songs, Duke Ellington and Thelonious Monk compositions, as well as freely improvised pieces (sometimes incorporating live electronics), all performed on the koto, a traditional Japanese string instrument.

George Lipsitz has suggested that "[t]he principal practices that define jazz music originated in specific sites, but by privileging relentless innovation over static tradition they offered cultural, moral, and intellectual guidance to people all over the world" (178). The global importance of free jazz and improvised music to struggles for human rights is evidenced by the following comments by South African percussionist Louis Moholo upon his arrival in the UK:

> When we came here I started hearing some other vibes. I was away from South Africa and away from the chains. I just wanted to be free, totally free, even in music. Free to shake away all the slavery, being boxed into places—one, two, three, four—and being told you must come in after four...From then on I just played free...
>
> Free music is *it* man, it's so beautiful. The word 'free' makes sense to me. I know that's what I want; freedom, let my people go. *Let my people go!* (quoted in Scott 36)

German pianist Joachim Kuhn similarly recalls: "I remember the moment I first heard Ornette Coleman's music. Somebody in a bar told me his name, saying that this was the new man who plays without chord changes. I was very much interested, very much attracted, because at that time East Germany, where I lived, was not a free country. But this kind of expression—free expression—that is what jazz really meant" (quoted in Shipton 828). Clearly jazz has moved far beyond the national boundaries that Wynton Marsalis and Ken Burns argue are so central to jazz and to jazz history. This is not to deny the importance of the American experience, particularly the African American experience, to the history of the music, but rather to suggest that the implications of jazz, particularly "freedom music" and its derivatives, for human rights have been far more wide-reaching and far more profound than dominant histories of jazz would have us believe.

NOTES

1. This new mindset and its importance to cultural trends during the decades following the Emancipation Proclamation is further evidenced by the roughly contemporaneous development of two other important African American musical genres: blues and ragtime.

2. In the 1960s, free jazz was sometimes referred to as "freedom music." See drummer Arthur Taylor's treasury of transcribed interviews from the period published in *Notes and Tones* in which many musicians discuss their views of musical freedom.

3. See Saul's discussion of the State Department "Goodwill Ambassador" tours by African American jazz musicians beginning in 1956 (392). See also Radano (15).

4. It should be stated that both the prevention of human rights abuses and the promotion of human rights depend crucially on the actual *material implementation* of regulations governing patterns of human interaction. One of the things I will argue throughout this essay is that jazz has been an important site not only for the theorizing of new social possibilities but also for the realization and implementation of those possibilities. In my view, musical relationships *are* social relationships and they can have real political consequences and significance. Consider the title of a recent duo recording by saxophonist/pocket trumpeter Joe McPhee and percussionist Hamid Drake: *Emancipation Proclamation: A Real Statement of Freedom*. The second part of this title implies that the statement of freedom made by McPhee and Drake through music is every bit as real as the Emancipation Proclamation made by Abraham Lincoln in 1863—possibly more so. As Daniel Fischlin and Martha Nandorfy have suggested, "The rhetoric surrounding the abolition of slavery and servitude...is profoundly skewed by illusions of freedom that conceal severe restrictions" (122). To my mind, Drake and McPhee's music points to some of the concealed restrictions inherent in the 1863 Emancipation Proclamation (through titles such as "Hate Crime Cries" for example) while simultaneously asserting a new—and very real—vision of freedom through musical collaboration.

5. It should be noted, however, that the political content of such recordings was sometimes filtered to protect the interests of the largely white-owned recording establishment. Consider, for example, Columbia Records' refusal to record a version of Charles Mingus's "Fables of Faubus" that featured lyrics ridiculing Arkansas governor Orval Faubus for his racist anti-integrationist policies. See also Frank Kofsky's discussion of the Riverside label's handling of Sonny Rollins's 1958 recording *Freedom Suite* (50-1).

6. See Monson (1999) for a discussion of Thelonious Monk's rather complex relationship to the Civil Rights movement. Her forthcoming book *Freedom Sounds: Jazz, Civil Rights, and Africa 1950-1967* will no doubt shed more light on this important period of jazz history.

7. The relationship between "freedom music" and black nationalist thought has been the source of much speculation. See, for example, Kofsky. It is important to note that many African American free players, including Marion Brown, Anthony Braxton, and others, have expressed discomfort with oversimplifications that link African American improvised musical performance to black nationalism. This discomfort is evident even in Kofsky's 1966 interview with John Coltrane, transcribed in *Black Nationalism and the Revolution in Music*. Coltrane repeatedly frustrates Kofsky's attempts to goad him into making oversimplified black nationalist remarks.

8. Lewis compares "Afrological" models of improvisation with "Eurological" trends. He suggests that setting up a free jazz/free improvisation binary along racialized lines is deeply problematic given the profound influence of Afrological models on European improvisers and the fact that many Afrological improvisers (including Cecil Taylor, Roscoe Mitchell, Anthony Braxton, Lewis himself, and many others) have drawn considerably on European forms.

9. See Radano (269-76) for a detailed and critical account of this development.

10. There are, of course, many other examples of this trend. Think, for example, of Joe McPhee's deconstructed version of Wayne Shorter's "Footprints" recorded on *Linear B,* or of Anthony Braxton's radical reworkings of Thelonious Monk or Lennie Tristano compositions (not to mention his numerous operas that include improvisation).

11. Through an examination of the work of Duke Ellington, Sun Ra, and Anthony Braxton, Lock identifies two major impulses in African American music: "... a utopian impulse, evident in the creation of imagined places ... and the impulse to remember, to bear witness ..." (2). The term "Blutopia," drawn from a Duke Ellington composition of the 1940s, signifies these impulses in its inference to both the blues and a utopian vision of society.

12. Ajay Heble has written extensively on the political implications and significance of dissonant musical practices in *Landing on the Wrong Note.* See also Attali (1985).

WORKS CITED

Attali, Jacques. *Noise: The Political Economy of Music.* Minneapolis: University of Minnesota P, 1985.

Bailey, Derek. *Improvisation: Its Nature and Practice in Music.* New York: Da Capo, 1992.

Baraka, Amiri [LeRoi Jones]. *Blues People.* New York: Morrow Quill Paperbacks, 1963.

Beauchamp, Lincoln T. Jr. *Art Ensemble of Chicago: Great Black Music—Ancient to the Future.* Chicago: Art Ensemble of Chicago Publishing, 1998.

Berlin, Isaiah. *Two Concepts of Liberty.* New York: Oxford, 1958.

Berliner, Paul F. *Thinking in Jazz: The Infinite Art of Improvisation.* Chicago: University of Chicago P, 1994.

Drake, Hamid. Personal interview. 4 September 2002.

Fischlin, Daniel and Martha Nandorfy. *Eduardo Galeano: Through the Looking Glass.* Montréal: Black Rose Books, 2002.

Gutman, Amy. Introduction. *Human Rights as Politics and Idolatry.* By Michael Ignatieff. Princeton, NJ: Princeton UP. vii-xxvii.

Heble, Ajay. *Landing on the Wrong Note: Jazz, Dissonance, and Critical Practice.* New York: Routledge, 2000.

Hentoff, Nat. Liner Notes. *We Insist! Freedom Now Suite.* By Max Roach. Candid, 1960.

Ho, Fred Wei-han. "'Jazz,' Kreolization & Revolutionary Music." *Sounding Off! Music as Subversion/Resistance/Revolution.* Eds. Ron Sakolsky and Fred Wei-han Ho. Brooklyn: Autonomedia, 1995. 133-143.

——. "Jazzing Away Prejudice." Editorial. *Chicago Defender* 10 May 1919: 20. Rpt. in *Keeping Time: Readings in Jazz History.* Ed. Robert Walser. New York: Oxford, 1999. 15-16.

Kelp, Larry. Liner Notes. *Tiananmen!* By Jon Jang and the Pan Asian Arkestra. Soul Note, 1993.

King, Daniel. "Fire Music." *Village Voice.* 12-18 March 2003. 06 April 2003 <http://www.villagevoice.com/issues/0311/king.php>.

Kofsky, Frank. *Black Nationalism and the Revolution in Music.* New York: Pathfinder, 1970.

Lewis, George. "Improvised Music after 1950: Afrological and Eurological Perspectives." *Black Music Research Journal* 16.1 (Spring 1996): 91-122.

——. Liner Notes. *Homage to Charles Parker.* By Lewis. Black Saint, 1979.

Lipsitz, George. *Dangerous Crossroads: Popular Music, Postmodernism and the Poetics of Place*. London: Verso, 1997.

Litweiler, John. *The Freedom Principle: Jazz After 1958*. New York: Da Capo, 1984.

Lock, Graham. *Blutopia: Visions of the Future and Revisions of the Past in the Work of Sun Ra, Duke Ellington, and Anthony Braxton*. Durham, NC: Duke UP, 1999.

Monson, Ingrid. *Freedom Sounds: Jazz, Civil Rights, and Africa 1950-1967*. New York: Oxford, forthcoming.

——. "Monk Meets SNCC." *Black Music Research Journal* 19.2 (Fall 1999): 187-200.

O'Meally, Robert, ed. *Living with Music: Ralph Ellison's Jazz Writings*. New York: The Modern Library, 2002.

Parker, William. "Freedom." E-mail to the author. 22 Feb. 2003.

——. Liner Notes. *Sunrise in the Tone World*. By William Parker & the Little Huey Creative. Music Orchestra. AUM Fidelity 1997.

Porter, Eric. *What is This Thing Called Jazz?: African American Musicians as Artists, Critics, and Activists*. Berkeley: University of California P, 2002.

Radano, Ronald *New Musical Figurations: Anthony Braxton's Cultural Critique*. Chicago: University of Chicago P, 1993.

Rose, Tricia. *Black Noise: Rap Music and Black Culture in Contemporary America*. Middletown: Wesleyan UP, 1994.

Saul, Scott. "Outrageous Freedom: Charles Mingus and the Invention of the Jazz Workshop." *American Quarterly* 53.3 (September 2001): 387-419.

Scherman, Tony. "The Music of Democracy: Wynton Marsalis Puts Jazz In its Place." *Utne Reader* 74 (March-April 1996): 29-36.

Scott, Richard. "Call Me Mr. Drums (An Interview with Louis Moholo)." *The Wire* 85 (March 1991): 34ff.

Shepp, Archie. "An Artist Speaks Bluntly." *Down Beat* 32 (16 December 1965): 11, 42.

Shipton, Alyn. *A New History of Jazz*. London: Continuum, 2001.

Small, Christopher. *Music of the Common Tongue: Survival and Celebration in African American Music*. London: Calder, 1987.

Taylor, Arthur. *Notes and Tones: Musician-to-Musician Interviews*. New York: Da Capo. 1993.

George Elliott Clarke

4 / Gospel as Protest: The African-Nova Scotia Spiritual and the Lyrics of Delvina Bernard

Although African-Nova Scotians are descended principally from the 3,400 African-Americans who fled post-revolutionary America in 1783 and another 2,000 who were summarily liberated by British troops and dispatched to British North America during the War of 1812, African-Americans themselves are frequently surprised to learn of the existence of these northern, saltwater 'exiles.'

GEORGE ELLIOTT CLARKE is an acclaimed poet and an English professor at the University of Toronto. His pioneering study, *Odysseys Home: Mapping African-Canadian Literature*, was published by University of Toronto Press in 2002. In 2001, Clarke received the Governor-General's Award for English Poetry.

Canadians, too, especially those who live in the central and western provinces of the world's second-largest country, are often mystified to discover, amid their ranks, blacks whose roots are not recent-immigrant Caribbean or African or traceable to the Underground Railroad exodus, but, rather, extending back to the eighteenth—or even the seventeenth-century. This general ignorance about the existence of African Nova Scotia—a 30,000-strong polity I call "Africadia"—has had two consequences: 1) their culture is dismissed as not being 'black'—i.e., not recognizably African-American—'enough'; 2) or it is seen as a displaced, stranded, cast-off of the American South. Thus, the history of African-Nova Scotian—or "Africadian" (to use my 1991 neologism)—musical expression, including the singing of spirituals and gospel songs, is often misunderstood as constituting either a simple extension of African-American practices or rejected as a rather 'pale' imitation of them.

Examples of these attitudes are legion. When the African-American anthropologist Arthur Huff Fauset came to tour the province and collect 'Negro' folklore in the mid-1920s, he was disturbed by his subjects' apparent lack

of familiarity with the minstrelized, Uncle Remus tales (popularized by Joel Chandler Harris), and asked his U.S. readers, "What would you think of whole groups of Negroes who had never heard of Brer Rabbit?" (vii). Fauset felt that Africadians should more closely mimic African-Americans, pointing out that "Even in a locality like Preston [located approximately ten miles northeast of the provincial capital, Halifax], where the Negroes live for all the world like plantation folk, in their rickety cabins (not log cabins), off to themselves … I could not find persons who knew the [Uncle Remus] stories" (viii).

Fifty years after Fauset's 'Grand Tour' of Negro Nova Scotia, another anthropologist, the Canadian Frances Henry, conducted a similar investigation with respect to music, and, in a 1975 article titled "Black Music in the Maritimes," argued that none existed, really, because the War of 1812 refugees had been so "demoralized" and "brutalized" (12) that neither "the folk-music tradition springing from its religious source" nor "the traditional importance of the [African-American] church" (15) remained essential to the culture. For Fauset and Henry, Africadians were defective African-Americans, who were unable to carry a tune (so to speak). In contrast, the Canadian magazine writer Edna Staebler opined in 1956 that some Black Nova Scotians "had a broad Southern accent" (Dillard 517); while fifty-plus years earlier, the visiting American writer Margaret W. Morley felt that "the Negroes are not yet reconciled to the climate of Nova Scotia—small wonder that they are not!—and though many of them were born there, they sigh for the palms of the traditional land of their ancestors and have little zest for the fir trees of the North" (144-5). For Staebler and Morley, Africadians were accidental Canadians, folks who were still, really, indelibly African-Americans or misplaced Africans.

And yet, *History* tells, in opposition, an apt story regarding the survival of 'African-American'-like, but distinctive, Africadian musical traditions, especially that of 'church' music—the gospel songs and spirituals. Indeed, the talent for, interest in, and production of music was always a constant in Africadian existence. So powerful was Africadian dedication to 'musicalizing' and 'instrumentalizing' that, in 1789, the white government of the Loyalist settlement of Shelburne passed a by-law "forbidding negro dances and frolics" (Smith 77). Moreover, if it is true that, as John Lovell proclaims in his magisterial study of the spiritual, African-Americans "belonged to a singing tradition that was centuries old" (96), why would they stop singing just because they crossed the border into colder—but freer—'Canada'? Of course, they did not.

Further proof for this point appears in the homely yet inspiring fact that the first Africadian publications include two collections of hymns and spirituals: The Reverend F. R. Langford's *A Call from Zion: Jubilee Songs and Old Revival Hymns* (1882) and the Reverend Wellington Naey States's *Hymns Sung at the Services* (1903). Remarkably, neither collection offers song titles or musical notation, suggesting that the intended purchasers of these anthologies already knew the music (or would 'pick it up' through oral instruction in church). Even Fauset recognized that

Africadians possessed "religious customs and even habits of living distinctly their own" (viii). The Nova Scotian folklorist Helen Creighton recorded the 'folk songs'—generally spirituals—sung by William Riley of Cherrybrook (an Africadian settlement) in 1942 and published several of them in a 1950 book (Clarke, Introduction 19). Africadia's first international singing star was Portia May White (1911-68), a contralto whose repertoire consisted of French, German, and English *bel canto* and spirituals. Lovell tells us that he experienced the spontaneous singing of "fourteen Afro-American spirituals," including "Steal Away," "Swing Low, Sweet Chariot," "When the Saints Go Marchin' In," and "Gettin' Ready for That Great Day," at a 1967 wake for a just-deceased Black Nova Scotian woman (557, 556). Henry appended to her article several "Spirituals Recorded by Group of Family Singers" (20), thereby acknowledging, implicitly, that *some* degree of propensity for 'African-American'-like music-making existed among Africadians, despite their despised descent. Newfoundland folklorist Neil V. Rosenberg records that in an interview with Ed Bailey, an Africadian singer, he volunteered the songs he performed as a boy were "mostly gospel" (144).[1]

To sum up, and to contradict scholars like Fauset and Henry, 'African-American' song never died out or faded away among Africadians. Instead, the religious music became part of the commonly held *folk* knowledge of the community. As I have written elsewhere, "Africadian folk music is...religious music" (Introduction 19). No other music could suffice to fill such a role—there is no *extensive* blues or jazz or soul tradition—because Africadia's only significant institution, for most of its pre-1960s history, was the African (United) Baptist Association, a group of two dozen or so churches founded officially in 1854. In the absence of any potent, secular, musical temptation, the *black* songs sung popularly were those bearing the imprimatur of the "Church."[2]

First Movement

Enter Delvina Bernard. Born in Halifax, Nova Scotia, in 1958, Bernard grew up in the Africadian settlements of Lake Loon and Cherrybrook, approximately eight miles from the city that is also the provincial capital. At Africadia's height, it boasted some forty-three separate communities, generally conceived as an archipelago of churches. Out-migration, "urban renewal" (destruction), and the end of school segregation (in the 1950s and 1960s) have served to reduce the size of most of these communities and to practically close some of the churches, but Cherrybrook remains a significantly, mainly black locale.[3] To grow up there, as Bernard did, was to be surrounded by black elders, parents, children, workers, teachers, and churchgoers (even the hypocritical ones). In this microcosmic world, her imagination would have been shaped by Canadian, Nova Scotian, African-American, and next-door influences, but also moulded profoundly by the song and singing of the Cherrybrook (African) United Baptist Church.[4] Bernard is learned; she graduated from Saint Mary's University in Halifax with a Bachelor of Commerce degree in 1982.

Delvina Bernard

A year earlier, she joined with three other women to form an *a capella*, gospel-based quartet, "Four the Moment," whose repertoire, influenced by the African-American women's group, "Sweet Honey in the Rock," was composed of anti-racist, anti-sexist, essentially progressive material stressing black history, black women's history, Third World struggles, and human rights. The quartet arose in opposition to the stated plans of an Ontario-based, anti-('coloured') immigrant splinter of the Ku Klux Klan to begin a recruitment drive in Nova Scotia. Thus, in late 1980, Bernard and three other women were asked to sing at an anti-Klan rally in Halifax; they did so to rousing success; and continued to perform at other progressive events throughout 1981, then constituted themselves formally as a group in 1982. The group's composition, despite personnel changes over the years, always involved three black women and one white, with Bernard always at the helm. During the quartet's heyday, in the 1980s and 1990s, Bernard and her 'sistren' toured widely across Canada and the United States, performing at colleges, universities, folk festivals, and protest events. Before its disbandment in the late 1990s, Four the Moment released three recordings, *We're Still Standing* (1998), *Four the Moment-Live!* (1993), and *In My Soul* (1995). Bernard produced each album (the first received several award nominations), and she eventually received a long-overdue East Coast Music Award in 1998 in recognition of her work. Bernard's song, "Freedom has Beckoned," was included on a CBS-Much Music recording, *Soul in the City*, featuring African-Canadian popular music. Bernard also wrote the music for Africadian filmmaker Sylvia Hamilton's first film, *Black Mother, Black Daughter* (1990). Four the Moment may be gone, but its music goes on, especially in terms of play on campus radio and on the Canadian Broadcasting Corporation radio network. Bernard, too, has gone on, to assisting her husband, Harvey Millar, with his recording initiatives, to helping to raise their children, and to work as a Haligonian civil servant.

While Bernard was a dynamic leader and persuasive producer of Four the Moment, as well as a powerful vocalist, she also brought songwriting savvy to the group, which had begun by re-iterating the Sweet Honey in the Rock songbook. Asked, however, to focus more on Afri-can-Nova Scotian historical experience, Bernard began to compose songs that commented on the lived realities of the local audience as well as on aspects of its history. These songs reveal Bernard to be a significant lyricist, one who blends the supernatural realism of biblically oriented song—the spirituals!—with the bluesy 'news' of black and women's and worker's experience. Her melodies are haunting, but not ethereal; there is soulful grit in what she sings and how she sings it. There is earth in her notes and then, sometimes, blood inside that.

Second Movement

Let us consider two of Bernard's writings, beginning with her signature lyric, "I Love You Woman" (also known as "Black Mother Black Daughter"), composed in 1986. As sung by Four the Moment, the song itself is stately, elegiac, an oral monument to the heroic transmission of strength from mother to daughter, woman to woman. But it is also archetypically Nova Scotian and universally applicable: the lyric opens with a chorus that depicts a woman, standing at a shore, speaking of other women. This imagery is suggestive of a passage through trouble and strife—crossing of the Jordan River or, for that matter, the crossing of the Atlantic, via slavery, to, in the words of African-American poet Robert Hayden, "life upon these shores" (54):

> we're here, standing at the shoreline
> made it through some hard times
> Black mother, Black daughter
> made it through some hard times
> Black mother, Black daughter (126; italics in original)

The atmosphere of the piece is anthemic: the unadulterated—but quiet—joy and triumph of survival is affirmed. Such may seem a barren victory to others, but for Bernard's women—and for too many black and brown people everywhere—it is fruit-bearing success of the most succulent sort: the continuation of culture and family *despite* all odds to the contrary.

In her next stanza, Bernard seems to signal to two other African-American poets thereby referring to the literary genealogy of survival so insistently voiced in Afro-diasporic texts:

> I see reflections of a past staring at me
> of hard work, and women kneeling to pray
> from the dusk, to the dawn
> each day hard, each day long
> giving me, my claim
> I love you woman (126)

Bernard's water-mirror reflective of labour and yearning conjures up the famous image that closes Waring Cuney's Harlem Renaissance-era poem, "No Images" (ca. 1924):

> She does not know
> Her beauty,
> She thinks her brown body
> Has no glory.
>
> If she could dance
> Naked,
> Under palm trees
> And see her image in the river
> She would know.
> But there are no palm trees
> On the street,
> And dishwater gives back no images. (98-9)

Naturally, Bernard replaces dishwater with the suggestion of a river or an ocean. More hero-ically, her speaker-singer in the chorus and the lyric recognizes her inheritance of a hard-won glory, that gift allowing her to say to long-gone ancestors, "you have prepared the way for me, and my presence honours your sacrifices and redeems your sufferings, while your *history* de-mands I add to our legacy of struggle." Bernard's speaker recalls, then, yet another storied Afri-can-American reflection on water, namely, Langston Hughes's Harlem Renaissance anthem, "The Negro Speaks of Rivers" (1921):[5]

I've known rivers:
I've known rivers ancient as the world and older than the flow
of human blood in human veins.

My soul has grown deep like the rivers...
I've known rivers:
Ancient, dusky rivers.
My soul has grown deep like the rivers. (63-4)

While Bernard's song may speak back to African-American forerunners—or ghosts (a technique not unknown to African-Canadian artists)—it is also located in a present tense that is specifically Nova Scotian: "I see waters of east shores wearing you grey.../of tides white...But never wear-ing you down" (126; ellipses in original). Not only does Bernard refer here to Nova Scotia's "Eastern Shore," a mainly white, often frankly anti-black part of the province (one located only a few miles from Cherrybrook), but her images may also allude to the first Africadian woman to publish a book (really, a chapbook) of poems, Gloria Wesley-Desmond, and her 1975 poem, "The Sea at Night":

Listen to the splash
Of the waves, white-
Capped, frothing, impenetrable!
Waves thundering,
Thundering! Crashing
To their death.
How deep the night! (68)

These cold, coastal, Nova Scotian waters—for both Bernard and Wesley-Desmond—represent challenge, turmoil, danger, and testing, which are, also, the trials presented by racism and sex-ism. Bernard writes, near the conclusion of her lyric, "I'm a woman Black, and a woman first / cause I know what I have to meet / fire and thunder...waters of courage / are the gifts you've given me" (127; ellipsis in original). Here one encounters imagery lifted from the religious spiri-tuals, but put to fresh use in Bernard's secular version.

Bernard's poem "We Women," written six years after "I Love You Woman," extends her interest in interweaving natural *cum* biblical imagery, black history, feminism, and Nova Scotian references. It merits quotation in full:

we women—Black, Beige, and Brown
have loaded-up…slave ships, ox carts…and guns,

we have walked through fire, returned from sinking sand
chopped wood, moved stone, fetched water, as women we will stand

we've cast lines to our sisters…yellow, white, and red
stained with blood of witches, voodoo queens, and heretics

we wrote the symphony, that makes the white man sing
we wrote the blues…bebop, jazz, and swing
we wrote the lullaby, when massa's baby cried
we wrote the negro spiritual…each time a black man died

Sojourner, Harriet, Ida, …………Zora Neale Hurston
Rose Fortune, Edith, Portia, …………Lydia Jackson

with tartan-tainted kente
we've tugged and tried, and spun
200 years of women
and wove them into one (127-8; ellipses in original)

This poem affirms crucial elements of Bernard's lyrical work. Again, there are allusions here, possibly, to African-American poems, such as Paul Laurence Dunbar's "We Wear the Mask" (1895) and Margaret Walker's "For My People" (1937, 1942). Again, Bernard rings changes on these poems. Dunbar's tortured cast and bitter tone ("We wear the mask that grins and lies" [14]) is replaced by a nearly triumphalist feminism. Walker's Whitmanesque, Carl Sandburg-like, and socialist ode which ends, "Let a race of men now rise and take control" (130), is modernized and democratized so that *races* of women—Aboriginal, African, Asian, European—are acknowledged as deserving empowerment and recognition of past inventions, works, and endurance.

Indeed, the choral speaker in Bernard's poem is dramatically, provocatively pro-active: she notes that women have had to load up many items in the epoch of patriarchy and slavery, including "guns" (and the elongated ellipsis preceding its announcement is deliberately Machiavellian in its malice). The choral speaker insists that she and her 'sisters' have "cast lines" to other women, meaning, I believe, not only ropes of rescue, but also, metaphorically, lines of inspirational song, prayer, and verse. The speaker allows for the possibility of violent resistance by women to patriarchal oppression (see the reference to guns), and connects the 'penning' of spirituals to passive resistance against lynching and other race-hate crimes. She also audaciously binds together the history of African-American women—as exemplified by abolitionist feminist Sojourner Truth, slave liberator Harriet Tubman, anti-lynching crusader Ida Wells-Barnett, and trailblazing novelist Zora Neale Hurston—with that of lesser-known, but exemplary Africadian women—North America's first policewoman Rose Fortune, the celebrated basket weaver Edith Clayton, acclaimed singer Portia White, and escaped slave Lydia Jackson,[6] who fled from Nova Scotia to Africa. The speaker's later assertion that two centuries of Africadian women's history is symbolized by the interweaving of Scottish "tartan-tainted" and Ghanaian (African) kente cloth enacts another union.

In her poem, "We Women," Bernard recapitulates themes that also occur in "I Love You Woman." Her apparent citations of the African-American literary canon refer mainly to figures and texts of the Harlem Renaissance period, which was essentially the 1920s. Bernard may have been won to these texts because Africadia was undergoing its own "Black Cultural Renaissance" from the mid-1980s to the end of the 1990s, a period which coincides with the group's creation and cessation.[7] Although Bernard's compositions, both lyrically and musically, borrow from spirituals and gospel music, there is a markedly Marxist orientation in her expression of the unity of the oppressed and her allowance for violence as a legitimate political tool. Additionally, Bernard's lyrics move toward the status of anthems: they are 'nation'-defining songs for the borderless nations of women, black people, and other constituencies of struggle, but also for the citizens of Africadia—a nation of the imagination.

Coda

All her interests meet beautifully in Bernard's stirring lyric, "Freedom Has Beckoned" (1986), which is strongly reminiscent of U.S. Civil Rights Movement songs:

I won't stop until the weak become the strong
I won't stop until the weak become the strong
I won't stop until the weak become the strong
cause freedom has beckoned me to come

And we won't be free
until the humble women speak!
and we won't be free
until the humble women speak!

I won't stop until Black people stand as one
I won't stop until Black people stand as one
I won't stop until Black people stand as one
cause freedom has beckoned me to come

I won't stop until the Pentagon has fallen

I won't stop until the Pentagon has fallen
I won't stop until the Pentagon has fallen
like Jericho its walls come tumbling down

And we won't be free
until the trumpet sounds for peace
and we won't be free
until the trumpet sounds for peace (132-3)

One hears in this lyric the reference to Joshua 6:4-5 (the fall of Jericho) as well as another allusion to spirituals, namely, one of those sung by the family recorded by Henry during her visit to Nova Scotia in the early 1970s: "When the Trumpet Sounds" (Henry 20-1). Certainly, Delvina Bernard's referencing of that spiritual, whether conscious or not, speaks to the continuance of the African-American cultural connection amongst the two-century-lost, African-American "colony" in Nova Scotia—just as it speaks to the shared, spiritual-based music of Africadia. Yes, and it also speaks to the steady relevance of spirituals as 'resistance song'—at least for those who have ears to hear.

NOTES

1. I must add the personal anecdote that, during a 1979 youth multiculturalism conference, in Dartmouth, Nova Scotia, I found myself with another six or seven Africadians who felt alienated and just downright angry because our concerns about anti-black racism were being ignored. Our group of high school or university students began to sing spirituals *spontaneously*: conveying our opposition to the structural racism of the conference in a way that uplifted ourselves and *shamed* the others, for we were implying that they were no better than the slave masters of yore.

2. I capitalize deliberately.

3. It is, for instance, the site of the provincially funded Black Cultural Centre for Nova Scotia.

4. Founded in 1854 as the African Baptist Association, a generation-long schism in the organization resulted in its reconstitution as the African United Baptist Association in the early twentieth century. Thus, individual churches are not cited as "African," but as "United."

5. Bernard has an acquaintance with Hughes's work, for one of the songs that Four The Moment performs on its debut album is "Dream Variations" [sic], a Hughes poem (1924, 1926) set to music by C. Mann.

6. The subject of another Four the Moment song titled "Lydia Jackson," with music by Bernard.

7. For more information on the Africadian Renaissance, see my article, "The Birth and Rebirth of Africadian Literature."

WORKS CITED

Bernard, Delvina. "Freedom Has Beckoned." *Fire on the Water: An Anthology of Black Nova Scotian Writing, Volume Two*. Ed. George Elliott Clarke. Lawrencetown Beach, NS: Potterfield Press, 1992. 132-3.

—. "I Love You Woman." *Fire on the Water: An Anthology of Black Nova Scotian Writing, Volume Two*. Ed. George Elliott Clarke. Lawrencetown Beach, NS: Potterfield Press, 1992. 126-7.

—. "We Women."*Fire on the Water: An Anthology of Black Nova Scotian Writing, Volume Two*. Ed. George Elliott Clarke. Lawrencetown Beach, NS: Potterfield Press, 1992. 127-8.

Bontemps, Arna, ed. *American Negro Poetry: An Anthology*. New York: Hill and Wang, 1963.

Clarke, George Elliott. "The Birth and Rebirth of Africadian Literature." *Odysseys Home: Mapping African-Canadian Literature*. Toronto: U of Toronto P, 2002. 107-125.

—. Introduction. *Fire on the Water: An Anthology of Black Nova Scotian Writing, Volume One*. Lawrencetown Beach, NS: Pottersfield Press, 1991. 11-27.

Cuney, Waring. "No Images." *American Negro Poetry: An Anthology*. Ed. Arna Bontemps. New York: Hill and Wang, 1963. 98-9.

Dillard, J. L. "The History of Black English in Nova Scotia-a First Step." *Revista Interamericana Review* 2.4 (Winter 1973): 507-20.

Dunbar, Paul Laurence. "We Wear the Mask." In Bontemps. 14.

Fauset, Arthur Huff, comp. Introduction. *Folklore from Nova Scotia*. Comp. Fauset. New York: American Folk-Lore Society, 1931. vii-xi.

Four the Moment. "Dream Variations." *We're Still Standing*. Recording. FTM 1987. JAM Productions Ltd. 1988.

—. *Four the Moment-Live!* Recording. FTM10-1. JAM [Just A Minute] Productions Ltd. 1993.

—. *In My Soul*. Recording. 02-50494. JAM Productions Ltd. 1995.

—. "Lydia Jackson." *We're Still Standing*. Recording. FTM 1987. JAM Productions Ltd. 1988.

—. *We're Still Standing*. Recording. FTM 1987. JAM Productions Ltd. 1988.

Hamilton, Sylvia. *Black Mother, Black Daughter*. Film. National Film Board of Canada, 1989.

Hayden, Robert. "Middle Passage." *Collected Poems*. Ed. Frederick Glaysher. New York: Liveright, 1985. 48-54.

Henry, Frances. "Black Music in the Maritimes." *Canadian Folk Music Journal* 3 (1975): 12-21.

Hughes, Langston. "Dream Variation." In Bontemps. 66.

—. "The Negro Speaks of Rivers." In Bontemps. 63-4.

Langford, F. R. *A Call from Zion: Jubilee Songs and Old Revival Hymns*. Weymouth, NS: n.p., 1882.

Lovell, John, Jr. *Black Song: The Forge and the Flame: The Story of How the Afro-American Spiritual Was Hammered Out*. New York: Macmillan, 1972.

Morley, Margaret W. *Down North and Up Along*. New York: Dodd Mead, 1900.

Rosenberg, Neil V. "Ethnicity and Class: Black Country Musicians in the Maritimes." *Journal of Canadian Studies* 23.1 2 (Spring/Summer 1988): 138-56.

Smith, T. Watson. "The Loyalists at Shelburne." *Nova Scotia Historical Society Collections* 6 (1888): 67-89.

States, Wellington Naey. *Hymns Sung at the Services*. Halifax: n.p., 1903.

Walker, Margaret. "For My People." In Bontemps. 128-130.

Wesley-Desmond, Gloria. "The Sea at Night." *Fire on the Water: An Anthology of Black Nova Scotian Writing, Volume Two*. Ed. George Elliott Clarke. Lawrence Town Beach, NS: Potterfield Press, 1992. 67-8.

Ray Pratt

5 / The Blues: A Discourse of Resistance

The blues is an historic American song form. Developed by African-Americans, it has influenced, if not laid down the foundations for, much of 20th century popular music—rock and roll, rhythm and blues, Motown, soul, jazz, country. And it continues to delight and inspire new generations who, as the founding and second generations of blues men and women have died, have turned to recordings to discover its stylistic diversity and its incomparable performers (AMG).[1]

RAY PRATT is Professor of Political Science at Montana State University. He has hosted a blues/jazz radio program for 25 years and is the author of *Rhythm and Resistance: Political Uses of American Popular Music* (Praeger, 1990; Smithsonian, 1994) and *Projecting Paranoia: Conspiratorial Visions in American Film* (UP Kansas, 2001).

Historically the blues has had important *political* functions as a *discourse of resistance*. It has also functioned as an important form of popular music, but perhaps now is more a specialized musical subculture, one that remains significant in both African-American and white culture as standing for so much more—as an *interpretive metaphor* and as an expressive force, with explicit things to say about the civil conditions and rights that are part of the African-American and white experience in America.

For Amiri Baraka (LeRoi Jones), in his classic *Blues People*, the blues is the cultural expression of an African-American *meta-society* (50-59), an emergent unity existing in opposition to the mainstream repressive white culture and political economy. *Blues People*, named on one list as one of the 100 most significant American books of the 20th century, was an important expression of *black nationalism* in the 1960s, and a precursor of the Black Arts Movement, in which Baraka was a central figure (Neal 31-32). Historian Eric Foner defines black nationalism not simply as a denial by blacks of a society that has rejected them, but also especially "an *affir-*

mation of the unique traditions, values, and cultural heritage of black Americans" (11). A major element of the worldview of black nationalism was pride in cultural heritage—a heritage that has become in the 21st century, in the rich diversity of what is now known around the world as *American* music, virtually synonymous with the culture of the United States.

Houston Baker, in describing the blues as a "matrix"—a key element of the black "vernacular"—states in *Blues, Ideology and Afro-American Literature* that Afro-American culture is "a complex, reflexive enterprise which finds its proper figuration in blues conceived as *a matrix*—a point of ceaseless input and output, a web of intersecting, crisscrossing impulses always in productive transit. American blues…are the multiplex, enabling *script* in which Afro-American cultural discourse is inscribed" (3-4). For Baker, the blues are an "always synthesizing" synthesis—"Combining work songs, group seculars, field hollers, sacred harmonies, proverbial wisdom, folk philosophy, political commentary, ribald humor, elegiac lament, and much more, they constitute an amalgam that seems always to have been in motion in America—always becoming, shaping, transforming, displacing the peculiar experiences of Africans in the New World" (5).

A Blues Discourse?

Discourse refers to the social process of making sense, of saying something, of reproducing reality and fixing meaning in language. The blues, seen in light of its development over 125 years, is a complex of discourses—telling stories through lyrics and sound. While the blues may be described as a discourse, there are also discourses *about* and *around* the blues—scholarly, fan, blues society newsletters, magazines, radio shows, and others. Blues discourses make sense of, and reproduce someone's view of, reality and attempt to fix meanings. Since vocal musical discourses over the decades of the development of the blues are products and constituents of constantly evolving historical realities, they both reflect and reinforce ideologies and reflect and inflect power relations, constituting a form of *semiotic power* (Fiske 175).

The ideas outlined here owe a great deal both to Baraka's *Blues People*—especially the extension, elaboration and development of its central argument—and insights in Ben Sidran's *Black Talk*. There is an identifiable continuity in the blues over time, yet there is also such periodization, stylistic variation, a diversity of individual performing styles, historical and regional traditions, that it is always difficult to make broad generalizations not violated by cases evident to other knowledgeable observers. My comments in this essay are one personalized reading of some of the meanings of the blues in so far as they relate to emergent rights discourses and resistant musical practices. Others will inevitably find or project onto or read back into the increasingly rich body of historical texts (books, recordings, videos, personal recollections and memories) other meanings and make other connections.

Origins and Roots of the Blues

The roots of blues music lie in the unrecorded past of African and American culture, and especially in the frustrations encountered in the first generation of black freedom in the United States in the late 19th century. In a white-dominated culture, in which contending versions of possessive vs. expressive individualism have warred, the blues (and its derivatives and successors), as a music of individual expression in a group context, has, perhaps ironically given its origins, also exerted a continuing appeal to successive generations of *white* minorities who, like its original creators, find elements of the music that speaks to their psychological needs. Critic Greil Marcus, writing about rock—of which the blues is a major constituent—once observed that popular musics can "catalyze the desires of an era" (80-81). Resonant with meaning for successive generations, the blues have for over a century catalyzed the existential and expressive needs of a society of increasingly atomized individuals, embodying unfulfilled longings that a series of societies and cultural moments neither effectively met, nor perhaps ever could. From the early 1920s on, successive generations of white mediators—producers and talent scouts (after some early initial reluctance to record the music precisely as performed by the black people who created it) (Levine 24)—have appreciated both its market appeal and the ultimate sustaining powers of its aesthetic, always there when needed: "those 12 bars inviolate, self-contained, eternal" (Goldstein 208).

Cultural components of the blues "matrix" lie in the past centuries of the black experience and the creative subjectivity of individuals—in work song and field hollers, performances of early songsters and itinerant singers, and the cries and proclamations of sanctified preachers. Several generations of black artists developed a rich and complex variety of blues styles and subcultures in the Mississippi Delta, Memphis, New Orleans, Atlanta, Dallas, Houston, St.Louis, Kansas City, Oakland, Los Angeles, and especially Chicago (Russell, Ostransky, Palmer, Evans, and Barlow). Each of these locales produced a complex, complementary underworld of pleasure, music, and borderline illegality as well as outright criminality that flourished and continued evolving though the 20th century (Sidran 78-115; Kelley 153-182).

Those who know the blues appreciate its simplicity of form, rich ambiguity, irony, irreverent commentary, but above all, its potent directness, imagery, and its unique capacity to capture and fuse hard realism with exultant sensuality, creating a cultural practice of cathartic emotional release. Literary references to "feeling the blues" go back several centuries, but there is general agreement that the music began in the Deep South, perhaps in a levee camp or logging camp, or, more likely, on a plantation in Mississippi between 1870 and 1890, though some suggest an earlier date. A situation of *polygenesis* probably existed, given the wide distribution of former slaves, black migrants, similar social and labor situations and the dispersion of cultural components of blues style throughout the South (Titon 29; Malone 42).

Polygenesis simply means the blues began in *many* places where black men and women sang about themselves, played guitar with a knife blade, or blurred, embellished or "bent" notes when singing. There are journal entries from the 1830s describing "extra-ordinarily wild and un-accountable" songs. William Cullen Bryant in South Carolina in 1843 commented on the "singularly wild and plaintive air" sung by slaves husking corn. Others, such as W.C.Handy, who heard references to "the blues" as early as 1892, described the emotional impact of the strange sounds produced by a knife blade applied to guitar strings by an old Negro guitarist sitting in a train station in Tutweiler, Mississippi in 1903. While the banjo and fiddle were in wide use throughout the 19th century, they soon gave way to the guitar, which provided the warmer and deeper resonance today associated with the blues (Oliver, *Story* 9, 11, 26-27). Recent 1980s recordings of a 5-string banjo played with a bottleneck suggests that commonly-played 18th and early 19th century instrument could well have been used for "country" blues sounds 100 years *earlier* than usual dates scholars suggest for the origins of the blues.

Nonetheless, those who sought out black music in the South and Border States immediately after the U.S. Civil War do not report what today is called "blues" until the last decade of the 19th century, coinciding with the adulthood of the first generation of blacks born after Emancipation (Levine 301). Here were people cast adrift from the well-defined, if brutally oppressive, social roles established during slavery. The subsequent course of development of the music follows the migration patterns (Rowe 26-39) of blacks out of the old Deep South toward northern cities where local blues subcultures would flourish around every major black community. This aspect of an evolving black underground has been described by Barlow, Sidran, Baraka, Ostransky, and Russell, among many others.

Profound *demographic* changes taking place in the nation, as both blacks and whites moved off the land and out of the South, were reflected in such local traditions and subcultures. In 1900, 77.4 percent of the black population lived in rural areas, 22.6 percent urban. By 1960 only 26.8 percent of the black population of the nation lived in rural areas, 73.2 percent in urban areas (Rowe 26-39). As blacks moved off the land they brought the blues to urban areas—Memphis, Atlanta, Houston, Dallas, St. Louis, Cincinnati, Indianapolis (see Barlow), and especially the objective of the greatest number of migrants, Chicago (Rowe). New York, though the recipient of most of the Southeastern migrants, was much more a *jazz* center, with Harlem the now-celebrated legendary heart of an emergent African-American cultural renaissance. The influence of the New York area specifically on the blues was notable for the development of blues and stride piano traditions, and arrival of guitarists out of the Southeastern states. The white "folk" movement of the 1950s and 1960s would arise there, with significant black influence and participation of numerous black "folk" blues men from the Piedmont region in its earlier formative years (Bastin). Later, local traditions developed in the 1930s around such cities as Kansas City—really one of the greatest musical melting-pots, the 24/7 bars and saloons providing continuous employment and nurturing many of the best instrumentalists, especially saxophonists such as Lester Young, Ben Webster, and Charlie Parker, and the shouted vocals basic to rhythm and blues and swing. The saxophone and theories of improvisation developed by Parker were central, eventually, to bebop, the new jazz art (Russell). During and after World War II, Detroit, Los Angeles, and the Oakland-San Francisco Bay area became important centers of blues because of the massive influx of black workers (Lipsitz). The relation between these large-scale migrations of African-American labour and the difficulties the migrants faced played a crucial role both in the emergent civil rights discourses of the period and the musical forms that gave expression to these discourses.

Blues Forms: Freedom and Community

To speak of blues "form" is to do so in a more expansive sense than a technical definition of 12 (and often 8 or 16) bars or measures of music, the blues scale, and particular "blue notes." These are set usually as a progression of three chords through 12 bars: the Tonic (I) in the first 4; the Subdominant (IV) in the second 4 bars; and the Dominant (V) in the concluding 4 measures, repeating the progression through each chorus. There is an elusive quality fusing meaning and feeling in blues. The musical scale utilized, containing a flatted third and seventh, places it outside the major-minor diatonic system of other Western musics. These flatted notes are actually "bent" or partially flatted, giving the blues its unique sound—a peculiar kind of "tension" generated by playing these blue notes against or over major chords (Shaw 113ff; Evans 15-105; Koch).

It is misleading to speak of the blues as *sad*-sounding music. The moaning or "cry" of the rural blues men might be mistaken for sadness, but because the three chords used are resolute major chords, there is no way the overall mood of the music itself can be considered "sad." Rather, the hearer senses *tension* arising from "the paradoxical or ambiguous relationship between the chords and the flatted melodies" (Shaw 114). This tension, musically, is as characteristic of the blues as it was in the lives of those who created the music. It is here that one finds "secrets" of the *encoded meaning* and appeal of the music to generations of hearers and performers, particularly in the "free space" within the form for exercise of the creative imagination.

The blues became a significant *poetic* form through development of the three line (AAB), 12 bar (4 measures of music per line) form, reflecting the poetry of West Africa, allowing the singer to set out a line, repeat it while thinking of a rhyming line (and, it would appear) inciting the expectations of listeners, who are in effect "invited" to "receive" the succeeding line. A "call" and "response" pattern, probably in the case of the blues derivative of work songs under slavery (but African in origin), is thus established. The form combines individual expressiveness and communal group context (Charters, *Poetry* 25). The singer directs the song expressive of individual feelings toward the audience members, who take those feelings as their own—the phenomenon of "substitute imagery." As Texas blues man Melvin "Lil Son" Jackson (1915-1976) once put it, " . . . If a man sing the blues it come more or less out of himself, if you know what I mean, see. He's not askin' no one for help. And he's not really clingin' to no one. But he's expressin' how he feel" (Oliver, *Conversation* 25). The blues singer in this way speaks *individually*, but does it toward a *collective* audience.

Interpreting the Meanings of the Blues

Anthropologist Charles Keil once suggested that concepts of "the blues" are a form of "*projective tests*"—people of varying pigmentation and political persuasions essentially hear in the blues what they *want* to hear and find in the blues ethos what they expect to find (*Urban* vii). Yet it is my conviction that a particular *kind* of content has been *invested in* the blues. Speaking to, for, and about unmet needs, representing a musicopoetic synthesis of the desire for a kind of freedom as yet unfulfilled, and perhaps not even fully conceived, the music invites participation and experience of its particular *feeling* as influenced by the social art contexts in which it is generated. Contemporary blues bar audiences may appreciate the good feelings generated by the music, interpreting it simply as party music. But blues texts speak with many more voices. Because of limits imposed by their own experience, most listeners may fail to appreciate the *other voices* present in the music—the memories (of slavery, of oppression, of resistance) that went into the music in its formative period and were reinvested by succeeding generations of creator-performers. Appreciating the more sophisticated, expressive uses of the form requires sensitization to the voices that resonate in the history of the blues—voices of the first generation of "free" blacks in the era of "Jim Crow" laws—the frustrating and depressing, massively *repressive* aftermath of Emancipation in the United States. To them, the blues said, "I am somebody, listen to my story!" Today's audience must be initiated into that history, sensitized to the collective and individual histories embodied in the music—a pedagogical and aesthetic project wholly in line with understanding the civil rights contexts in which the blues participates.

The 1928 recording *Empty Bed Blues,* written by James C. Johnson and fervently sung by Bessie Smith, demonstrates how the form is not intrinsically pessimistic, as the melancholy aspects of the lyrics are dialectically redeemed and overcome through the forceful, exultant, life-affirming sensuality expressed in Smith's ebullient rendition:

> *I woke up this morning with an awful aching head (X2)*
> *My new man had left me just a room and an empty bed*

A succeeding verse, accompanied by the robust and bawdy trombone of Charlie Green, expresses the most exultant and (apparently) unrepressed sexuality: "He's a deep sea diver and his wind holds out so long." This recording, heard by multiple generations since, expresses the essential dualities and sometimes disconcerting ambiguities of a music embodying both joy and sorrow, realism and expectations. For its biographical connotations in Smith's own life, one must look to other studies (Albertson; Davis).

Shouters Jimmy Rushing (1903-1972) and Big Joe Turner (1911-1985), of Kansas City origin, would both often sing the line, "Baby, you're so beautiful, but you gotta *die* someday." Or, Texas/California blues man Aaron "T-bone" Walker (1910-1975), "I love my baby, she *hurt* me all the time." Evans in *Big Road Blues* described such examples of *contrast* in the blues as a "basic structural principle." In itinerant Atlanta-based street singer Blind Willie's (1901-1959) "Death Cell Blues" (1933) observers as early as 1903 noted the line "They got me charged with murder, [But] I ain't never harmed a man." While a few writers have criticized traditional country blues for the apparent incoherence of its stanzas, they may miss an underlying "emotional association" (Evans 46) in which the space for social commentary with explicit rights dimensions, as is the case with McTell's lyrics, is opened up. The greatest of the classic blues—of whatever regional or local tradition—have an elusive quality in their lyrics, musically conveying a simultaneity of feeling and social context that may be their most significant legacy to subsequent popular musics, especially rock and roll, but carrying contemporary rap lyrics, too, which must also be heard at multiple levels (Potter).

Recordings and the Blues

The wide dissemination of the blues owes a great deal to the development of the phonograph record. The first so-called "blues" *recordings* were actually done by whites, many of them specialists in Negro dialect material. It was nearly a decade after the first blues "craze" (W. C. Handy published the "Memphis Blues" in 1912 and the "St.Louis Blues" in 1914) that practicing black country "folk" blues men began to be recorded (Oliver, *Story* 6-30; Dixon and Godrich). This required overcoming company resistance to recording black artists. Initially, several black women singers were recorded, singing vaudeville versions of the blues. The push to record blues artists happened because white entrepreneurs, finally made aware of the 14 million black persons of the potential "race" market, reluctantly decided to do it. Part of what today is known as the blues began as a *stereotype* of blacks created by whites. As with a good deal in black culture in the United States, the forms and stereotypes that whites initiated and fostered eventually were transcended by black artists, though it took over a decade, Keil suggests, "to adapt the white stereotype, work it through, master it and turn it into a black identity" (Keil, "True Blues" 15, 22).

One should never underestimate the significance of the *free space* the recording industry provided for black artists during the first decade of blues recording. Not only did the "Negro" market exist, but "it was able to *impose its own tastes* upon the businessmen who ran the record companies" (Levine 225). Those who ran the companies really did not understand much about the music, consequently giving virtually complete artistic freedom to those they recorded. Since the objective of the companies was maximization of sales, artists brought to the various recording studios were considered to be the best judge of what would sell in their regions. John Fahey points out, "virtually *anyone* who could make any kind of musical sound could make at least one audition record for Paramount, Vocalion, or Victor" (14). Such non-directive and wide-open practices quite effectively documented local country blues tradition in Mississippi in the late 1920s and early 1930s. Literally hundreds of Southern black artists were thus allowed the freedom to audition, be recorded, and have records issued of songs they had been singing for decades (see Dixon and Godrich and Fahey, especially, 14-16 for the names and stories of some of these pioneering recording artists.

This phenomenon would be repeated without such striking degrees of openness over the history of the recording industry, demonstrating the cultural freedom possible within a system that treats popular culture as a commodity for sale. Where some critics of mass media assume popular cultural commodities are somehow imposed on a passive mass of consumers, practices of the early years of the "race" recording industry suggest a significant variation from this supposed pattern so far as initial access is concerned. While the aims of companies have been to sell recordings, they also provided a significant degree of access to whatever they thought might sell. In this manner a significant degree of creative free space was essentially "squeezed out" of a system with virtually no formal ideological commitment to providing it. Between 1927 and 1962, Fahey suggests, "the commercial recording industry did an infinitely better job of collecting, preserving and making available to the public" native folk music, especially *black* folk music, than did American scholars of folk music (Fahey; Levine).

The Blues as Expressive Communication

In the more than two decades since he published it, Ben Sidran's description of the blues remains one of the best ever written. Sidran discusses the blues as a form of communication, combining a *"galvanization of meaning and pitch"* (*The Blues* 13) into a single kind of vocalization with multiple voices, building an interpretation on Baraka's (1963) conception. As Gunther Schuller argues in *Early Jazz*, the blues has never been 'art music.' It was (and remains) in his view "an essential *mode of expression*, through which a minority could render…suffering," but also happiness (36). Rather than merely expressing sadness, the blues is a way of laying sadness to rest, providing insights into the highly complex and varied dimensions of human suffering fused with joy and sensual exultation.

As a form of expressive communication, the blues is a manifestation of an *oral* subculture, opposed to *literary* modes of thinking so characteristic of white American society. As "modes of perceptual orientation," oral and literate cultures articulate radically different views of what constitutes "practically useful information." Oral cultures employ only the spoken word and its oral derivatives (including musical representations of basic vocal styles). As Sidran puts it: "to paraphrase McLuhan, the message is the medium." The oral tradition encourages a greater degree of emotional, and perhaps even physical, involvement in the environment, which in turn allows for a more developed sense of community as well as a heightened collective awareness and even "collective unconsciousness" (Sidran 2-3, 3-6).

Advantages of the oral mode are manifest in the ability of groups to carry out spontaneous, improvised activity. Music in American history was one of the legitimated outlets for socially repressed black people—indeed, under slavery it was virtually the *only* outlet. The vocalized tone and rhythmic approach allow for non-verbal, heavily coded communication. This African and black cultural tradition, then, constitutes a *negation* of the entire European tradition, which is rooted in a pattern of structure and regularity. Borneman conceptualized this phenomenon in technical terms as follows: "While the whole European tradition strives for regularity—of pitch, of time, of timbre and of vibration—the African tradition strives for precisely the 'negation' of these elements" (17). In language, "the African tradition aims at circumlocution rather than at exact definition. The direct statement is considered crude and unimaginative; the veiling of all contents in ever-changing paraphrases is considered the criterion of intelligence and personality" (17). In music, "the same tendency towards obliquity and ellipsis is noticeable: no note is attacked straight; the voice or instrument always approaches it from above or below, plays around the implied pitch without ever remaining on it for any length of time, and departs from it without ever having committed itself to a single meaning." Timbre is thus "veiled and paraphrased by constantly changing vibrato, tremolo, and overtone effects. The timing and accentuation finally, are not 'stated', but 'implied' or 'suggested'" (17).

In oral culture, music is created *by the group* as a whole and the individual is integrated into the society at such a basic level of experience that individuality "flourishes in a group context." Rhythm plays a major role in this process, not only creating and resolving tension, but conveying information. Whereas literate culture stores information through writing, oral culture stores it through physical assimilation, thus itself constituting (to paraphrase Baker again) a "matrix of information." Within the music, therefore, the subject-object dichotomy is eventually transcended so that performer and listener enter into the same process. Ideas and acts are unified. *The process of communication becomes the very process of building community* (Sidran 8-14).

Within the blues one especially sees the "blue" notes, the melisma or vocal smears—the cries and moans of field hollers and gospel songs and, later, the unique, personalized *sound* of each of the great jazz saxophonists—Hawkins, Young, Webster, Parker, Coltrane, Rollins—all carrying nonverbal information. In their performances there is, again, that "galvanization of meaning and pitch" into a single vocalization. Musically, this is expressed by the unique "voice" of each instrument or vocalist culminating in development of an individualized "sound." This quality of blues and jazz, moreover, is inseparable from specific contexts—social, historical, performative, and otherwise. Initially, even if the message carried *seemed* one of resignation, there was more—not only a longing for escape and freedom, but *resistance* and even revenge. This intonational communication was intensely emotional—more basic even than human speech. The use of cries and melismatic (note 'smearing') techniques was a means of bringing out the individualism in otherwise repressed personalities, beginning when slaves expressed themselves as individuals, *through music* (Sidran 8, 11, 13-16). Could it be that these vocalizations represent the emergent voice of an emergent discourse in which the "right" to speak was (and remains) paramount?

Blues as Music of Individuality and Resistance

Herein lies part of the quality of black music as resistant social practice. The origins of unique "cries" went beyond "mere stylization." It was the basis on which a mass of people could commit themselves to action, *together*, while retaining individuality. After Emancipation and Reconstruction (1863-1876) and through the Jim Crow period (1877-1954)—but especially and originally in the years of Slavery—this action took place in the face of some of the most overt kinds of oppression, including physical bondage, destruction of families, denial of personal and political rights, rape and coerced sex, murder and—especially in the Jim Crow era—the ritualized collective white murder of black men known as lynching (over 500 documented cases in the State of Mississippi alone). Music has always been a social act of great subversive and expressive power within African-American culture. To the extent each person was involved in the music produced by this culture—and especially the blues and jazz—they were involved, effectively, in a process of resistance and personal and cultural transformation. From this perspective, black music could be seen as "revolutionary," if only through retaining an African approach to perception and communication in the face of extraordinary repression. Beginning with work songs and spirituals in the era of slavery, black music took on an *oppositional* or counter-cultural meaning as slaves created an immense and unique "culture of resistance" under the very eyes of their masters (Sidran 14-16; Lomax).

The result: in a society otherwise seemingly atomized, musical forms helped provide outlets for group action, a form of semiotic power, relatively free from the influence of otherwise physically dominant whites. The essentially revolutionary aspects of vocalization, expressed by a leader and encouraged by the responses of a chorus—the basic antiphonal (call-and-response) pattern of almost all Afro-American music—were central to these songs, which were significantly communal, *social actions* by black people during an era when other sorts of mass activity were outlawed. Thus, music became not simply a leisure activity, but *a way of life*—a way of asserting the rights coincident with being alive. In periods of the most oppressive forms of cultural suppression, then, music was a powerful means of self-affirmation.

The blues has been a most significant source for subsequent black music and much white popular music over the past century. Jazz in its various forms is perhaps best seen as resulting from a merging of circus and minstrel bands with the blues tradition: "a product of a peculiarly black voice (blues) in a peculiarly white context (Western harmony)." The blues tradition, first and foremost, has been an idiom of simultaneous individual expression and social activity. It has been, and remains today, through a structure that invites improvisation and spontaneity, a music of freedom, social criticism, and individual expression with an enormous and largely unexamined pertinence to rights discourses in America (Sidran 16-17, 34).

Women and the Blues: A Black Feminist Tradition of Resistance

Women have played a significant role in the development and spread of the blues. In the 1920s and 1930s, such black women as Gertrude "Ma" Rainey (1886-1939), Bessie Smith (1894-1937), and Lizzie "Memphis Minnie" Douglas (1897-1973) were some the most distinctive figures among scores of singers introducing the world to the blues through their 78rpm recordings played on home Victrolas. While African-American women moved into a wide variety of other areas of popular music during the Swing Era (1930-45) and after, over the past 6 decades in the United States, there have been innumerable outstanding blues and rhythm and blues singers such as Helen Humes, Dinah Washington, Willie Mae "Big Mama" Thornton, "Little Esther" Phillips, Koko Taylor, and many great female *jazz* vocalists, such as Sarah Vaughn, who could deliver compelling renditions of classic and contemporary blues songs (notably, Vaughn's 1958 blues performance of "No Count Blues").

Arguably, in no other music as in the blues do women chronicle and confront so well their social position and the range of relations between the sexes, something resulting in an identifiable women's discourse in music. While, as we have noted, the blues as an identifiable musical form had its origins in rural black music of the last quarter of the 19th century, women's contributions in that era came largely through singing spirituals, part of the distinctive division of labor in the black church, which had male preachers and female singers, a division that continued throughout the 20th century. But in the urban blues of the "classic" era of the 1920s and 1930s, women played the most significant roles. As the blues became known throughout the United States, it was significantly through the dispersion of phonograph records by such classic era women as "Ma" Rainey, Bessie Smith, or Ida Cox (1896-1967) and Victoria Spivey (1906-1976). Among blues performers of the period, while men such as Lonnie Johnson and Leroy Carr became widely known and identifiable, the great women singers are the people who first made the African-American blues known throughout the United States.

In the earliest women's blues, common themes include, besides sex and love, male cruelty or infidelity or the sense of loss at the often abrupt departure of a lover. Such themes of loss and attendant travel frequently occur, reflecting the tremendous migrations of African Americans from the rural areas to cities and back again, if only temporarily. There was significant movement between cities of the North as well. In the blues of the 1920s and 1930s, there is a strong explicit sexuality and sexual objectification, though many (certainly not all) of the most explicit and risqué lyrics were written by men. Even so, great singers such as Bessie Smith and Victoria Spivey could sing the "dirtiest" blues one could imagine, verging on the pornographic, with thinly-veiled *double entendre* songs an important part of their repertory.

The earliest women's blues sometimes present an almost desperate unhappiness fused in often disconcerting exuberant sexuality that is initially puzzling to contemporary consciousness, black and white, male or female. Sandra Lieb's 1981 study of "Ma" Rainey, *Mother of the Blues*, considers Rainey's most erotic and violent sung text (written by a man; is this incidental?), the "Sweet Rough Man" (1928) with its graphic imagery related by a woman whose man beats her with five feet of copper coil, yet somehow also, problematically Rainey sings, "the way he love me, makes me soon forget" (119-121).

The explicit sexuality and imagery, while a constant element over the decades, was increased to sell more records during the early Depression years, though one can note as well an evolving sophistication and skepticism about men, followed by exasperation, even anger. As the resignation of the earliest women's blues lessened, more frequent expressions of acute insight into the ways men used women made their way onto records. And the expressions may be seen as an example of how the blues played a role in the critique of domestic injustice that remains so crucial to conceiving of human rights generally. This is evident in such blues recordings as "He'll Come Back, Some Cold and Rainy Day" (1928, Bertha "Chippie" Hill), which suggests that just when a woman thinks she has rid herself of a predatory, good for nothing lover, he'll show up at her door some rainy night looking for a handout and a bed. Another proclaims, "I Can't be bothered with no sheik" (1931, Rosa Henderson), in which the singer expresses her exasperation at the lack of sexual commitment of her man. These themes were combined with the sexual explicitness of blues metaphors and similes extolling men's "stingers," or my "bumble bee" (Memphis Minnie); "my kitchen man," my "sausage man" (Bessie Smith), men's "black snake" and "organ grinder" (Victoria Spivey); or, suggesting "I need a little sugar in my bowl" (Bessie Smith), and many similar images. Whether such themes were always endorsed by the women singing them is open to question, but—from the evidence of extant recordings—the invariably enthusiastic nature of the performances of such raunchy lyrics, many written by the women singing them, is not. It is often said the blues through the decades—especially among classic era women singers—has been obsessed with sex, but it might be more accurate to say that *most people* in the years of the classic blues and since were intensely preoccupied with sex, if in repressed ways (Garon).

Women's Blues Literature

While many of the scholarly and popular works on the blues, written almost exclusively by men before the 1980s, talked knowledgeably about the role of women in the development of the blues tradition (Baraka; Oliver, *Story*; Shaw; Charters, *Sweet*), and there were several sympathetic studies devoted to profiling blues women, such as Derrick Stewart-Baxter's 1970 British paperback *Ma Rainey and the Classic Blues Singers,* it was not until the 1981 publication of Sandra Lieb's *Mother of the Blues: A Study of Ma Rainey* that a truly scholarly study by a woman author appeared. Focusing on Rainey's songs and examining blues expression of women's attitudes about sex and love, Lieb's is a meticulously documented study of early-20th-century women's blues. The author argues that "the body of Ma Rainey's recorded songs constitutes a *message* to women" and demonstrates "women aggressively confronting or attempting to change the circumstances of their lives" (xvi). 1988 subsequently saw the publication of *Black Pearls: Blues Queens of the 1920s* in which Daphne Duval Harrison comprehensively investigates such blues women of the 1920s as Rainey, Bessie Smith, Ida Cox, Alberta Hunter, Sippie Wallace, and Victoria Spivey. Harrison argued her study provides an opportunity for its readers to see such blues women as "pivotal figures in the assertion of black women's ideas and ideals from the standpoint of the working class and the poor" (10). Indeed, she suggested, the texts of the singers' songs illustrate "an emerging feminist perspective," asserting persuasively that their

> interpretation and analysis are a critical key to understanding the general nature of black cultural expression and the movement of black women toward self-determination and independence. Although the blues women sang about the same topics that men did, they provided new slants. They dealt openly with the issues that were of particular concern to black women in the urban setting—freedom from social and religions constraints, sexual and economic independence, alcoholism, and drugs. Issues of sexuality

and sex were addressed directly in their lifestyles and their blues. Lesbianism was practiced by such diverse singers as Bessie Smith, Ma Rainey, and Gladys Bentley—the last known as a tough-talking, singing piano player who some believed to be a male transvestite and others, a lesbian. (13)

Other significant analyses of women's blues include Hazel Carby's 1986 essay, "It Jus' Be's Dat Way Sometime: The Sexual Politics of Women's Blues," which situates the blues of Rainey, Bessie Smith (there were *several* other "Smith" women who sang blues, including Clara, Mamie, and, much later, Carrie), and Ida Cox in the sociopolitics of the early 20th century, where women's music becomes a response to the Harlem Renaissance and its presentation of black culture. Paula Giddings's *When and Where I Enter: The Impact of Black Women on Race and Sex in America* explores the interrelation of racism and sexism in black women's experience, illuminating, as Woldu points out (90-95), their efforts to transcend what was in effect double discrimination. Additionally, there were studies of individual women in jazz, popular biographies of such singers as Alberta Hunter (Taylor), and continuing biographical profiles of several women in diverse studies of rock, rhythm and blues, soul—too numerous to note here—and in collections of shorter pieces dealing with jazz by such writers as Gary Giddens, Whitney Balliett, and Martin Williams.

Angela Davis's Blues Legacies and Black Feminism

Angela Davis's 1998 study, *Blues Legacies and Black Feminism: Gertrude "Ma" Rainey, Bessie Smith, and Billie Holiday,* incorporates insights from much of the earlier literature but attempts to illuminate, through examination of recorded performances of Rainey, Smith, and Holiday, what she describes as "unacknowledged traditions of feminist consciousness in working-class communities" (xi). While some earlier studies (and simply aficionados of women's blues, such as the present writer, who has for 25 years regularly presented radio programs on women's blues and specials on the great historical blues women) have recognized these traditions, none have made the argument so clearly as Davis. Moreover, Davis makes a still more original and significant contribution in demonstrating there are "*multiple* African-American feminist traditions" (xix), evident through exploring the body of recordings by Rainey, Smith, and Holiday.

Davis's chapter "Blame It On The Blues" is specially pertinent from the perspective of this essay's exploration of potentially liberatory political implications of blues as a complex historical tradition containing diverse discourses of protest, resistance, or cultural revolt. Davis there critiques some earlier arguments by Paul Oliver, Samuel Charters, and others, calling attention to the importance of larger socio-political *contexts* for understanding blues texts. A key contribution of Davis's study is the recognition that *protest* in music need not assume explicit political characteristics, necessitating "an organized political structure capable of functioning as a channel for transforming individual complaint into effective collective protest" (113), to be *effective* protest. Rather, she argues compellingly, through *aesthetic forms*, oppressive conditions can be identified and change exhorted:

> Rainey's and Bessie Smith's songs may be interpreted precisely as historical *preparation* for political protest. They are certainly far more than complaint, for they begin to articulate a consciousness that takes into account social conditions of class exploitation, racism, and male dominance as seen through the lenses of the complex emotional responses of black female subjects. While there may not be a direct line to social activism, activist stances are inconceivable without the consciousness such songs suggest. (119)

Davis correctly calls the reader's attention—as noted earlier—to traditions going back to the era of slavery, in which messages were *encoded*, a practice that has continued through decades of the blues. Attentive and knowledgeable listeners of the blues of whatever period will hear messages that others, listening casually, may miss completely. Certainly among the thousands of blues recordings by African-American women over the decades there is a significant diversity of statements from which to sample the ways black women have negotiated and re-articulated their socially constructed realities. Davis notes how previous approaches, concentrating on the individual biographies of the blues women, who often led painfully conflicted personal lives, "tend to foreground their subjects as 'characters' and often fail to situate the individuals in the larger historical/social/political contexts in which they live or lived" (121). There are problems with such an approach, including the contested meaning of *authorship* and issues of attribution. Are the lyrics written by the singers? If the songs are written by others, usually men, do the women singers endorse the lyrical content, or are they simply producing a product for a possible market, as suggested by recording producers, who might simply supply them with a sheet of lyrics? This seems particularly so with the sexually explicit "dirty" blues, with detailed objectification of images of male sexual organs and technique that make up a small but significant portion of classic women's blues, but it also might apply to situations where a song contains lyrics making detailed comment on economic conditions.

The section of Davis's study dealing with the songs of Billie Holiday, two chapters totaling a scant 37 pages, bearing the titles "When A Woman Loves A Man" and "Strange Fruit," highlights some of the authorship issues. Holiday—aside from the relatively few actual blues songs she performed or recorded, such as "Fine and Mellow" and "Baby, Get Lost"—sang and recorded almost exclusively so-called jazz "standards," written originally by male composers for shows or as part of the manufactured song production of "Tin Pan Alley" (unfortunately, probably because of onerous and sometimes costly permissions process, Davis does not include as many detailed song lyrics for Holiday as she does for Rainey and Smith). Yet every jazz book, chapter, or set of record notes I can recall that mentions the importance of Holiday notes her incomparable phrasing and inflection of lyrics. Instrumentalists such as Miles Davis have noted her influence on his and others' playing, as have others (Crouch). Admittedly, while her work took place in a virtually totally masculinist context and from a masculine view point (recognized by Davis, 178, noting Michele Wallace's comments), Holiday could still create, through her incomparable delivery of lyrics composed by others, her own *authorship* of a song (Margolick; Williams; Crouch). Arranger and bassist Bob Haggard, music director for some of her Decca sessions, once said to John Chilton, "Billie could take a standard tune and add her Midas touch to the existing melody—giving the song a whole new value" (Lasker). Her performance could thus amount to a kind of authorship in the same way great instrumental stylists could deliver a unique interpretation of a standard tune. In fact, by comparing alternative versions of such standards, one can clearly sense the unique voice, style and creativity of improvising artists. Similarly, one might compare and contrast the delivery and virtual re-composition of songs, while speaking the same lyrics, of great blues and jazz singers.

Nonetheless, the retrospective analysis of such song texts, based on historical recordings, does run the risk of ascribing or attributing ideological meaning to a performance that the performing artist never intended. But that does not mean the meaning is not *there*, properly contextualized, even when the artist did not see, hear, or intend it. Intentionality is an issue far too complex to treat here, but one I have discussed elsewhere in some detail (see *Rhythm and Resistance*). Nonetheless, Davis's study demonstrates some of the potential payoffs, along with potential hazards, of using performed musical texts of the past as prime sites for investigation of the social and political ideologies evident in classic and more recent women's blues.

Three Models of Blues Resistance: Johnny Shines, J. B. Lenoir, and Memphis Minnie

Johnny Shines

Johnny Shines's (1915-1992) best recordings crackle with energy. In person he was a magnetic performer whose slashing slide guitar embodied the spirit of his 1930s sometime running mate, the legendary Robert Johnson. While the Johnson association was evident in his performances of such songs as "Ramblin" and "Dynaflow Blues," which sound like the very best of Johnson's work of the 1930s, Shines had his own vocal sound and guitar style. What made him such a powerful performer was his ability to combine a mastery of the spoken word with a performing style to conjure up the ghosts of the early 20th century Mississippi Delta. He was a gifted story teller who could rivet an audience with tales of the repressive era of slavery, making it seem a contemporary issue. Shines was also a powerful social critic who never ignored what he saw to be historical truth.

While now critically acclaimed, during the 1940s and 1950s, when he was at his performing peak, he only issued a very few recordings, working various jobs as a laborer and (later) as a photographer. He was "rediscovered" in 1964 by British researcher Mike Rowe, author of *Chicago Breakdown* and then recorded by Samuel Charters in 1965 for the much acclaimed Vanguard

Records series, *Chicago—The Blues—Today*. (I first heard Shines on these recordings in the late 1960s, but had the pleasure of actually spending a day with him and his long-time traveling companion and co-performer Robert Jr. Lockwood in early 1979, when the two performed at a Santa Barbara Blues Society concert and I acted as their chauffeur, guide, and dinner host).

Shines was born in Frazier, Tennessee April 25, 1915, spending most of his youth in Memphis and south into the Mississippi Delta. He acknowledged Howlin' Wolf as a first musical influence, but traveled and performed with Robert Johnson in the late 1930s until Johnson's mysterious death. Johnny Shines was always moving in new directions. He quit the music business completely in 1958—apparently disgruntled with the musicians' union over several matters, even pawning his all his equipment—only to return a few years later. In the early 1980s, Robert Jr. Lockwood told me in a phone conversation of his frustration with Shines, who was then recovering from a stroke, yet rather than practicing to regain his guitar technique, had taken a course in electric motor repair. Possessed of a fascinating conspiratorial and paranoid outlook and vision on the world and the history of the relations between the races, Shines said to me over dinner in 1979, "Do you know they've got *black* opera singers—in Italy! And *they*'re not telling *us* about it." He was apparently seeing it as part of the long conspiracy on the part of the white power structure to keep black Americans from knowing the achievements of their sisters and brothers in other lands. He long aspired to travel to Africa, but never made it.

A rare, largely unknown, but powerful and characteristic composition and performance by Shines, embodying some of his unique vision, is his "Livin' in the White House" recorded for the J.O.B. label January 12, 1953, just prior to Eisenhower's succession to the Presidency:

[Now] I'm living in the White House
Just tryin' to help old Ike along (X2)
And tryin' to make amendment
for things Harry left undone

I don't need no police to chauffeur me to no jail (x2)
Because, I'm kinda in a hurry,
I have to write Space Cadet!

I want to live in Paradise,
Make servants outa' kings and queens
I want to live in Paradise,
Make servants outa' kings and queens

Now, don't shake me please, darlin'
This is one time
I want to finish my dream!
[on Paula Records CD PCD-4]

In this selection, backed by Sunnyland Slim on piano and J.B. Lenoir on guitar, Shines displays characteristic elements of his imagination, irony, and social criticism. In referencing the then extremely popular *Space Cadet* TV show (it ran on all four major networks in the early 1950s), Shines sardonically attempts an ironic linkage in the minds of his black listeners with an element of larger, repressively dominant, and ubiquitous white television popular culture of the day. More significantly, he anticipated the incoming Eisenhower administration, while adding to the long line of songs addressed exclusively to an African-American cultural audience about the (then-preposterous) incongruity of a black man actually advising—or, earlier in the 20th century, even *visiting*—the President of the United States.

One of the earliest examples of such tacit political knowledge and commentary directed at a racial in-group was Gus Cannon's 1927 topical blues, "Can you blame the colored man?" (once available on Yazoo LP 1022, *Memphis Jamboree*). Memphis blues man Cannon's topical blues was recorded originally under his nickname "Banjo Joe," and backed by the guitar legend Blind Arthur Blake. One of the few directly political blues, it was a comment on Booker T. Washington's famous White House dinner with President Theodore Roosevelt, October 16, 1901, which caused something of a national furor. Cannon's lyric milked the historical event for the laughs it would occasion among his black listeners:

Now Booker T., he left Tuskegee
To the White House he went one day,
He was goin' to call on the President
In a quiet and sociable way . . .

Now when Booker knocked on the President's door
Old Booker he begin to grin
Now he almost changed his color,
When Roosevelt says to 'Come in.'
'We'll have some dinner—in a little while'

Now, could you blame the colored man
For makin' them goo-goo eyes?

Shines's 1953 lyric, while it came before the U.S. Supreme Court's 1954 *Brown v. Board of Education* decision that desegregated public schools, not only anticipated the presence of an African American advisor at the highest levels 48 years later—when George W. Bush could name a (conservative) black woman, Dr. Condolezza Rice, as his National Security Advisor and another black/mixed race man, Colin Powell as Secretary of State—but looks far *beyond* that to a social/political world turned upside down in a wildly utopian, anarchist vision: "I want to live in Paradise, make servants outa' kings and queens." He does so while recognizing and sharing with his listeners what to all of them then would be the absurdity of his vision: "Now don't shake me darlin', this is one time I want to finish my dream!"

Johnny Shines was the personification of the conscience and visionary power of the classic country blues men, transported to the city in the 1940s, then touring the nation over the next 40 years. I recall vividly his 1979 Santa Barbara performance with Robert Jr. Lockwood (the "step son" of blues legend Robert Johnson—Johnson lived with Lockwood's mother). An apparently inebriated Joe Cocker (the English rock vocalist) was in the audience, and listeners urged Shines—who was not familiar with the artist, resident in Southern California—to let Cocker come up to sing with him and Lockwood and their band. Shines invited him to the stage. After a sloppy-drunk, semi-coherent mumbled blues, Cocker departed. Shines, clearly unimpressed, even insulted by Cocker, glared at the crowd members who had urged him to bring up the "star." Addressing them sternly, he reminded them that *this* music—his art—was much more than drunken party music: "Do you people know that *this* music came from *people who were slaves*?!" The audience quieted, and Shines then performed a furious extended acoustic slide guitar blues that might have come from a night 80 years before. The all-white crowd was riveted to their seats by the force of his performance, transported back to another era, across a racial divide. They might have been laborers back on some Delta plantation, gathered about a man whose music asserted their unique individuality—their ability to resist the commercial and cultural forces threatening the distinctiveness of their expressive vision.

J. B. Lenoir

Mississippi/Chicago blues man J.B. Lenoir (1929-1967) addressed tough rights issues in his songs as much or more than any other blues performer of his era. In the 1950s, in his politically-charged "Eisenhower Blues," he made comments on the economic recession of the time, identifying it with the national administration, which apparently—though much of this is hearsay—sent some "men in black" from Washington to his record producers and to his own home, questioned his motives and, with veiled threats, suggested he "watch" what he was doing to avoid trouble. (This was in the McCarthy era of Red Scares and repression of alleged communists.) Later, in May 1965 and September 1966, recording two albums of acoustic guitar and vocals to be issued in Europe by German promoter Horst Lippmann with Chicago legend Willie Dixon supervising, Lenoir composed some of the most striking anti-war blues and civil-rights-themed blues ever done by anybody, "Down in Mississippi," "Shot on Meredith," and "Vietnam Blues." "Vietnam Blues" is a riveting performance that remains one of the most striking statements by any black artist throughout the Vietnam War period. A prescient statement of what mass black opinion would become by the end of the 1960s, the song embodies all the critical power of the blues tradition, expressed *against* what, at that moment, was relatively overwhelming white and black *support* of the war. It is also an insightful commentary on the hypocrisy of the U.S. Johnson administration's public professions of their protection of "freedom" in Southeast Asia, especially hypocritical given the endemic racism at home.

Vietnam, Vietnam, everybody's cryin' about Vietnam (X2)
[but] These old lonely days, killing me down in Mississippi,
nobody seem to give a damn

Oh God [Lord] if you can hear my prayer now
Please help my brothers over in Vietnam (X2)
The poor boys fightin', killin', hidin' out in holes
May be killin' their own brothers they do not know

Mr. President, you always cry about peace,
But you must clean up your house before you leave

Oh, how you cry about peace
But you must clean up your house before...you go

How can you tell the world why we need peace
and you still mistreat and killin' poor me?

Lenoir's sentiments would become mass public sentiments three years later, though the war would continue to drag on, with U.S. financial support, through the Nixon-Ford administration—at least until the rout of the Saigon forces in 1975. J. B. Lenoir died suddenly and unexpectedly in 1967 from injuries received in an auto accident, with no sign of peace anywhere. His haunting final recordings on *Vietnam Blues* continue to express the critical power of blues discourse in relation to crucial civil rights issues.

"Memphis Minnie" and Women's Blues
While Bessie Smith carries the title of the Empress of the Blues and is generally recognized as the greatest of all the classic era blues singers, another exultantly strong female figure who sang, composed, and was a riveting instrumentalist is sometimes overlooked. "Memphis Minnie" was born in Algiers, Louisiana in 1897 as Lizzie Douglas, soon known as Minnie, and then "the Kid." She moved to Memphis, Tennessee as a girl, spending 20 years in the hectic musical life on Beale Street (with side trips to Mississippi to study with the legendary Willie Brown) before moving to Chicago. First known among blues men as "Kid Douglas," she hung out with the original Memphis Jug Band. Later she lived with Casey Bill Weldon, who was nine years her junior, one of the greatest of the Hawaiian-style steel guitar blues men and, as available recordings of Weldon suggest, a stunning instrumental stylist. She later married and recorded frequently with Joe McCoy, sometimes known as "Kansas Joe," (who had no connection to Kansas, but was given the name by a record producer). Her output of records, approximately 200 songs, mostly written by her, was at a consistently high level throughout her career which extended until 1960. She returned to Memphis with her third blues man husband Ernest Lawlers (known as "Little Son Joe"), with whom she had frequently recorded. She died in a Memphis nursing home in 1973, some years after a stroke.

What was, and remains, a striking quality of Memphis Minnie's recording persona as heard decades later on a number of CDs (see AMG), is the firm independence in her lyrics in scores of songs, such as "I Don't Need That Junk Outa You" (1931), in which she takes her man to task for taking her money, which would be fine—if he came home (but he doesn't): "I stood on the corner lookin' for you all night long." This leads Minnie to declare, "Lookit here, man, you can't be mine and somebody else's too!" And, "Man, I don't need that junk outa you." Other themes among the some 200 recordings were classics like the sexually objectifying "Bumble Bee," covered in later years by Big Mama Thornton, and reworked into Muddy Waters' classic "Honey Bee," and "Black Rat": "you are one black rat; someday I'll find your trail, and bury my shoe—close to your shirt tail!" The latter was again covered in a notable version by Big Mama Thornton in the 1960s. In 1941 Minnie recorded one of her biggest hits, "Me and My Chauffeur," with memorable lines about her not wanting her chauffeur man to be "driving" those other girls around, instead wanting him to drive *her* "around the world"—which carried *double entendre* meanings to schooled listeners. Her 1930s composition "Lonesome Shack" was notable for its sensitivity to the likely leaving of men and the necessity of being prepared by having her own place, a "lonesome shack" in which she would put her bed "in the southeast corner." Of course, as Charters (*Sweet* 83-95) notes, most of her women listeners, living in urban tenements with limited financial resources, would have no such opportunities and probably could not have located where the "southeast corners" of their rooms were!

Yet, metaphorically, Minnie's song suggested that women had to think for and about themselves in their relationships with men, to be prepared for the possibility they might be left—alone. Among Memphis Minnie's recordings, I have always especially appreciated her "In My Girlish Days" and "Nothin' in Ramblin'" from the early 1940s, in which she looks back on her life of freedom and carousing and, while not regretting anything, suggests she is also very happy with who she is now, at that moment. Some of her happiest-sounding late-period recordings were for the short-lived Regal label in 1949 (available on a Biograph CD collection), on which she plays some searing electric guitar, her vocals interspersed with laughter at the good times she seems to be having in the studio recording "I'm a Down Home girl" (she had, of course, lived in Chicago for at least 15 years), and an hilarious couple of takes of "Night Watchman Blues," in which she is obviously so enjoying herself, perhaps with drink or weed, that she gets her tongue twisted into "Wight Natchman, Wight Natchman" but punches out some sharp, percussive chords at the words, "Time for you to punch your clock!" (Biograph CD).

Johnny Shines recalled the wild club scene in Chicago he found when he arrived there in the early 1940s, and Memphis Minnie's place in it: "Any men that fool with her she'd go for them right away. She didn't take no foolishness off them. Guitar, pocket-knife, pistol, anything she get her hand on she'd use it; y'know Memphis Minnie used to be a hell-cat...(H)er and Son Joe, Roosevelt Sykes used to work together...boy! They'd have some of the terriblest rows but Memphis Minnie'd be the winner every time—she'd have it her way or else!" (Rowe 43).

Minnie was a terrific guitar player, blues lore has it, who could cut *any* male guitarist, winning club guitar contests on the strength of her searing early electric guitar technique, which obviously benefitted from the intricate blues finger-picking and phrasing she had learned over the two preceding decades, including several years apprenticeship (during her late teens) in Mississippi, where she had gone from Memphis to learn from the legendary country bluesman Willie Brown. Minnie's prodigious technique earned the overwhelming applause of the patrons in the Chicago club audiences. Big Bill Broonzy summed up the views of the top rank of Chicago blues men of her era when he said she could "pick a guitar and sing as good as any man I've *ever* heard" (Briton 2). Broonzy's language, which might seem condescending, obscured the truth that Memphis Minnie was a phenomenal and pioneering blues musician who, according to some accounts, played a ferocious stand-up electric guitar live on stage in Chicago at least a year *before* Muddy Waters even began playing electric, and five years before Muddy's first major electric blues single,"I Can't Be Satisfied" on Chess Records (1948). Sadly, Memphis Minnie was never *recorded* playing guitar that way, though one gets a few flashes of her electric style in the 1949 Regal sessions (on a Biograph CD). When most blues guitarists still performed from a chair, Minnie began standing up, her guitar slung down on her hips. She played electric guitar with a fierce power, virtually unparalleled in her time. Some of the other early electric guitar blues and jazz players, such as T-Bone Walker or Eddie Durham, both out of Texas, were much more restrained or laid back in their styles. Minnie was clearly an early "guitar killer," and her years during the 1920s married to Casey Bill Weldon undoubtedly contributed to her performance style.

Early in 1943, poet Langston Hughes saw Minnie play at the 230 Club and was overwhelmed, devoting his column in the January 9, 1943 *Chicago Defender* to her performance:

> Memphis Minnie beats out blues on an electric guitar…She grabs the microphone and yells, 'Hey now!' Then she hits a few deep chords at random, leans forward ever so slightly on her guitar, bows her head and begins to beat out a rhythm so contagious that it makes the crowd holler out loud…All these things cry through the strings on Memphis Minnie's electric guitar, amplified to machine proportions—a musical version of electric welders plus a rolling mill. (quoted in Briton 3)

Memphis Minnie, clearly one of the strongest, most assertive of any of the blues men or women of the classic era, always presented an image and recording persona of a woman with a clear sense of who she was, in control of her own life, and unwilling to take any crap from anybody—especially the men who said they wanted to do things *for* her (Garon, *Woman*). Her life and career as a woman performer—in effect, her resistance to social practices that had traditionally excluded women from achieving a public presence—suggest the important role she and other female blues artists played in emancipatory rights discourses.

The Blues and the Psychology of Resistance

As discussed earlier in the essay, the blues was a product of the era after Reconstruction in which blacks were formally freed from bondage to the land, but found themselves increasingly repressed on every side in economic terms, as was evident in the conditions which fostered the emergence of the sanctified churches and engendered gospel music in the late 19th century (Pratt, *Rhythm and Resistance: Explorations* 47-74). This situation produced a growing psychological tension and thwarted personal expectations as the promise of Emancipation gave way to the harsh realities of racism and Jim Crow legislation. Out of these conditions, the blues continued to grow as an intensely *personalized* music, as evidenced in the earliest eyewitness accounts from Mississippi and Texas and the recordings of the major figures of country blues in the 1920s and 1930s. Their songs expressed an increasingly rich and complex creative subjectivity, evidence both of the possibilities of the free space that the music provided for the creative expression of the personality of the performer and of the innate artistic powers of the most oppressed members of society.

The music created was thus a response to new forms of thwarted individuality, by those who both performed and heard the music. Some writers on the effects of slavery stressed the atomization of individuals and crushing of spirit that the system intentionally sought. Yet, as Baraka makes central to his interpretive history *Blues People*, the very *opposite* was the historical result. As Albert Murray pointed out, rather than asserting the inevitability of some indelible "mark of oppression" (as expressed by Kardiner and Ovesey, 1951; see critique by Thomas and Sillen 45-56), a more accurate description of the powerful legacy might be "a disposition to confront the most unpromising circumstances and make the most of what there is to go on, regardless of the odds," while "finding delight in the process...[and] forgetting mortality at the height of ecstasy" (Murray 69-70).

Rather than dwelling on what was done *to* the creators of the blues, it might be far more fruitful to consider what they did with what was done to them, to consider how they seized from their apparently limited and oppressive world the opportunities to create a music that persists through generations, remaining one of most significant of world rebel musics, informing and influencing much of the popular music of recent decades. There is an important *political* lesson: oppressed people fight with resources they have, entering arenas to which they have access. In the case of black people in the United States, to engage in *cultural* action was/is rational and effective action given the context in which they had to work and the absence of organized movements and parties that would advance their interests, at least until the first Civil Rights legislation was proposed as late as the 1940s during the Truman Administration and the subsequent emergence of several organized movements during the 1950s and 1960s (Morris).

As young black people of each generation encountered anew the brutal reality of racist oppression, the encounter culminated for many in a psychic wounding of character and withdrawal—as black children found that beyond a certain age they were no longer acceptable playmates, or could not drink from "whites only" water fountains, or could *not*, as Martin Luther King's young daughter found out in the mid-20th century, visit a widely-advertised amusement park (Oates 181-2), simply because of the color of their skin. But interestingly, the predominant response has been an affirmation: the creation of *an alternative culture of resistance*. In the years since the first generation of supposedly emancipated blacks produced the blues, there have been many political and social expressions of resistance. Some—a minority—have moved toward actual radical political activism (Morris; Evans and Boyte). Yet black *music*—in all its rich varieties from classic country blues through rap and the varieties of jazz, from Armstrong to Coltrane, to the fusion of "space" music and jazz of Sun Ra—remains the most profound and affirmative *cultural* embodiment of such resistance. As the decades pass, it may constitute a more *enduring* "political" response—in the sense of providing an available and evolving cultural resource—than more formally-organized movements, which rise and fall, come and go.

The blues was and remains an affirmational response to psychological needs the system of racism over the decades sought to deny. The music communicates expectations, desire, indignation, joy, and sensuality in a fusion of enduring power and appeal, allowing "things to be *sung* that could not otherwise be expressed." The blues are *ritualized* to a high degree, with forms and conventions that function psychologically, John Szwed notes, with the intention of "easing or blocking" the stress associated with what A.F.C. Wallace has termed "transformation of state." Such ritual events help to restore a sense of social equilibrium under conditions producing severe individual psychological stress (Szwed 223-5). Thus the old notion that the blues ease the "troublin' mind." A large number of songs embody those words, the best known being Richard M. Jones's 1926 formalization of traditional materials into the blues "Trouble in Mind," which itself has since become a part of the oral folk tradition:

I'm blue,
But I won't be blue always,
…the sun's gonna shine in my back door some-day.

The St. Louis blues man Henry Townsend (born 1909), interviewed by Paul Oliver, demonstrated acute insights into the psychological mechanisms involved in the appeal of the blues:

There's several types of blues—there's blues that connects you with personal life—I mean you can tell it to the public as a song, *in* a song. But I mean, they don't take it seriously which you are tellin' the truth about. They don't always think seriously that it's exactly you that you talkin' about. At the same time it could be you, more or less it would be you to have the feelin'. You express yourself in a song like that. Now this particular thing reach others because they have experience [sic] the same condition in life so naturally they feel that what you are saying because it happened to them…Because people in general they takes the song as an explanation for themselves— they believe this song is expressing their feelings instead of the one singin' it. (Oliver, *Conversation* 164-165)

The blues serve a cathartic function, providing a means of psychological release through the "substitute imagery," which is an important way that popular music functions to meet the needs of the mass audience.

Another psychological approach to the blues conceives the music as the return of all that society has *repressed* in the minds of people seeking their fullest individuality. Herein lies another reason for the appeal of the blues among a stratum of college educated, yet alienated, intelligentsia as well as among significant numbers of white radical intellectuals who find themselves "outsiders" in American society. Proceeding from a surrealist-psychoanalytic perspective, Paul Garon, in *Blues and the Poetic Spirit,* hears the blues as a form of *poetic revolt* against all the repressions of society: for Garon, "the blues is the musical and poetic expression of working-class black Americans, and as such it has served and continues to serve a specific function in a specific social context" (15). He regards the blues as "the poetic voice of a people distinctively victimized by the whole gamut of the repressive forces of bourgeois/Christian civilization" (16). In this view, the blues in the present era can still play a significant role in releasing the human mind from the repressions *all* experience as humans in civilization.

The blues, Garon argues, are also a kind of "spontaneous intuitive *critical method.*" Through free association and expression of some of the most passionate inner feelings, "the imaginative possibilities" of existence are hinted at—a key element underlying rights discourses, yet one neglected in the legal and political discourses of actual rights legislation. Nowhere is this more evident than in the treatment of sexuality and eroticism. These possibilities are the first thing that strikes many listeners about the blues. As a teenager in the 1950s, I first heard records of blues shouters Jimmy Rushing and Big Joe Turner, with lines as:

Some like 'em tall and mellow,
Some like 'em short and brown,
You can't tell the difference
When the sun goes down.

(Rushing, Jimmy. "Jimmy's Blues." With Count Basie Orchestra. New York: Columbia Records, 1944)

Or,

Tell me pretty baby, how you want your rollin' done.

(Turner, Big Joe and Pete Johnson. "Tell Me Pretty Baby." Arhoolie CD333)

I was stunned and delighted by their directness, especially compared with the sexual repression buried deep in pop lyrics or even the evident sexuality in performances by Elvis Presley. Writers such as Samuel Charters have long extolled this quality, remarking with regards to his initial attraction to the black blues tradition that, "white culture had developed…defensive hypocrisy toward so many elements in its life, from sexuality to more personal mores. In the black expression I found direct-ness, an openness and an immediacy I didn't find in the white" (Charters, *Country* ix).

Garon sees a similar directness and immediacy, suggesting "the search for erotic love lies at the core of the blues—indeed at the core of all authentic poetry—just as sexuality lies at the core of every individual" (*Blues* 66). To those who stress an obsessive preoccupation with sexuality in the blues (usually expressed in far more subtle terms than contemporary rock and certainly rap lyrics), he counters with the notion that "all *humanity* is preoccupied with sexuality, albeit most often in a repressive way; the blues singers, by establishing their art on a relatively non-repressive level, strip the 'civilized' disguise from humanity's preoccupation…" (66). Here the interpretation of the erotic goes beyond the merely sexual toward the more expansive conception of human liberation found, say, in Herbert Marcuse's 1955 classic *Eros and Civilization* (Bokina and Lukes).

In Garon's interpretive reading the rich varieties of the blues hint at "new realities of non-repressive life, dimly grasped in our current state of alienation and repression," but revealed by treatments of sexuality in the blues. Previously unimagined desires are evoked, poetically tran-scending existing morality. The truths revealed are not simply imaginative; while the blues ex-press both frustrated and satisfied sexuality, this is paradigmatic for the whole human condition. Blues people—singers and instrumentalists—become *poetic tribunes*, not just on behalf of a re-pressed social minority, but on behalf of those who feel "the dynamic interrelationship of pro-jected gratification and actual frustration," which is "the key to the essence of the blues" (67).

Garon argues that the appeal and critical power of the blues, and a basis of its continuing attraction is that "what is possessed is not wished for—what is not possessed is wished for." This capacity for *fantasy*—allowing listeners to address frustrations and repressed desires—creates a cultural form embodying simultaneously *reflective* and *projective* potential: "the capacity for fantasy becomes the crucial function in the ability to finally overthrow reality and the displea-sures that accompany it, to unleash desire in truly non-repressive situations of gratification and joy" (*Blues* 67).

Conclusion: Politics and Resistant Consciousness in the Blues

The blues are not primarily concerned with civil rights or obvious political protest: they are an art form and thus a transcendence of those conditions created…by the denial of social justice. As such they are one of the techniques through which Negroes have sur-vived and kept their courage during the long period when many whites assumed…they were afraid. (Ellison 251)

Garon's effusive ardor illuminates, at a rhetorical level, a certain subversive character—evident if one wishes to search back over a century of blues lyrics and recordings. In a similar way, as I noted earlier, Angela Davis's *Blues Legacies and Black Feminism* reveals the possibility of using blues texts retrospectively in the contemporary formulation of a kind of "revolutionary" discourse. But the task is complicated and problematic and can amount to a cultural cherry picking and selection out of context, becoming perilous in its validity if one tries to generalize about the whole tradition. None of the works discussed in this essay effectively demonstrates that the blues is—except among a minority of radical intellectuals and *aficionados*, despite the electrifying performances one can nightly encounter in a Chicago club or at many festivals—still a living and subversive cultural form in the contemporary period. One can say, however, that the enthusiasm of writers such as Garon or Davis is valid, if only for the fact that virtually *every* form of contemporary popular music in the United States, from jazz to rock to rap to country-and-western, has been shaped or influenced by the blues. Yet, other than Davis's arguments, there is no effective demonstration in all of the blues literature of how the rebellious, subversive, poetic elements in the historical examples of the music—fantasy, desire, imagination, irony, humor, satire, criticism—*necessarily* lead to or support any organized, continuing, identifiable political or revolutionary tendency. Lacking in all such approaches attributing *political* influence is a distinction between a kind of *culture of revolt,* which the historical blues certainly was, versus a conception of *organized movement* as revolutionary force, in which one cannot say the blues has ever been directly involved. This is not to ignore that many political radicals—black and white—over the years in the United States have loved the blues. Nor is to ignore that the blues is a fundamental constituent of African-American cultural nationalism. In much blues literature there is a reading back into or projecting *onto* the body of historical blues texts of critical political perspectives that develop out of a diverse variety of influences.

The blues, like all forms of popular music, has run the risk of being integrated into the commodity culture of the cultural-industrial complex. Many radical enthusiasts of *rock* in the 1960s seemed to believe an emotionally charged and progressive musical culture, in part created out of cultural alienation and in part out of what seemed to be an emergent "counter-culture," would somehow contribute to the mobilization of human commitment and goals of political organization aimed at transforming U.S. society. Yet rock declined, transformed largely into a cultural commodity, though many musicians from the era remain committed to "progressive" causes decades later.

So, where does the "revolutionary" *political* power of the blues lie? Lawrence Levine, in *Black Culture and Black Consciousness,* notes how, in many discussions of the blues, "group consciousness and a firm sense of self have been confused with *political* consciousness and organization" (239). The oral (Sidran) and poetic/poetry of revolt (Garon) motifs examined here arguably incorporate powerful kinds of *general* assaults on capitalist culture and social relations in ways beyond the immanent critique of racism embodied in the music (a critique itself rarely explicit in blues lyrics). In the history of the blues one can often see elements of a *general* antipathy to the whole system of white-dominated capitalist culture and social relations, combined with an irreverence and critical orientation generally toward traditional values—of uncritical patriotism and organized religion especially—that are often upheld in other forms of popular music. As pointed out by Boggs and Pratt, that these critical elements of the blues never became linked to *concrete* political objectives does not contradict this or deny the *expressive power* of the blues. Nor does it ignore the power of the *model* of cultural commentary, critique, and resistance evident in past blues performances for inspiring contemporary generations. Yet "the leap from a 'subversive' cultural form to an organized socio-political movement is an enormous and complicated one, and blues historically has exercised little, if any, [direct] radicalizing influence on the black community or on American politics in general" (Boggs and Pratt 289). This fact does not detract from the cultural integrity and expressive power of resistance embodied in historical blues traditions, nor does it detract from the possibility of contemporary inspiration for civic consciousness that can be derived from historical blues recordings. In these special, delimited historical senses, the blues still functions today as a significant discourse of resistance.[2]

NOTES

1. References made in this way throughout this essay refer generally to the works in their entirety as cited in the bibliography.
2. For more on blues recordings, readers are directed to *The All-Music Guide to the Blues* (San Francisco: Miller Freeman Books,1999), edited by Michael Erlewine et.al, and the frequently up-dated website <www.all-music.com>. This essay draws on courses taught by the author over many years and the author's years as producer-host of blues radio programs: weekly during 1978-79 on KCSB-FM, Santa Barbara, CA, as "The Good Morning, Blues Show"; and weekly, from October 1979 through January 1999, as "The Blues Tradition," and then later from September 2001 to the present, as "Blues in the Groove," on KGLT-FM, Bozeman, MT. The author wishes to thank the editors and Carl Boggs for valuable discussions on the political implications of the blues.

WORKS CITED

Albertson, Chris. *Bessie.* New York: Stein & Day, 1972.

AMG, *All Music Guide to the Blues.* Eds. Thomas Erlewine et.al. San Francisco, Miller-Freeman Books, 1999.

Baker, Houston A., Jr. *Blues, Ideology, and Afro-American Literature.* Chicago: U of Chicago P, 1984.

Baraka, Amiri [LeRoi Jones]. *Blues People.* New York: William Morrow, 1963.

Barlow, William. *Looking Up At Down: The Emergence of Blues Culture.* Philadelphia: Temple UP, 1989.

Bastin, Bruce. *Red River Blues: The Blues Tradition in the Southeast.* Urbana: U of Illinois P, 1986.

Biograph CD. *Early Rhythm & Blues, 1949.* #B000003HLY.

Boggs, Carl and Ray Pratt. "The Blues Tradition: Poetic Revolt or Cultural Impasse?" *American Media and Mass Culture: Left Perspectives.* Ed. Donald Lazare. Berkeley: U of California P, 1987. 279-292.

Bokina, John and Timothy J. Lukes. *Marcuse: From the New Left to the Next Left.* Lawrence, KS: UP of Kansas, 1994

Borneman, Ernest. "The Roots of Jazz." *Jazz.* Eds. Nat Hentoff and Albert J. McCarthy. New York: Da Capo, 1978.

Briton, JoBeth. "The Forgotten Queen: Was Memphis Minnie the Mother of Electric Blues Guitarists?" *The Worcester Phoenix* 20-27 June 1997: 1-4 <www.worcesterphoenix.com/archive/music/97/06/20/MEMPHIS_MINNIE.html> [accessed on-line Feb.2003].

Cannon, Gus. "Can you blame the colored man?" *Memphis Jamboree* Yazoo LP 1022, 1927.

Carby, Hazel. "It Jus' Be's Dat Way Sometime: The Sexual Politics of Women's Blues." *Radical America.* 20:4 (1986): 9-22.

Charters, Samuel. *The Country Blues*. New York: Da Capo, 1975.

——. *The Poetry of the Blues*. New York: Avon Books, 1970.

——. *Sweet As the Showers of Rain: The Bluesmen, Vol.II*. New York: Oak Publications, 1977.

Crouch, Stanley. Liner *Billie Holiday: All Or Nothing At All*. New York: Polydor Inc.,1978.

Davis, Angela. *Blues Legacies and Black Feminism: Gertrude "Ma" Rainey, Bessie Smith, and Billie Holiday*. New York: Pantheon Books, 1998.

Dixon, Robert M.W. and John Godrich. *Recording the Blues*. London: Studio Vista, 1969.

Ellison, Ralph. "Blues People." *Shadow and Act*. New York: Signet Books, 1966:241-250.[Rpt. of "The Blues." Review of *Blues People* by Leroi Jones. The *New York Review* 1.12 (6 Feb. 1964).

Evans, David. *Big Road Blues: Tradition and Creativity in the Folk Blues*. Berkeley: U of California P, 1982.

Evans, Sara and Harry Boyte. *Free Spaces: The Sources of Democratic Change in America*. New York: Harper & Row, 1986.

Fahey, John. *Charley Patton*. London: Studio Vista, 1970.

Fiske, John. *Television Culture*. London: Methuen, 1987.

——. *Understanding Popular Culture*. Boston: Unwin, Hyman, 1989.

Foner, Eric. "In Search of Black History." *New York Review of Books* 22 October 1970: 11-15.

Garon, Paul. *Blues and the Poetic Spirit*. London: Eddison Bluesbooks, 1975. San Francisco: City Lights Books, 1999.

Garon, Paul. *Woman With Guitar: Memphis Minnie's Blues*. New York: Da Capo, 1992.

Giddings, Paula. *When and Where I Enter: The Impact of Black Women on Race and Sex in America*. New York: William Morrow, 1984.

Goldstein, Richard. *Goldstein's Greatest Hits*. New York: Tower Publications,1970.

Harrison, Daphne Duval. *Black Pearls: Blues Queens of the 1920s*. New Brunswick: Rutgers UP, 1988.

Hogue, W. Lawrence, *Discourse and the Other: The Production of the Afro-American Text*. Durham, NC: Duke UP, 1986.

Kardiner, Abraham and L. Ovesey. *The Mark of Oppression*. New York: W.W. Norton, 1951.

Keil, Charles. *Urban Blues*. Chicago: U of Chicago P, 1966.

——. "True Blues."Rev. of *Deep Blues* by Robert Palmer, and *Roots of the Blues* by Samuel Charters. *New York Times Book Review* 27 September 1981: 15, 22.

Kelley, Robin D.G.,"The Riddle of the Zoot: Malcolm Little and Black Cultural Politics During World War II." In Joe Wood, ed., *Malcolm X:In Our Own Image*. New York: St. Martin's, 1992: 153-182.

Kellner, Douglas. *Media Culture*. New York: Routledge, 1995

Koch, Lawrence. "Harmonic Approaches to the 12-Bar Blues Form." *Annual Review of Jazz Studies* I (1982): 59-72.

Lasker, Stephen. Liner notes. *Billie Holiday: The Complete Decca Recordings [1944-1950]*. New York: GRP Records, 1991.

Lenoir, J.B. *Vietnam Blues*. Evidence CD, ECD26068-2, 1965-1966.

Levine, Lawrence. *Black Culture and Black Consciousness*. New York: Oxford UP,1977.

Lieb, Sandra. *Mother of the Blues: A Study of Ma Rainey*. Amherst: U of Massachusetts P, 1981.

Lipsitz, George. *A Rainbow at Midnight: Class and Culture in 1940s America*. Revised Edition. Chicago: U of Illinois P, 1994.

Lomax, Alan. Liner *Roots of the Blues*. New York: New World Records CD. New York, 1992. <http:www.newworldrecords.org/cgi-bin/search2/disc.cgi?disc=80252>

Malone, Bill C. *Southern Music-American Music*. Lexington: UP of Kentucky, 1979.

Marcus, Greil. "Critical Response." *Critical Studies in Mass Communication 3* (1986): 80-81.

Marcuse, Herbert. *Eros and Civilization*. Boston: Beacon, 1955.

Margolick, David. *Strange Fruit: Billie Holiday, Café Society, and An Early Cry for Civil Rights*. Philadelphia: Running Press, 2000.

Morris, Aldon. *The Origins of the Civil Rights Movement: Black Communities Organizing For Change*. New York: The Free Press, 1986.

Murray, Albert. *Stomping the Blues*. New York: Vintage Books, 1982.

Neal, Mark Anthony. *What the Music Said: Black Popular Music and Black Public Culture*. New York: Routledge, 1999.

Nicholson, Stuart. *Billie Holiday*. London: Victor Gollanz, 1995; Boston: Northeastern UP, 1995.

O'Meally, Robert G. *Lady Day: The Many Faces of Billie Holiday*. New York: Da Capo Press, 2000.

Oates, Stephen. *Let the Trumpet Sound: A Biography of Martin Luther King, Jr.* New York: Harper& Row, 1982.

Oliver, Paul. *Conversation With the Blues*. New York: Horizon, 1965.

—. *The Story of the Blues*. New York: Chilton Publications, 1969.

Ostransky, Leroy. *Jazz City: The Impact of Our Cities on the Development of Jazz*. New York: Prentice- Hall, 1978.

Palmer, Robert. *Deep Blues*. New York: Penguin Books, 1982.

Potter, Russell. *Spectacular Vernaculars: Hip-Hop and the Politics of Postmodernism*. Albany: State U of New York P, 1995.

Pratt, Ray. *Projecting Paranoia: Conspiratorial Visions in American Film*. Lawrence, KS: UP of Kansas, 2001.

—. *Rhythm and Resistance: Explorations in the Political Uses of American Popular Music*. New York: Praeger, 1990.

—. *Rhythm and Resistance: Political Uses of American Popular Music*. Second Edition. Washington, D.C.: Smithsonian Institution Press, 1994.

Rowe, Mike. Rpt. of as *Chicago Blues*, New York: Da Capo Press,1981 *Chicago Breakdown*. New York: Drake Publishers, 1975.

Russell, Ross. *Jazz Style in Kansas City and the Southwest*. Berkeley: U of California P, 1971. New York: Da Capo, 1997.

Schuller, Gunther. *Early Jazz: Its Roots and Development*. New York: Oxford UP, 1968.

Shaw, Arnold. *Black Popular Music in America*. New York: Schirmer Books, 1986.

Shines, Johnny. *Chicago—The Blues—Today*. Vanguard Records series. Samuel Charters, 1965.

—. "Livin' in the White House." With J.B. Lenoir and Sunnyland Slim. J.O.B., 1953.

Sidran, Ben. *Black Talk*. New York: Da Capo Press, 1981.[orig. pub. New York, 1971]

Stewart-Baxter, Derrick. *Ma Rainey and the Classic Blues Singers*. New York: Stein and Day, 1970.

Szwed, John. "Afro-American Musical Adaptation." *Afro-American Anthropology*. Eds. Norman E. Whitten and Szwed. New York: The Free Press, 1970.

Taylor, Frank C. with Gerald Cook, *Alberta Hunter: A Celebration in Blues*. New York: McGraw-Hill Paperbacks, 1988.

Thomas, Alexander and Samuel Sillen, *Racism and Psychiatry*. New York: Bruner/Mazel, 1972.

Titon, Jeff. *Early Downhome Blues: A Musical and Cultural Analysis*. Urbana: U of Illinois P, 1977.

Vaughn, Sarah. "No Count Blues." *No Count Sarah*. Written with Thad Jones. With the Count Basie Orchestra. Emarcy CD 824 057-2, 1958.

Ward, Brian. *Just My Soul Responding: Rhythm and Blues, Black Consciousness, and Race Relations*. Berkeley: U of California P, 1998.

Williams, Martin. "Billie Holiday: Actress Without An Act." *The Jazz Tradition, New and Revised Edition*. New York: Oxford UP, 1983: 83-91.

Woldu, Gail Hilson. "Blues Legacies and Black Feminism." Rev. of *Blues Legacies and Black Feminism: Gertrude "Ma" Rainey, Bessie Smith, and Billie Holliday*, by Angela Davis. *Women & Music Annual* (1999): 90-95.

Norman Nawrocki

6 / Rhythm Activism: A "Rebel News Orchestra/Rock 'n' Roll Cabaret" Band

This essay describes and reflects on my own involvement with the Montréal-based rebel music group Rhythm Activism as well as with the various (and diverse) communities for whom we perform. It considers some of the ways in which our group has sought through music to foster critical consciousness and to empower our audiences to work for social change.

NORMAN NAWROCKI is a Montreal cabaret artist, author, and musician who tours the world promoting creative resistance. His latest book, about a band tour of Europe, was *The Anarchist & The Devil Do Cabaret* (Black Rose Books, 2003). His latest CD is *DaZoque!*, a collaboration with the group of the same name.

Beyond Buttonhole Band

Imagine 400 people, aged 6 to 76, packed into a soup kitchen in Montréal's impoverished east end, stomping their feet, hollering, laughing, and clapping with approval, while, on stage, members of a rock band—in drag—alternately go go dance, engage in slapstick, and roll out 1960s Québec hit pop songs, all rewritten into a radical "community cabaret" about welfare rights—a show aiming to prime the audience to fight for justice.

Imagine the same band, months later, on tour in Europe, wearing suits and ties, playing blistering sets of original, indie music in hardcore clubs, for dreadlocked, tattooed and pierced hardcore anarcho punks and crusties as part of a benefit tour to raise money for Zapatista schools and hospitals in Chiapas, Mexico. Finally, picture a 10,000 strong crowd seething with rage against a public gathering of extreme right-wing Right to Lifers strutting their stuff through the streets of Old Montréal, protected by 500 riot police, while in the middle of the protest demonstration, this band plays drums and horns and sings satirical songs in an attempt to help diffuse the electric,

cop-riot-ready tension. This is Rhythm Activism—a flexible, all-purpose, "you-want-some-beats-on-the barricades?" performance unit, specializing not only in songs for resistance, but also in music for weddings, divorces and perogie parties.

Rhythm Activism (RA) is an internationally acclaimed, Montréal-based "rebel news orchestra," sometimes "rock and roll cabaret," sometimes "giant talking cartoon," "musical newspaper," and "radical class clown ensemble." It's also an "indie" band with an ever-changing cast of musicians, actors and other performers. Since 1985, RA has taken its high-energy, topical and provocative, issue-oriented roadshows and "resistance cabarets" across Canada, the USA and Europe. Always ahead of the news, RA is known as an act whose shows can make national headlines. There is no major music label support behind RA. It's a DIY (Do It Yourself) phenomenon for the anarcho-nation.

Funny and hardhitting, RA isn't afraid to take on issues of the day. The band can use costumes, masks and vaudeville to turn serious politics into subversive but hilarious living theatre. RA performs a surprise packed, riotous brand of independent, theatrical music and song, in English, French and Polish, and has appeared on stage either as a duo, a four to seven piece band, or a full-blown, "Fuck poverty—Let's smash Capitalism," acclaimed, popular circus with a cast of 50 dancers, actors, jugglers, acrobats, clowns and musicians. RA has recorded over 40 CDs, LPs, EPs, cassettes and compilations worldwide, and has composed soundtracks for films and videos, radio and TV documentaries, and been filmed itself. The band has raised consciences and tens of thousands of dollars for social justice projects across North America, Mexico and Europe. Read the reviews in Cantonese, Polish, Hungarian and Italian. RA knows no boundaries, musical or otherwise; it prefers to smash them all, and have a good time in the process. If the cause of Social Revolution is advanced ever so slightly, then all of RA's broken strings, blistered fingers and wine-bottle hangovers were worth it.

The band has a reputation for working closely with community groups, but slips just as easily in and out of punk clubs, poetry festivals and traditional Ukrainian weddings. RA's work takes it beyond the usual "we are a band" mentality, into a frontier where few indie music acts go, where community suppers or cookie and tea question and answer sessions, or even workshops could follow the performance, where shows are deliberately crafted to reach the moms and pops of poor neighbourhoods with a message, where RA—on and off the stage—is not only playing music, but also helping

Les Frères Giguère (The Gigger Brothers):
a pair of experts about everything
(L) Sylvain Côté (R) Norman Nawrocki

to mobilize and organize. This is Rhythm Activism. Another dissident voice, another dissonant chord for freedom. The music, the words, however funny or twisted, straightforward or rearranged, are always subversive in intent. The aim: to entertain, inform, and ultimately, empower audiences to take control of their own lives. Preferably, with the last laugh.

RA—The Concept

RA's home-base, Montréal, is known as "the poverty capital of North America," where, unofficially, one-in-five scrapes by on either provincial social assistance or federal unemployment insurance, where French and English co-exist peacefully, drinking beer, and where the once fabulously cheap rent meant any artist—political or not—could survive and create without fear of a mind-numbing, wage-slave noose around his or her neck. Musically, Montréal is renowned for its continuing stranglehold on disco, its love of smoky dance clubs, its embrace of any trendy Euro-beat, its claim to host the world's largest jazz festival, its ability to tolerate esoteric experiments like *musique actuelle*, and most importantly, its irrepressible, vibrant underground music scene. The kind that can spawn a band like RA.

RA was born in 1985 as a two person, poetry/music, crossover ensemble, during the height of the "performance poetry" trend sweeping the literary world. Poets were no longer content to simply read their work—everyone wanted to perform. The more outrageous the show, the better. A visible minority of loud, raw, "punk poets," decked out in spikes, leather and studs, spilled onto and off literary and club stages, denouncing the traditional, pretentious, academic-dominated poetry scene as lame and dated. Among them were a handful of daring "political poets," like the Brit's Nick Toczek and Atilla the Stockbroker, who used music to help them storm the literary scene, and gain acceptance in the bars and clubs where only raunchy bands usually ruled. Best of all, the heavyweight radical Jamaican dub poets like Linton Kwisi Johnson, Mutabaruka and Oko Onu raised the bar and showed how marrying critical words to thunderous beats could produce a new, gut-grabbing and hypnotic poetics of protest. These are the artists who inspired the faraway, fledgling RA.

Because 1985 was also the height of the "do-it-yourself" credo sworn to by punk rockers, people everywhere were drawn to the possibilities of creating one's own "free zone" of creative expression. The "Home-taping is-killing-the-music-business" ethos popular in the international, underground music scene also encouraged acts like RA to give the finger to the corporate music world and focus on their own non-commercial, creative ambitions.

From the start, RA's combo of cutting-edge music and topical, provocative, spoken word pieces laced with humour took everyone by surprise. The duo's focus on current issues like city politics, the homeless, squatting, date rape, and direct actions of street kids to clothe and feed themselves, led poetry snobs to say: "That's not poetry!", or "This political stuff is so dated. There's no future in it." They frowned on RA's experimental approach as an irrelevant, "uncool," "too weird" new genre. Nonetheless, RA shows drew strong, approving crowds from the start. The band seemed to fill a void. A certain audience was hungry for a new, politicized act. Mainstream music critics were puzzled but intrigued. RA didn't fit the "rock and roll" mold. It was neither mindless, nor formula, neither pure pop, nor punk, but a sort of edgy "agit-prop-pop." RA didn't really sing songs; these were growl-speak, self-described "news poems," and the odd, off-centred ode to love. These weren't pop tunes, they were musical soundscapes, except again, for the wacko cover versions of something really obscure. Local music TV rejected RA with the excuse that it "wasn't a real band;" there were only two members, it had no drummer and it was too "minimalist." Bar owners were leery to book RA, hypothesizing that the band couldn't serve the dance or drinking set's needs. However, the ringing of the beer cash register during RA shows would prove them wrong. The unstated but ever-present assumption among early disbelievers was that because RA's *raison d'être* was partially "political," that somehow made it invalid as entertainment or art. And in hindsight, the choice of RA's name—a description of what the band thought it was doing—set off silent alarms amongst the general apolitical public against a potentially boring, cliché, humourless product, which of course wasn't the case.

In the mid-1980s and early 1990s, the band had no problem carving out its own little performance niche in "anything-goes" Montréal. RA was dubbed "gypsy anarcho punk rockers," even though neither of the duo was a "punk." But "punk" in the eyes of the critics seemed to sum up the intellectual and musical challenge of RA and the band's attitude. No one else represented themselves as a high-energy, fun time, provocative, "alternative electrified journalism" musical package with an unmistakably intense focus on social issues. Outside the Western world of politicized punk bands like DOA, The Dead Kennedys, CRASS, The Clash and company, who else could get away with this? Political folkies? Not really. It's a no-brainer to say that after all the initial confusion and lack of comprehension on the part of critics and public alike, RA's early work was marginalized even beyond the edges of the already marginalized underground artist scene. But that didn't stop the band. RA started releasing home recorded and duplicated cassettes with hand-coloured, photo-copied covers and liner notes. Each release charted on college radio across North America, the little home-jobs rubbing shoulders with albums from the major corporate labels, even charting above them. RA's material was topical, newsworthy, different. The word spread. Audiences grew. Critics warmed up.

Beyond the Bars

I admit that the idea of live, spoken poetry backed by improvised electric guitar didn't set me on fire, but jeez these guys are powerful! Nawrocki's poems never just sit there, they CRANK, like a suddenly radicalized news anchorman. The guitarist provides eerily perfect backdrops to his diatribes, wailing away in free-form nirvana and then suddenly snapping back to coherence to drive the message home. Topics include the mass murdering of chickens, Dow Chemical, and the contagious singalong of "Coors: Nastiest Brewery in the West."—*Option Magazine*, Los Angeles

RA toured the underground bars and clubs of Canada, the USA and Europe and discovered that its work fit into a huge, international, political band network that included kindred-spirits like America's Fugazi, England's Chumbawamba, and Holland's The Ex, the Dog Faced Hermans and more.The public response to RA affirmed that even though the band had no commercial hits, it was doing something right. Non-traditional audiences—people who never visited the standard bars and haunts of poets and rock and rollers because they were too poor, too busy, or never really interested, became fans of RA's populist approach. Audience members would exclaim: "I had no idea poetry could sound like this, that it could deal with politics." And even though people said they had never heard anything quite like RA, they accepted the irreverent and sometimes challenging, but well-played music. The demand for more RA performances and recordings grew. Rhythm Activism satisfied a curious appetite out there for political, poetical, music and was invited to perform in places where no traditional "poet" or band had ever gone before. Most poets were confined to their poetry circles, underground musicians to their lofts and bars. RA broke through to a new, untapped general audience in soup kitchens and church basements where neither poets nor rock bands had performed before.

Metro Rebels

For RA's very first public performance in 1985, the duo selected a thematic image for a poster that proved to be highly popular. The Montréal public transit authorities were trying to discourage transit riders from using the city buses and subway or "metro" system without paying. Fares had recently gone up, and the transit riding public was not happy. Phony monthly bus passes were circulating; people were jumping the turnstiles; sneaking onto buses with recycled transfers, doing whatever they could to make public transit affordable for themselves—those without much money. Transit authorities embarked on a campaign to discourage riders from "defrauding" the system. Their symbol: a masked fox in a running position, with the slogan beneath: "Fraud doesn't pay." RA took the masked fox, reproduced him on a poster with the phrase: "Rhythm Activism: for Metro Rebels" and turned him into a people's hero. Strangers would knock on doors where the poster was displayed and ask if they could sign up to become a member of the newest gang in town: "Metro Rebels."

> They call us "fare cheaters" the system's worst enemy
> They call it "fraud" 'cause their "un-fair" we refuse to pay
> No one bothered to see the crime
> of bleeding the moneyless one more time
> so now stand proud

We're fare fighters
we're no pack of fools
we're fare fighters
we'll outfox all their rules"
(RA, "Transit Justice: the Good News")

Hardcore Poetics

Early RA shows were trademarked: poetry of revolt and subversive string plucking. RA was the sound of flying arms and fingers on a guitar sharing the beat, the wavelength, with rants and poems about social injustice and what people could do about it. Critics called it "Hardcore poetics," from Montréal's premiere "ranting poetry/rebel orchestra" ensemble.

RA's second recorded release—*RA Live*—a home-recorded, 11 song cassette from 1987, charted on alternative, campus radio across North America and propelled the duo into the international spotlight. The 60 minute, live recording showed the double-edged performance unit at its best on stage from Montréal to Olympia Washington. The pieces were presented as "news from the alleyways, and direct action for survival," and included "rollicking ballads and fables, raging news poems and dream fantasies from urban badlands." It covered direct action pacifists who broke into arms factories; the racism and long-standing far right politics of the COORS brewery family; corporate polluters, a history of Canada's little known, first labour strike outside Montréal in the mid-19th century, where canal construction workers were massacred by the State, and more. With increasing radio play, RA now was reaching hundreds of thousands of listeners in North America and abroad. The reticence about the relevance of "Rhythm Activism" began to fade. The concept of wedding activist music to activist poetry was no longer an odd, cultural experiment. The RA machine kept churning out the recordings, and a fan base grew.

From Peace Activism to Self-Reduction

As activist artists, RA usually covered the news of the day long before corporate media got to it. RA was "plugged into" ongoing actions around Montréal, and beyond, making it a point of staying informed, so that the band in turn could inform others. The specific creative process involved taking the news from the street and converting it into "alternative electrified journalism"—with a performance twist. RA wrote about housing activism; anti-sexist activism—all the everyday activisms that result when basic inequities, little and big injustices, make life difficult. RA documented this, then re-wrote and re-told the stories to make them performance-ready, recordable, and with the right music, enjoyable. The duo tried to avoid the reductivist solution of simple sloganeering—the kiss of death for any thoughtful activism. At the same time, RA was always on the lookout—at least lyrically—for a way to tell it like it was: succinctly, imaginatively, intelligently, and when possible, with a healthy humorous twist.

A Musical Fax Machine

Montréal radio stations especially looked forward to RA supplying musical commentary on current events. The band, living up to its reputation as a "musical fax machine," would churn out radio-friendly and catchy hits against the war machine, the social cut-backs and reforms machine, the State terror machine, the corporate spin machine and others. Speed in a crisis—a RA specialty. RA's early "instant cassette" releases added a critical voice to any social or political drama. When striking post-secondary school students in Québec asked RA for musical backup, the band wrote a song on a Friday night, recorded it Saturday, mixed it and duplicated copies on Sunday, and by Monday morning, delivered the copies, on bicycle, to student picket lines, where it was immediately played, picketers singing along, the words memorized, then translated into French for striking francophone campuses.

The "OKA Polka," was a cheesy ditty with toe-tapping hooks and lyrics about a soldier who disobeys orders to attack First Nations people during Canada's "OKA Crisis" in 1993, during the height of the 78 day armed standoff between a handful of Mohawk Warriors and over 2,000 tank and Canadian troops. The song shot up to number one across Canada on alternative stations. As part of the psychological warfare waged by both troops and Warriors, the Mohawks blasted the RA song from their side of the barricades with speakers aimed at the army.

Before the first American initiated Gulf War of 1991, CBC Radio Canada International called RA to ask: "Do you have anything about this war?" The band promised an anti-war album in one week. Six days later, a four-song, self-produced EP, *War is the Health of the State*, was mailed to radio stations across the country. RA called the release "Our statement against the War and Canada's knee-jerk, kiss ass participation in it." It debuted on Montréal streets, blaring out of a portable sound system in the middle of an anti-war demonstration before it started charting nationwide. One of the songs was a tongue-in-cheek public service commercial for "Mutiny Aftershave" for men, and "Mutiny Hair Shampoo" for her—two new products that would "help bring soldiers home, alive and smelling good. Your honey back or your money back." Another, "Yo Ho Ho!" was described by critics as "a farty, swashbuckling song about rum, oil and sailors on a warship to Iraq."

One Hell of an Electric Guitar

RA's original, non-conformist music was a conscious expression of dissent, of questioning and challenging extant corporate rock music culture. It was key to helping make the political story-telling work. And it was never boring.

Sylvain Côté's electric guitar was a powerful tool in the original RA arsenal. The band co-founder used it more as a sonic laboratory or workbench for sound, rather than as a simple stringed instrument to strum. He pounded, twisted, hammered, stretched, rearranged and squeezed unbelievable sounds out of his battered, old, classic Fender Jaguar. Here was a guitar-ist who broke all the rules and did the unthinkable with a sacred object of rock and roll. As he said himself in the liner notes to RA's first self-titled release in 1986:

> Fine, long filaments of wound metal are attached to fixed and moveable parts held to-gether by dried maple and rosewood, from where sonic vibrations stimulate and excite the ear. Struggling to be free, these sounds are let loose with the help of match-book covers, beer bottle caps, stone and plastic, through emotion and liberty of physical movement. Creating atmosphere, cutting loose is what it's all about; poetry taken one step higher.

At times, spoken word pieces were layered on top of expansive, rhythmic soundscapes. Others followed more traditional song structures with verse and chorus. There was no set formula. Ori-ginally, the "grinding, nasty, minimal" guitar work of Sylvain was the only music available to RA to accomplish the job. He would use distortion pedals, feedback, rocks and pieces of handheld metal, matchbook covers, elastic bands, forks—anything to make his strings speak differently. Early comparisons to the ground-breaking improv guitar work of England's Fred Frith and the USA's Eugene Chadborne were accurate, since both had influenced Sylvain's personal musical evolution. The RA sound always tried to stretch the public's musical taste, going from minimalist soundscape accompaniment to full-out rock 'n roll. There was always a passing nod or a wink to other musical genres.

RA were big fans of musical satire through words and musical arrangements. The tone, mel-ody and reproduction of the music; the lyrics and vocalizations; the voices, the background noises, the spirit of *joie de vivre*—all components were equally important, as was the need to al low space for that wonder drug: humour. RA loved nothing better than to deliver hard hitting, critical messages interspersed with something sublimely ridiculous both musically and lyrically. The project was founded on a mutual appreciation of having fun—on stage, and for audiences. RA never lost sight of this. As one journalist commented on the *Perogies, Pasta & Liberty* RA re-lease of 1990, "The music is unpolished, the lyrics ludicrous and/or thoughtful, the ambience cheerful while poking fun with punk, folk, cabaret and rap styles. It's a pleasant change to hear social protest coming from people who quite enjoy life and prefer 'good food, music, friendship & freedom' to bleeding heart musical complaining" (*Option*, May 1990).

Minimalist Music

RA's music inspired hundreds of facile, journalistic labels: "urban rat jazz;" "folk punk;" "gypsy grunge." All were true. The band was constantly re-defining itself musically. The fixed precepts, though, that guided RA musically were simple: an underground, non-commercial, lo-fi, inde-pendent, non-mainstream and "alternative" sound, at a time when this word meant something, before it was coopted by the industry as another marketing tool. RA didn't have to try. Working with limited resources, like a four track recording set up and no major label money, the duo believed, as did thousands of other independent musicians, that home-recording would "kill big music business." This was the underground fantasy of the '80s.

RA kept the sound minimal as well for the ease of touring. It meant, too, the duo could experiment with guerilla performance techniques. Setting up and playing in a matter of a few minutes, with little equipment and few wires to cross, meant RA could conveniently do hit and run shows—a prerequisite for performing during demonstrations or in situations like an occupation where everyone was risking arrest. RA was also willing to experiment and take musical risks and never shy from on-the-spot improv. In fact, instant improv, musical poetry pieces became one of the band's trademarks. RA loved to pull into a new town, interview the hosts, then, as part of the set for the show, turn this info into a humorous improv "news" piece on local politics. This was one way to demonstrate how anyone with a bit of imagination could transform news and social commentary into a fun, creative, topical statement of protest.

"Eddy: The Guy Over There"

One example of RA's effective role within a larger community outside the underground music scene was its series of hilarious, radical, issue-oriented "community cabarets." These started in 1990. Even as a simple duo, RA was evolving into something more than just a "band." After four recordings and a few international tours, RA was outgrowing its original vocation as a straightforward music and poetry ensemble. All the touring, performing, and cumulative total of creative energy and experience meant it was time for something new artistically, something more challenging. It was time to add to the cultural tool chest and experiment with different art forms on stage. It was also time to redefine and expand the link between indie-music "art" and "politics." The band was also keen to reach people beyond the club and bar scene, to reach *monsieur* and *madame tout le monde*, the people out there who didn't follow "alternative" music or any "scene" other than the daily grind to survive. RA believed it could offer them something beyond the lure of their TV screens.

In 1989, RA had already created and performed a moving and somewhat poignant two-man musical theatre piece called "Eddy: the guy over there." This was a dreamlike story about an ordinary blue-collar working man who died, but who refused to attend his own funeral. His soul debates him about the merits of going, about his fears, his continuing doubts of the value of his earthly life, his successes, failures, loves and disappointments. In the conversation with his mirror imaged "soul," he touches on current economic and political events, memorable strikes, mass evictions and the changing face of Montréal. In this show, the two band members—now both actors and musicians—play the principal roles, their instruments, and they dance and sing.

"Eddy" was RA's first foray into the world of "theatre"—but it wouldn't be the last. Now convinced of the creative possibilities of twinning live music with live theatre, RA was ready for more experimentation, more challenges. There are limits—some self-imposed—to what rock bands, imitating other rock bands, can do. But RA was no ordinary rock act lusting after the elusive big label recording contract. It was an open-ended, anarcho-cultural project, without commercial or career-focused restraints. It was willing to go outside the music industry's recommended parameters, where typical rock bands never thought of going: into the community, armed with more than just live music and a "look." More specifically, RA wanted to work directly with activist groups in poor neighbourhoods and see if it could contribute anything substantial to their efforts. By now RA wanted to bring them something other than just a live music act. It was offering them a cabaret.

Community Cabarets

The band already loved to clown around on stage. Comedy was a given and effortless part of existing shows. And RA was already performing some songs as miniature pieces of theatre. The guitarist's playing was naturally highly theatrical as were the vocalized stories and poems. Since the band identified more with the avant garde, cutting edge, provocative and aesthetical tradition of European cabaret, than with any form of musical theatre, it decided to mine this rich history and adapt it for a contemporary audience. Even though the general public might think of cabaret as simply Liza Minelli's limited film portrayal of the genre, the tradition was much more. The world of late 19th century European cabaret was filled with anarchist poets, musicians and story tellers, who, in the 20th century, became outspoken anti-fascists, filling the stage with creative, biting social critiques. Because RA was based in Québec, any connection to a traditional, European art form made more sense to French-speaking audiences. RA decided to explore this world of cabaret and transform it into a contemporary agit prop cultural experience. The result: highly politicized, but funny theme shows that combined the best of European cabaret with the worst of American TV talk shows.

These cabarets became RA's legacy to the community. The shows, touring Québec's poorest neighbourhoods from 1990 to 1998, were hugely successful, garnering national and international media attention, and established RA's francophone fan base throughout the province. The first cabaret, "Un Logement pour Une Chanson" (A house for a song), dealt with tenant's rights. The second, "Deux Femmes; Une Tcheque" (Two women and a cheque)—promoted the rights of welfare recipients; the third, a variation of "Deux Femmes; Une Tcheque," covered the rights of impoverished, ex-psychiatric patients; and the last one, "Le Cirque en Ca$h" (The Money Circus) was an enormous, 50 person, circus cabaret about the roots of poverty and how to fight back.

In 1990, "Un Logement Pour Une Chanson" toured 25 Québec neighbourhoods, from Hull to Chicoutimi, Shawinigan to Chateauguay, reaching thousands of tenants face to face or via TV and radio broadcasts. The lively, satirical cabaret was a joint production between RA and a coalition of 43 Québec community groups called PROUD (People's Rights Over Urban Development, or FRAPRU in French). PROUD has always enjoyed a broad base of support province-wide among people directly concerned with housing and welfare issues: those on fixed and low incomes, who suffer the most from social program cutbacks and the shortages of affordable housing. PROUD continues to be the single, most active poor peoples" rights group in Québec, fighting every level of government, and private interests, too. They never shy away from militant, direct action occupations, sit ins, human blockades—highly creative protests of all sorts—aimed at capturing the public's attention and influencing government policies, and are well respected by the media as informed, experienced, credible sources about housing and related issues.

RA had approached PROUD months earlier with a proposal to create a tenant's rights cabaret, a show that would meet the needs of each of PROUD's sponsoring local groups, and to tour the province with it. PROUD accepted the offer and worked closely with RA to mount the show. The goal was to create a family-friendly cabaret as part of PROUD's province wide housing rights information campaign. The cabaret would also serve as an organizing tool, a new, fun, entertaining resource for each sponsoring group in each town to use as they wanted depending on their specific needs. It could help them liven up their regular meetings, reach new people, allow them another point of access to the media to cover their issues, or serve as a fundraiser. Best of all, they could tailor the show to highlight their particular concerns by participating actively, on stage, as part of the performance. (Outside of the large urban centres like Montréal and Québec City, most of PROUD's membership inhabited small towns where cultural resources can be scarce.)

RA and PROUD members embarked on a three-month long consultation process to determine the issues the cabaret would address. RA provided the "artistic" framework for the discussions; each group provided the specific information that found its way into song and theatre. For the participating groups, the focus ranged from how to fight unscrupulous landlords to how to get more support for a social housing project.

The challenge was familiar enough: create a show that worked aesthetically, and conveyed useful information. But this project also offered another curious hurdle for the band. Could an urban "rebel news orchestra" used to performing as an "alternative music" act in downtown, underground bars and clubs, break out of the ghetto of marginalized culture and reach a new audience, marginalized even more so economically socially, and geographically? The tour would take RA into the backwoods of Québec, deep into impoverished small towns coping with new unemployment problems, like "do we pay the rent, or do we go hungry—again?"As one journalist put it, the band "had to overcome the great cultural divide which normally separates the underground music scene and the everyday working stiff"(The Montréal Gazette, Feb 15 1990).

Could two characters from the fringe create something with mainstream appeal? Thankfully, RA's bottomless suitcases contained enough bad jokes, bad sight-gag material, and enough cheesy-music-familiarity to pull it off. The result: a fast-paced, low-budget cabaret, part music, part theatre, with giant cockroaches, blood-thirsty "condo-vampires," larger than life replicas of the Prime Minister and Premier—all singing and dancing their way through the housing maze that confronts Québec tenants. Armed with an acoustic accordion and violin, a ghetto blaster, and suitcases full of costumes, RA presented a cast of 14 loveable or despicable characters who raised questions about housing discrimination, neighbourhood gentrification, the failure of government housing programs, and the mysteries of tax shelters and the inadequate private housing market. It was a quick change performance, with RA darting behind a portable backdrop and reappearing seconds later in new costumes as they drove home a radical critique and offered alternative solutions.

The music was either original, somewhat offbeat, but not too esoteric, or simple, well-known tangos, waltzes, re-arranged popular Québec folk songs, and some 1960s fuzzy organ numbers sampled and chopped up. There were enough wacky costumes, sight gags and bad dancing, that even children in the audience loved it. Audience sing-alongs guaranteed everyone would feel part of the show. RA called it a "family show," saying "it's aimed at mothers, and people can bring their landlords." Thanks to the outreach efforts of the sponsoring groups, the church basements, community centres and elementary school cafeterias were packed nightly with the elderly, public housing tenants, welfare recipients, nuns, and tenants looking for new entertainment. The cabaret—always free—offered them a rare opportunity to leave their homes and see a show that was relevant to their lives. Some said this was their first ever exposure to "a live show." For the sponsoring community groups, the cabaret was a success. Unlike regular meetings which sometimes couldn't attract the masses, here was an excuse for people to come out with their kids, meet others, get entertained, and receive useful information, too. Sometimes the show also featured a low cost or free community supper. Because each performance ended with question and answer periods, audiences always left better informed, if not inspired—to get active.

The show also provided a novel hook for media coverage. One Montréal daily (Le Journal de Montréal, Feb 9 1990) actually wrote: " PROUD has found an original way to start its campaign denouncing the private housing market: they're using a provocative cabaret animated by the Montréal duo RA."

For the band, the experience was equally satisfying. It demonstrated that radical community groups outside the normal field of vision of the music world can appreciate and support the work of artists willing to cooperate in joint, artistic/social ventures. It also underlined the need for artists to offer their talents to assist these groups. Too often, either poor people's organizations are afraid to ask bands to support their work, or bands might not even consider the possibilities, or simply underestimate the importance and ultimate satisfaction of participating in social justice projects.

"Two Women and One Cheque": A Welfare Rights Cabaret to Expose Québec

Deux Femmes, Un Tcheque (L) Sylvain Côté (R) Norman Nawrocki

In the late 1980s, while Québec's economy was failing, city and provincial officials turned their backs on the province's poor and unemployed, while penny-pinching Parti Québécois bureau-crats were busy re-writing the welfare laws—a move guaranteed to pile on the misery and penalize the moneyless even more—ordinary people were hurting. Even though across Canada, the "nationalist debate" seemed to dominate public affairs and national news, behind the head-lines and manufactured crisis of identity, Montréal's reputation as "the poverty capital of North America" slowly started to take on new meaning. Experts testified: the city's poor are suffering from malnutrition because they can't afford to pay the rent and eat at the same time; children are going to school hungry, or not at all, because their parents don't have enough money for food or proper winter clothing; pensioners are starving and unable to afford their medication; welfare recipients are unable to survive because of the high costs of basic amenities; single mothers are being terrorized by "welfare police" looking for pretexts to terminate their benefits. This was neither national nor provincial news. These were the stories circulating in working class and poor neighbourhoods across the province, in community health clinics, in women's centres, in soup kitchens, and in tenant's and welfare rights offices. The number of people living on so-cial assistance at this point was 600,000 and growing. But the provincial government was pre-paring to subject them to even more indignities.

Share an apartment with someone to split the rent? The new welfare reform law would punish you and trim $100 from your monthly welfare cheque of $400. Under 30 years of age and on welfare? The law would slice your benefits in half and suggest you live "at home." Need a job? The new law would subsidize multinationals like McDonald's to hire you on as cheap labour to "top off" your welfare cheque. The attack on the poor was vicious, hurtful and widespread. Critics denounced it as "draconian, inhuman and intolerable." Officially, one-in-five in the city of Montréal were directly suffering the consequences. Among them, friends, neighbours and fans of RA, already reeling from lost jobs, and RA members themselves. The social safety net was being ripped apart. Something had to be done.

A province-wide coalition of 40 trade unions, women's groups, community organizations and anti-poverty groups—"La Table nationale contre la loi 37" (The National Coalition against Law 37)—sounded the alarm. They debated rent strikes, consumer strikes to refuse to pay provincially owned Hydro bills, a wave of occupations of government offices, banks, welfare offices, and more. The debate was covering new ground of heightened discontent and an equally bump-up-the-stakes of the necessary public "civil society" response to the attack on the poor. But people were not ready to hit the streets. Despite dissenters, the cautious and not too confident majority wanted to "educate the public first," with a public awareness campaign. Tell people the truth. Embarrass politicians into taking some sort of action. Get the media to write stories about this law. How to accomplish this was the question.

Among the coalition members were activists who remembered RA's popular and effective "housing rights cabaret" from the previous year. RA's phone rang: "Can you create a new radical community cabaret to tour the province?" The band said "yes" and started work on a hilarious but hard hitting bilingual "welfare rights cabaret" that would eventually rock the public laugh meter and draw provincial and national attention to the real crisis plaguing Québec. But first, the band had to do its research.

The coalition wanted a factual, family-friendly show in French that could play church basements and soup kitchens, that was portable, that could travel to the furthest corners of the province, off the beaten track. It had to appeal not only to people on welfare who needed to see it to learn about their rights, but also to potential political allies, the middle-classes, the Québec intelligentsia and church goers. The coalition requested a show that would not offend church allies—since many anti-poverty groups in Québec received the support of the church—but also, a show that "would tell it like it is," and deliver a radical critique of existing social policies. This show would spearhead a public relations campaign that included collecting 37,000 signatures of protest on postcards, workshops about rights, and a "surprise" political action in the year to follow. In other words, RA was being asked to put together a highly political, entertaining, critical, respectful, family and church friendly cabaret that would deliver the message and keep kids and grandparents happy. This would be RA's fifth piece of musical theatre, the third in a series of "community cabarets," and the most challenging to date.

RA attended rowdy meetings of the welfare rights coalition, asking questions and taking notes. Opinion was often divided on how to contest a new provincial law, from the "let's not rock the boat, it's too risky" line to "rock it hard, or people will continue to suffer and die from poverty." As invited artists with a social conscience, RA—the "creative hired guns"—had to create a middle road for the cabaret that respected the wishes of the coalition—itself divided—without upsetting either one side or the other on the tactical debate. Some wanted to confront the authorities and risk arrest; others were not prepared to embark on any kind of direct action. RA had to write a show that would create the maximum impact without offending the sponsors or potential allies, or without downplaying the level of debate about how to fight this reform. The agit popsters wanted to also inspire—not dissuade—people on welfare to take a stand and participate actively in the campaign. This material was fleshed out with facts and figures about being poor in Québec and about people's rights. Community organizations had difficulty helping welfare recipients understand their basic rights, especially if these people were being constantly terrorized with the threat of losing their benefits if they dared speak up for themselves.

After a summer of research RA presented a series of rough sketches to a "Cabaret Consultative Committee, " a group of all-women welfare rights activists who agreed to work with the band to refine the show. "Right on! Not true! Too exaggerated! This is touchy! Ah yes!" Week after week the band returned for feedback. A giant, talking, dancing turkey was cut from the script. Too surreal. A priest was cut. Too sensitive. One scene involved a single mom welfare recipient forced to take a low-paying, ridiculous job stocking shelves, mopping floors, cleaning windows as a "job skill enhancement program" in order to receive her monthly welfare cheque. She is constantly abused verbally and sexually harassed by the "boss," represented by a giant, foam, talking clock face. At one point, she turns to deliver a windup punch to the clock face after the "boss" paws her "breasts." Half of the Consultative Committee yelled in approval while the other half expressed shock. The problem: some women didn't want the female character to risk being charged with assault on the job. Others argued, punching the boss demonstrates a logical response to his continued sexual aggression.

It shows guts and a willingness to say no. The scene provoked an hour-long debate among the women, who, finally agreed, in the interests of "the show," the single mom protagonist could turn to the audience and express her thought process: "If I hit him, I could be charged with assault and lose my job. If I don't hit him, he'll keep harassing me because he doesn't respect me." She concludes in a moment of Brechtian truth as she addresses the audience: "Well, it's only theatre!' and slugs the clock. The Committee agreed, and in every performance thereafter, at the punch, audiences would roar their approval.

Like many marginal artists, each of RA's three members had first hand experience living on welfare, so the true life horror stories about the indignities, the hard times, the frustration and the anger were close to home. So were the fantasies about fighting back.

Musically, RA decided to play it safe and stick to rearranging popular Top 40 Québécois hits from the 1950s, '60s, and '70s. Québec has its own unique pop heritage, its own Elvis Presley, Doris Day, Englebert Humperdink, and Patsy Cline. This was the music of a generation now retired, or unemployed, stuck between once plentiful blue collar work in resource industries and manufacturing, and the reality of a withering economy. These were people now forced onto welfare, but denied their rights. They were also the people who made up the bulk of the Coalition members: middle-aged and aging. RA needed a musical "in" that would carry the message, yet be fun to perform. A show soundtrack that could be played by three musicians/singers/actors, with one electric guitar, one violin and a set of drums and a keyboard. The old hits could do the trick.

RA re-wrote the lyrics of these unforgettable love songs, dance favourites, road music that contained the words every Québécois of a certain age already knew, and transformed them into mostly funny, but sometimes poignant new songs with the same melodies, but rewritten lyrics. The technique is ancient "cultural jamming" and probably dates back centuries. It was best used by the IWW (Industrial Workers of the World) song meister, Joe Hill, in the early 1900s when he transformed preachy but recognizable Christian hymns into sidewalk class struggle anthems; it continues to be used today by groups as diverse as the Radical Cheerleaders and The Raging Grannies. Take a popular song—a Celine Dion song—and rewrite it into an anarchist singalong.

For the welfare rights cabaret, RA churned out the re-written hits and audiences loved it. Sixteen songs and sketches traced the life of two single moms. They lose their jobs, meet in a welfare office, suffer through the bureaucracy, the censure of family and the community, become friends, and learn how to fight back, joining a welfare rights group along the way. They even get physically flirtatious with men in the audience. During one show, a RA band member in drag, playing a divorcee with three kids, unknowingly cruised a blushing priest—out of his collar—as he sat in the audience. Among the songs were tear-jerkers about the strained relations between a single mom on welfare, and her embarrassed, elementary school son, who asked her why she couldn't find a job like other mothers. There were kick-out-the-jams, go go dancing numbers, where enthusiastic women in the audience jumped to their feet to twist and "mash potato" with the RA members in drag, on stage in a number about how to say "No! Get lost!" to the welfare police when they ring the doorbell for a surprise house inspection visit. At almost every performance, at least one woman audience member would spontaneously jump up in the middle of the show, point a finger towards the stage, and shout out "That's me!" The musical arrangements were simple, but effective. The costumes and sight gags, cheap and colourful. It all added up to a stinging, but sensitive vaudevillian romp through the province's revamped welfare system—a veritable Alice in Wonderland chamber of horrors for those unlucky enough to be part of it.

RA's cabaret in drag exposed the contradictions and hypocrisy of the reform bill, and why, in the interests of human dignity, it should be scrapped. The show also motivated audiences to join the local welfare rights organization and send in postcards of protest. This tour took RA far from downtown Montréal punk clubs to pinpoint bush towns in the outreaches of Québec where a dozen local community volunteers, including the odd nun, in her habit, would be waiting, ready and eager to help the band unload and set up. When the show was in a church basement, the dressing room was often the confessional upstairs, or between the pews. As one community organizer put it, "RA's show helped explain in simple terms basic rights for people on welfare who before couldn't understand the information we were trying to give them."

A Community "Circus"

By the late 1990s, Montrealers without money were hurting more than ever before. RA decided it was time to mount a new production—one that would go beyond its previous concerns and address the worsening effects locally of the "globalization of capital," and the "globalization of misery." Social program cutbacks, business closures and re-locations to the Third World were devastating sections of the population. Food banks were straining to feed the hungry; tenants' rights groups were overwhelmed with victims of ongoing gentrification; the elderly, the sick, were being written off by hospital closures and cutbacks of medical assistance.

The new faces of poverty were everywhere. RA responded with a proposal for a "community circus cabaret," "Le Cirque en Ca$h" ("The Money Circus").

"Le Cirque en Ca$h"

Given the successes of the first two community cabarets, PROUD accepted again to work with RA. The result was a giant, theatrical, topical, musical "circus," offering a critical—but comical—perspective on the roots of poverty—"Why are we poor?"—with suggestions about how citizens could organize themselves to fight back. The 80 minute French show grew out of months of renewed consultation with front-line anti poverty groups across Montréal. Not content with a little three-piece production, RA put out a call for volunteers and ended up with a monstrous cast over 50 local artists. There was a 7 piece circus band, *"L'orchestre des elephants,"* which performed new, original music composed by the musicians and directed by RA's guitarist, Sylvain Côté. There were troupes of dancers, jugglers, acrobats, clowns, actors, and community participants from neighbourhood groups who contributed to and hosted the show.

This "circus" was conceived as a giant, musical, talking cartoon, both entertaining and educational, lyrical and satirical, combining audience sing-alongs and dancing with provocative, hard hitting information about current economic affairs. It featured "the highest paid clown in the world;" a stunning dance troupe, "Les Grands Balais Canadiens" (The Big Canadian Brooms), a troupe of office cleaning women who choreographed their mundane, but sometimes dangerous work; "academic kangaroos" (hired by corporations and the State and parachuted into the public consciousness to sell cutbacks and privatization schemes); "human curiosities" (like the single mom with 4 part-time jobs struggling to feed her kids); an entrepreneurial "ringmaster" always trying to make a deal with the audience; a"menagerie" of untamable, domestic and exotic animals (from the local poverty-stricken neighbourhoods—the rats, cockroaches, alley cats, stray dogs, squirrels); plus corporate "magicians" who could make jobs and exorbitant profits disappear with the push of a button, the juggling of a book.

On the most obvious level, the free circus was a huge success. There were only three Montréal performances, in the poorest neighbourhoods of the city. Hundreds of people were turned away at the doors. Hundreds more were on their feet inside giving standing ovations for a radical, political circus, advocating direct action solutions to local problems. Radio France International's correspondent compared and contrasted "Le Cirque en Ca$h" to the newest production of the renowned "Cirque du Soleil"—where the budget was a few million dollars, the admission tickets up to $100. RA's circus worked with a few thousand dollars, and admission was free. Critics called it "passionate," and "astonishing political cabaret."

Using simple songs, dances, sketches, slapstick, slides, video and audience participation numbers, the show addressed issues normally left untouched on the stage. It demystified "the deficit;" "the debt;" and government rationalizations of cutbacks. It examined the disparity between rich and poor, political promises and official doubletalk, government and corporate propaganda, and the reality of growing numbers of impoverished, suffering, frustrated and angry citizens trying to survive in the shadow of record bank and corporate profits. It presented concepts as complex as "privatization, commercialization, and de-regulation" in terms comprehensible to ordinary people. The IMF, the World Bank, spreading globalization, the route of a cleaning woman's meagre pay cheque from a bank machine to the banker and around the world was investigated, with help from a helpful talking bank machine.

Considering the despair and growing poverty of the previous ten years plaguing Montrealers, the circus took RA's work to the next, logical level. People living on the edge economically were feeling overwhelmed, looking for ways to cope with a staggering decline in their standard of living. In meeting after meeting pre-production, RA heard the same refrain: people are going hungry, homeless, without medication, and are desperate for solutions. Tired of "charity," they're prepared to do whatever is necessary to overcome the despair and change the reality of poverty.

People who would never call themselves "anarchists" talked about raiding supermarkets for food; "squatting" empty buildings to house the homeless; raiding drug stores for drugs for the elderly. It was a new level of public discourse in community groups that RA hadn't heard before. RA hoped that the circus would help serve once again as a mobilizing tool, to encourage audience members to become active in local action groups, to stand up and fight for their rights. The show worked on different levels. It received international media coverage that focused on people's concerns. Community organizers and sponsors were bowled over with the overwhelming positive public response. The circus reached a new group of normally unreachable single moms, isolated families and others in the neighbourhood who otherwise wouldn't come out for meetings. How far these people were willing to go once the show was over was, as always, the question. For one night only, many people experienced a sense of solidarity, a sense of celebration of their community, a sense of affirmation that they were not alone feeling the need for far-reaching change. Kids and adults alike were entertained and given new ideas about potential new approaches to change things. Some signed up to get involved with local community groups. Others took home information pamphlets and memorable songs and sights. And a small group, already well into the planning stages, went out and raided a chic downtown hotel lunch buffet to feed the hungry. RA was later incorrectly identified by a national newspaper headline as the potential inspiration for this raid.

RA's Bid for the Airwaves

How can a so-called "radical" band counter the lies, disinformation and distortion caused by local and world leaders monopolizing the airwaves and corporate media? Is it possible to use music, poetry, the wonders of recording technology, and live shows to produce products, sounds, shows that will be heard by the same people listening to official propaganda? Although the RA approach was, by necessity, low budget and low fi, this never stopped nor stymied the spirit of creativity and the desire to produce music and shows that had something to say. It can be said that RA developed a local, Canadian, and international reputation as a group with original re-sponses to pressing political crises. That the band's music travelled around the world, from the jungles of Chiapas, to poor inner city neighbourhoods in North America and beyond. That this music, though never "commercially successful" in terms of "unit sales," nonetheless was heard by people on a few continents. There is no question that RA's music contributed in unmeasur-able ways to helping listeners, fans, and others in efforts to move forward towards radical social change.

Why Should Bands Get Involved?

Often musicians from other bands asked: "What is RA doing? Isn't this contrary to what musi-cians should focus on? Why get involved in political projects or even think politics is relevant? Why believe that music can help change anything?" And always, RA's answer: musicians with a social conscience have a responsibility—to themselves, and the public—to try to use their music as a tool to effect radical social change. Music can play a role. It can shift people's thinking. Move them from inaction and couch potatoism to becoming socially engaged. This much, countless RA friends, acquaintances, fans and strangers over the years have attested to:

"Listening to (insert the name of any favourite, memorable radical musical personality or re-corded project here): Joe Hill, Woody Guthrie, the MC5, Bob Dylan, Phil Ochs, Paul Robeson, Joan Baez, Pete Seeger, DOA, Mecca Normal, The Dead Kennedys, Bob Marley, Mutubaruku, Gil Scott-Heron, The Subhumans, The Clash, Rage Against the Machine, Propaghandhi, The Ex, The Indigo Girls, Fugazi, Ani DiFranco, Utah Phillips, Warsaw Pact, The Weakerthans, Bakunin's Bum, and even Rhythm Activism made me curious, motivated and inspired me to question my lifestyle, my views, my apathy, to talk, read and get involved." RA fans have said that RA's music specifically encouraged them to:

- go door-to-door in their apartments and organize to fight rent increases;
- learn about their rights as welfare recipients, tenants, or underpaid, overworked workers;
- join international solidarity movements (with the Zapatistas), boycotts (against COORS beer), protests;
- learn more about local, national and international politics;
- join radical social movements;
- meet new friends who share the same musical tastes, and form a group of like-minded music fans with new political projects;
- get involved in environmental, anti-war, anti-sexist protests;
- share classified information they have access to, to help inform public opinion about po-lice practices, eco-disasters in waiting, irresponsible employers and manufacturers;
- organize benefit concerts to raise money for humanitarian aid projects, for immigrant workers, for battered women;

• stay on picket lines during strikes fighting for their rights;

• leave unhealthy relationships, quit dead end, deadening jobs, or just say no to any madness around them;

• create their own political music, films, artwork; engage in "cultural jamming."

RA received fan mail describing how the music, the lyrics, an entire album or even one particular show contributed to someone's political awakening, their becoming aware of issues beyond the obvious work-pay bills-watch tv-sleep-eat-work again-lifestyle. People would travel miles to see RA live, to get their anarcho rock and roll cabaret fix. They came not only to be entertained, but to recharge their activist batteries. They bought albums to share with friends and family, to help do the vacuuming, and for those moments later when they needed a political, musical boost, and RA wasn't in town.

RA never realized a commercial breakthrough, despite having many of its albums chart in the top ten on Canadian or American college radio. In the days before NAFTA and the FTAA became a reality, RA was already churning out harshly critical, but humorous, pieces about the jingoistic violence of American imperialism, drawing attention to the USA's aspirations for world domination. RA brought to its music a global and a historic vision. One album, *Blood and Mud*, based on the roots of the Zapatista uprising in Chiapas Mexico in 1994, was recommended by the American music magazine, *Option*, as "mandatory listening for members of Congress."

By rewriting international news stories and forgotten people's history and making them accessible and memorable the band never faltered in a drive to share information that could help someone, somewhere, take action to address some injustice and fight for their rights. The band's prolific repertoire of over 1,000 pieces was written to help address issues that corporate media and music culture ignored. RA used the air waves of non-commercial radio to spread messages about do-it-yourself direct actions to lower the cost of living, about taking control of your own housing, about how to rebel on the workplace floor and more. Music as a wake up call. Music as a tool to help popularize "radical ideas that people don't have access to in the mainstream media." This is Rhythm Activism.

DISCOGRAPHY

Rhythm Activism

Rhythm Activism. (cass) Montréal: Les Pages Noires, 1986.

Rhythm Activism "Live." (cass) Montréal: LPN,1987.

Resist Much–Obey Little. (cass) Montréal: LPN, 1987.

Louis Riel in China. (cass) Montréal: LPN, 1988.

Un Logement Pour Une Chanson. (cass) Montréal: LPN, 1990.

Fight the Hike! (cass) Montréal: LPN, 1990.

Perogies, Pasta & Liberty. (cass) Montréal: LPN, 1990.

Oka. (cass) Montréal: LPN, 1990.

War is the Health of the State. (cass) Montréal: LPN,1991.

Oka II. (cass) Montréal: LPN, 1992.

Tumbleweed. (cass) Montréal: LPN, 1993.

Blood & Mud. Montréal:LPN 1994./ (cass) Konkurrel, Amsterdam:/Warsaw, Poland: Nikt Nic Nie Wie: LPN, 1997.

More Kick! Montréal/Konkurrel, Amsterdam: LPN, 1995.

Buffalo, Burgers & Beers. (cass) Montréal: LPN, 1995.

Jesus Was Gay. Winnipeg: G-7 Welcoming Committee Records, 1998.

Compilations

*Expo Hurts Everyone,*Vancouver: Sudden Death Records, 1986.

Voice of Americanism. (cass) New York: Bad Newz, 1988.

CIA Tapes. (cass) Bradford, UK: Blurg Records, 1988.

Theft of Paradise. (cass) Ottawa: Technawabe Sounds, 1988.

Sur La Guerre Des Sexes [About Sex War]. Paris: P.A.I. 1990.

Les Mystères Des Voix Vulgaires. LP, (cass) Milano, Italy: Divergo, 1990.

Just Listen. (cass) Waltham, MA: All Genre, 1991.

Brain Battery. (cass) Limesay, France: Broken Tapes, 1991.

Nightmare on Albion Street. LP, Bradford, England: 1 in 12 Records, 1992.

*Zwolna Tapes Vol.*1. (cass) Metz, France: Zwolna T & R, 1992.

Bittersweet Canada. Toronto: Word of Mouth Records, 1992.

Pogo Avec Les Loups. Paris: On a Faim!, 1992.

Mais Où Est Passé l'Anarchie? (cass) Limesay, France: Broken Tapes, 1994.

Crises. Limesay, France: Broken Tapes, 1994.

Uniracial Subversion. HongKong: Blackbird, 1995.

Zoocompilation. (cass) Budapest, Hungary: Trottel Records, 1996.

King Kong 2. Konkurrel, Amsterdam: 1996.

Up To D.A.T. Saint-Etienne, France: Mad's Collectif, 1997.

Keskideez. California: Broken Ear, 1997.

Less Rock More Talk. San Francisco/Edinburgh: AK Press, 1997.

Les Mystères Des Voix Vulgaires #2. Milano, Italy: Art as Hammer Records, 1997.

Les Mystères Des Voix Vulgaires #3 (cass) Milano, Italy: Art as Hammer Rec, 1997.

Folkophobia. Chambery, France: Tranzophobia, 1998.

*Pasazeer.*Warsaw, Poland: Pasazer Records, 1999.

Return of the Dead. Winnipeg: G-7 Welcoming Committee Records, 1999.

More info: www.nothingness.org/music/rhythm

Martha Nandorfy

7 / The Right to Live in Peace: Freedom and Social Justice in the Songs of Violeta Parra and Víctor Jara

Violeta Parra and Víctor Jara are musical emblems of revolutionary and visionary social commitment in Chile during an extraordinarily troubled period in that country's history. While both wrote music that has been described as "protest," the range of themes and the combination of traditional rhythms and original creativity characterizing their musical works invite multi-disciplinary, historicized responses.

MARTHA NANDORFY is the author of *The Poetics of Apocalypse: García Lorca's Poet in New York* (Bucknell UP, 2003) and co-author (with Daniel Fischlin) of *Eduardo Galeano: Through the Looking Glass* (Black Rose Books, 2002). She is Associate Professor of Latino/a and Chicano/a Literature at the University of Guelph.

Such labels as "protest" music tend to evoke lyrical and sonic effects associated with that genre in the specific context of the United States, especially during the student protests against the war in Vietnam.[1] A historicized approach to the context of Chile in particular, and Latin America in general, requires that clear distinctions be drawn, especially between dominant and subordinate cultures. "Protest" means one thing in the most powerful, affluent, and economically and culturally dominant country in the world. And it means quite another in a culture that differs radically in its racial and ethnic features, as well as in the precarious status of its economic dependence and political subordination to that dominant power.

The primary focus of this essay, then, is the popular musical expression of a collective call for human rights that takes into account the native indigenous and working class inheritance—its cultural richness, economic poverty, and extreme marginalization. What Víctor Jara preferred to call "revolutionary" as opposed to "protest" music demands re-evaluation with a view to identifying how internal and external factors in Chile interacted to erode democratic values to the point of complete erasure. That erasure turned Chile into a terrorist fascist state, which lasted nearly three decades and whose legacy remains.

Instead of discussing theoretical texts on social justice and human rights issues in relation to music, I propose to reconstruct the historical framework for this essay by drawing from testimonial literature and biographical writing that I relate to the songs of Violeta Parra and Victor Jara. This approach reflects my belief that the expression of popular culture, especially in its artistic "*sentipensante*" forms brings us closer to intuitive knowledge of justice than theories written by specialists. I borrow the term "*sentipensante*" [feeling-thinking] from the Uruguayan writer Eduardo Galeano, who in turn borrows it from Colombian fishermen who understand that heart, soul, spirit are inseparable from mind and reason (*The Book of Embraces 121*). I also examine at some length political scientist Mark Mattern's work on the intersection of music, community, and political action, *Acting in Concert: Music, Community, and Political Action*. Mattern's study of the political power of music in support of democratic social practices is one of the few sustained works of criticism to look at music's role in cultural survival and political activism and thus warrants, especially in his treatment of Chilean *nueva canción*, a thorough evaluation.

Cultural Survival in Song: Music and Liberation

Tío Ho, nuestra canción	*Uncle Ho, our song*
es fuego de puro amor	*is fire of pure love*
es palomo-palomar	*is dove-dovecote*
olivo del olivar	*olive of olive grove*
es como el canto universal	*it is like universal song*
cadena que hará triunfar	*bond that will make triumphant*
el derecho de vivir en paz	*the right to live in peace*

("El derecho de vivir en paz" ["The Right to Live in Peace"] Victor Jara)[2]

Yo canto a la chillaneja	*I sing Chillán style*[3]
si tengo que decir algo	*if I have to say something*
y no tomo la guitarra	*and I don't pick up my guitar*
por conseguir un aplauso.	*to get applause.*
Yo canto la diferencia	*I sing the difference*
que hay de lo cierto a lo falso,	*between what's true and false*
de lo contrario no canto.	*Otherwise, I don't sing.*

("Yo canto la diferencia" ["I Sing Difference"] Violeta Parra)

I was first introduced to the music of Violeta Parra, Victor Jara, and other Chilean groups like Inti Illimani and Quilapayún by the many Chilean refugees who arrived in Ottawa after the coup d'état in 1973. These people regularly organized what they called *"peñas,"* where musicians performed a combination of revolutionary political music and traditional Andean music to which their audience actively sang along and danced the *cueca*.[4] These were always family gatherings even though they tended to last late into the night. They served hot *empanadas* and wine and other Chilean specialties to recreate the atmosphere of popular Latin American get-togethers and to raise money for solidarity organizations. Anyone who was interested in hearing these people's stories of exile from the terrorist state inaugurated by Augusto Pinochet on that other horrendous September 11th, as well as their hopes of one day returning to a just society, was warmly welcomed and encouraged to participate. The memories that circulated at these lively events in both conversation and song were overwhelming in their nightmarish depictions of narrow escape from death. But they also expressed the passionate nostalgia of the exiled, not for an irretrievable past, but for a future that they envisioned as a possibility. A future that was continually conjured up as a horizon, homeland, utopia, past and future, where the exiles and the disenfranchised would resume the project of building a democracy—guaranteeing freedom, equality, and justice—that had suddenly been aborted.

These memories and hopes confronted the young Canadians who attended the *peñas* with a reality that seemed to belong to some secret society in that it was spoken about only within that community, while those who relied on television and other mainstream media seemingly knew nothing about the concentration camps, the disappeared, the CIA involvement and general U.S. support for fascism in Chile and elsewhere in the Americas. Popular ignorance of the details of the coup and its aftermath is not surprising given the collusion between U.S. foreign policy and the news media. In his introduction to *Chile's Days of Terror: Eyewitness Accounts of the Military Coup*, José Iglesias offers his own eyewitness account of media censorship in the United States. He had been asked by Puerto Rican television director José García to participate in an hour-long talk show for the educational television station in New York City. The program was to be structured in accordance with the typical U.S. media approach to create the impression of impartiality, even when that means giving equal time to proven mass murderers and violators of human rights. García's superior, who "knew nothing about Chile or South America," decided to include a representative of the militarists, who cancelled half an hour before the show and was not replaced, though both Chile's United Nations Mission and Washington embassy were contacted in search of a substitute speaker. Despite heavy-handed intervention from the television station officials, García finally managed to have his program televised and the station received the greatest viewers' response in recent history.[5] In Yglesias words (16):

> The station officials were not heartened by this: they fired José García and erased—yes, erased—the tape of the show. Unlike other programs on that station it was never repeated, and colleges that called to rent the tape were refused. More important, erasing

the tape ensured that it would not be shown nationally. One would think that this incident of censorship is news, but no newspaper ever reported it. *Variety*, the weekly devoted to show business, carried a big article on its front page. For them it was a show biz scandal, but it is ironical that they should have been the only publication in our country to point out that this program was the only 'in-depth' report on Chile carried by television.

This kind of subterfuge is carried out seemingly without jeopardizing the reputation of North American democracy as the fount of rights discourse. Those who take pride in the constitutional amendment guaranteeing freedom of speech clearly fail to question whether all citizens have equal access to media in order to exercise that freedom, and whether their fellow citizens consequently have reasonable access to uncensored information regarding North American involvement in human rights abuses. The largely unexamined belief that U.S. society is governed according to democratic principles is especially disturbing when viewed in light of the absolute disregard for human rights that occurred in Chile with U.S. support and virtually no media coverage:

> Over 350,000 workers have been fired from their jobs for political reasons, according to the former vice president of Chile's labor federation, Edgardo Rojas. Trade unions have been banned and any worker showing the least sign of dissatisfaction faces firing or arrest. Thousands of people have been driven out of Chile, forced to seek asylum or to wander from one country to another in search of a home.
>
> The toll in human life is staggering. Church and legal sources in Chile report between 18,000 and 20,000 killed and over 65,000 jailed since the September 11 coup. Many were summarily executed. Others died from torture and maltreatment in prison. Ten to twelve thousand political prisoners still languish in Chile's jails and concentration camps. (Yglesias 11)

The direct contact we Canadians had with Chilean refugees transformed the words "democracy," "freedom," "justice," "equality" from theoretical abstractions (which mass media expects us to take for granted) into tangible experiences. People whom we now knew personally had fought for those ideals in a struggle that had cost them their homeland and the lives of friends and family. This intercultural exchange revealed that the democracy that we were taught to pride ourselves for representing as Canadians fell drastically short of what those words meant to the exiles. It wasn't just the cold weather and reserved attitudes that made them despair and long for their country. Even if it was a refuge—hopefully a temporary one—Canada was no promised land.[6]

I return in this essay to the songs of Violeta Parra and Victor Jara after many years of working on Latin American literature, knowing that most of those Chileans I met in Ottawa have stayed in Canada. They are struggling to make sense of a life that, despite its material advantages, safety, and small successes, resembles basic survival, and not the full life that they had once envisioned and worked for in Chile. And yet this somewhat depressing realization is not limited to their reality. It implicates all those who believe, like the Guaraní Indians of Paraguay,[7] that the world wants to be born again, since the current state of affairs is not acceptable (even for those of us who live in the privileged pockets of the first world). And that we are still a long way from any democracy that ensures basic human rights for all.

The decision to work on the music of both Violeta Parra and Victor Jara, instead of focussing on one of them, first presented itself to me simply as a way of increasing the body of work in which to examine the place of social justice in relation to music, folklore as cultural survival, and the envisioning of radical democracy. Once I started to research and write about these two Chileans, however, I was struck by some significant differences in their visions of the social role of artists and the power of music to liberate. And I found myself struggling to resist setting these two musicians up in a contrastive, reductive way: Anarchist versus Marxist, woman versus man, feminism versus male dominance in the *nueva canción* movement, outcast and independent versus representative of the Left in general and Allende's government specifically. There are so many factors to complicate such schemes. Is it fair to judge or even to examine how a piece of music affects us as listeners divorced from the moment and the context in which it was created? While much of this music continues to resonate, seemingly free to circulate in time and space, the emotive and physical effects of some of their pieces can perhaps no longer be reconstructed or imagined once the political urgency of the moment has passed, has been brutally buried, or nostalgically enshrined. Yet their approaches to promoting social justice and democracy need to be examined in order to appreciate their individual reactions to social and political circumstances. Without losing sight of the complexities of each musician's circumstances and art, differentiating their politics leads to interesting questions about theory and practice, urgency and goal orientation, leftist revolutionary music and anarchic rebel music.

While Violeta Parra was Victor Jara's senior by fifteen years, there are numerous significant intersections in their musical careers and general cultural formation. Both started their lives in the Chillán area and lived a childhood of poverty. Both gave creative expression to their experiences of marginalization and their vision of a better world in a variety of artistic media. At the age of 27, Victor Jara directed his first theatrical piece after graduating from the school of drama at the University of Chile. Like Violeta Parra, he gathered, recorded, and researched folklore, and was encouraged by her in 1957 to continue with his musical career.[8] His university degree and involvement in professional theatre changed Jara's material circumstances significantly. He left the slums to live in one of the upper class neighbourhoods of Santiago with his British wife Joan, a dancer who collaborated actively in cultural projects with her husband and other leftist Chileans in support of Allende's government. I say "leftist" because Joan Jara's biography of her husband makes it clear that social and political differences in Chile ran so deep that tolerance and collaboration between people of diverse ideological perspectives was difficult.[9]

The deaths of both Violeta and Victor were extremely traumatic. Victor was tortured and assassinated at the hands of the military junta on September 16, 1973. But before he died, he managed to pass the lyrics of a song he wrote as testimony of the capture of approximately 5,000 people held with him in the Chilean Stadium to a fellow prisoner, who lived to write it down, and give it to Victor's wife Joan. Like Allende's death in the Moneda Palace during the siege by Pinochet's junta, Jara's death was a highly public event, not only because it was publicized, but also because they both died in a massacre in which thousands of people were brutally killed. Victor's songs became emblematic of the hopes and triumphs shared by Chileans with a social conscience, and even his death song *"Estadio Chile"* is open-ended or unfinished, as Joan Jara suggests in the title of her biography: *Victor: An Unfinished Song*:

La sangre del compañero Presidente
golpea más fuerte que bombas y metralletas.
Así golpeará nuestro puño nuevamente.
¿Canto que mal me sales
cuando tengo que cantar espanto? (sic)
Espanto como el que vivo,
como el que muero, espanto.
De verme entre tanto y tantos
momentos del infinito
en que el silencio y el grito
son los metas de este canto.
Lo que veo nunca lo vi,
lo que he sentido y lo que siento
hará brotar el momento... (Jara Vol. 4)

My comrade president's blood[10]
beats stronger than bombs and sub-machine guns
That's how our fist will beat once more.
Song, how badly you turn out
when I have to sing terror
Terror like the one I am living
like I'm dying, terror.
Seeing myself in the midst of so much and so many
moments of infinity
in which silence and the cry
are the aims of this song.
What I'm seeing I never saw,
what I've felt and what I'm feeling
Will germinate the moment...

Despite the horror attested to by this song, the chain of symbols (the juxtaposed images of the comrade's blood, the collective fist of defiance, the cry of protest conflated with silence) opens the poem/song to a future moment. This opening is achieved by the imagery culminating in the last verse in the verb *"brotar,"* suggestive of sprouting vegetation or flowing water. While that moment trails off into the silence signaled by ellipsis, the accumulated imagery evokes continued resistance and promise.

Violeta's suicide, like most suicides, was a solitary act of desperation. One of the most understanding and like-spirited writers to give testimony of her life and death, Alfonso Alcalde, sums up her contradictory character on the back cover of his anthology *Toda Violeta Parra*:

> Cuando se suicidó, disparándose un balazo el 5 de febrero de 1967, estaba sola y desesperada como era más o menos su costumbre y parte de su oficio humano. No es que cultivara la incomprensión, pero era bastante hosca por naturaleza y odiaba sin piedad a los imbéciles. Ella misma confesó una vez que era una de las mujeres más feas del mundo, lo que era cierto y también una gran mentira. Porque cuando iba cantando, cuando se la escuchaba, nacía otra mujer cuya hermosura iba creciendo como una tempestad incontenible.

> When she committed suicide, by shooting herself on February 5th, 1967, she was alone and in despair, which was more or less her way of being and part of her humanity. It wasn't that she sought incomprehension, but she was, by nature, quite gruff and hated imbeciles, without pity. She herself once confessed that she was one of the ugliest women in the world, which was true and also a big lie. Because when she would sing, when you would listen to her, another woman was born whose beauty would grow like an uncontainable storm.

Alcalde repeats a similar image evocative of her dynamic nature in an anecdote about how Violeta discovered tapestry making when confined to bed due to a serious illness: *"Era como querer atar el mar a un palo"* (39) [It was like wanting to tie the sea to a stick]. Coincidentally echoing the image of the beat in Jara's *"Estadio nacional,"* Alcalde describes Parra's suicide in keeping with her fiery temper: *"Cuando le llegó la fama de golpe, se fue. Como quien pega un portazo, pero con tanta dignidad que su acongojado hijo Angel al conocer la noticia dijo: 'Yo respeto lo que hizo mi mamá, yo respeto la dignidad de su suicidio"* (50). [When she suddenly became famous, she left. Like someone slamming a door, but with such dignity that her distressed son Angel upon hearing the news said: 'I respect what my mama did, I respect the dignity of her suicide.]

*Violeta Parra
(Chile, 1917-1967)*

*(Below) Contra la guerra (Against War),
from Décimas de Violeta Parra*

The contrasts between these two musicians in terms of social acceptance must be examined in light of their distinctive contributions to and battles with Chilean culture, and the contexts leading to their deaths. I suspect that Violeta slammed that door on more than just one man, and that the material and psychological effects of the deep division in Chilean culture drove Violeta to her death, as surely as the fascist torturers murdered Victor because of the politics of his music.

The Nueva Canción Chilena [New Chilean Song]: Representing "El Pueblo"

The musicians affiliated with the genre "nueva canción" played key roles as community organizers, forging significant links between musical expression and communities seeking to exert influence on political process:

> During the 1960s, nueva canción musicians played key roles in the formation of a group of democratic socialists that emerged as a community of resistance and opposition. In other words, the formation of community and the use of confrontational forms of political action occurred simultaneously. The constituent elements of this community included a commitment to resistance and opposition to the political right, to cultural degeneration within Chile, and to other countries viewed as imperialists. (Mattern 39)

Leading up to and during the three short years of Allende's Popular Unity government, Victor Jara assumed the role of cultural ambassador both nationally and internationally, composing songs like "El Alma Llena de Banderas" [Our Hearts are Full of Flags] and "Venceremos" [We Shall Win] that achieved the status of national hymns. He also collaborated with other artists on theatre and epic dance pieces that retold the history of oppressed and marginalized communities. These pieces were sometimes performed by the protagonists themselves, who re-presented important historical events of political persecution and resistance. Joan Jara makes it clear that in the period leading up to Allende's election and during the Popular Unity government, committed artists could not conceive of their value in any terms other than political. This vision of the social significance of art sprang from the urgency to change Chilean society in order to ensure human rights and empower the working class. In reference to the performances Victor, Joan, and others regularly presented in the urban slums and impoverished countryside, Joan's testimony reveals that these played an important part in Allende's political campaign. But it is also clear in what she says that they were not considered forms of cultural exchange motivated by the recognition that everyone needs art as a form of creative expression and interchange:

> In those intimate performances we also managed to reduce our focus to the real people sitting in front of us. It would have been easy to get depressed about what we were doing in the sense that we might feel that it was useless or irrelevant to the priorities of their lives and needs, but their reaction was so warm and enthusiastic that we realised that there was something we could give them, even if at that moment it was only an expression of solidarity. Our best way of fighting was to do everything in our power to en-

sure the victory of a president who would make the neglected and under-privileged people the protagonists of history. (144)

Violeta Parra's political affiliations and eminence as a socio-political icon are more ambiguous. While her artistic production far exceeded that of most other musicians, she was seen as an outsider by both the upper class and the leftists, as the following quotation of Victor Jara's assessment of her indicates:

None of us could say, while Violeta lived, that she was an artist of the people. We even criticized her. But time and the people themselves will recognise her. She lived the best years of her life among them—the peasants, miners, fishermen, craftsmen, the indigenous people of the Andes in the north, the islanders of Chiloe in the south. She lived with them, shared their lives, their skin, their flesh and blood. Only in that way could Violeta have created songs like "¿Qué dirá el Santo Padre?" or "Al centro de la injusticia" and others which will remain in the history of our country as the birth of a new type of song… (J. Jara 105)

Given this description of Violeta's life viewed in the light of her own and others' accounts of the poverty she lived in, and the traditional roots and commitment to human rights expressed in all her artistic endeavors, it seems unreasonable not to consider her an artist of the people. It is also unclear who "us" and "we" refer to in the first two sentences of this quotation, since many people expressed openly the impact Violeta had on their lives. Furthermore, several of her acquaintances have left accounts of how she even managed to gain acceptance in Mapuche[11] communities where she traded her own songs or clothing in exchange for their music.[12] We may also ask why recognition of her by the people would be relegated to some future time, when it is clear that she interacted successfully and genuinely, especially with rural people, perhaps begging the additional question of whom exactly Jara refers to as "the people." While Joan Jara's biography is written in English, it is likely that Victor would have used the term "el pueblo" in the sense of "working class and peasants," again begging the question of whether the indigenous communities were adequately recognized as being an important component in a consensual concept of majority rule.

   In response to whether the people would recognize Violeta in the future, two anecdotes can be cited to support the view that women and disenfranchised peasants openly expressed their solidarity with her. The first refers to the massive funeral march held on the 7th of February 1966, dominated by the crowd numbering 10,000 people who made it impossible for the official orators to pronounce their farewell speeches. Several people jostled to get close to the coffin onto which a group of women threw themselves weeping "Nosotras te comprendemos, Violetita" (Sáez 13) [We understand you, dear Violet]. Violeta's son, Angel Parra, expressed disenchantment and hurt at this display for typically coming too late. It is clear from Sáez's study of press reports on Violeta's suicide and funeral that Chilean society was divided along cultural lines that ran much deeper than party affiliations. Violeta Parra was not actively involved in supporting any political party and was deeply mistrustful of politicians generally. Nevertheless, the popular press (left-wing) ran a long retrospective of her work and life, while the dominant newspaper *El Mercurio* published only three brief paragraphs the day after her death, never to mention her again (Sáez 14).

The second example of the people's recognition of Violeta Parra appears as an entry for the year 1984 in Eduardo Galeano's *Memory of Fire*: *Century of the Wind*: "The dictatorship of General Pinochet changes the names of twenty bone-poor communities, tin and cardboard houses, on the outskirts of Santiago de Chile. In the rebaptism, the Violeta Parra community gets the name of some military hero. But its inhabitants refuse to bear this unchosen name. They are Violeta Parra or nothing" (277). Clearly, choosing a meaningful name for their squatter's settlement is important to these people if they dare to defy the official name imposed on them by the military regime, which prohibited and severely punished any dissension.

The gap between the *nueva canción* artists and Violeta Parra seems to be a generational one to some extent, since her own children Angel and Isabel opened and ran a very important venue for jamming and performing this kind of music, and reviving Latin American folklore generally. The locale was dubbed *"Peña de los Parra"* and had a varied mandate. It was situated in a run-down neighbourhood in an old house, which in the art and entertainment world was highly unusual, given that singers were expected to dress like elegant nightclub performers in an equally elegant ambience associated with "showbiz." The Parras decided to change the élitist biases associated with performance, in hopes of attracting a working-class audience who could become actively involved in using the space to explore, recuperate, and create diverse cultural forms. At first, the audience consisted primarily of "writers, intellectuals, other artists, people from the university, politicians—even some Christian Democrats from the more progressive wing of the party—with lots of young people, mostly students" (J. Jara 84).

This was the atmosphere described by Joan Jara in 1965 when the *Peña* first opened, and where Victor Jara had a hugely successful début, culminating in his first recording, a single of *"La cocinerita"* [The Little Cook] and *"El cigarrito"* [The Cigarette]. The latter is a simple song whose lyrics were composed by a popular poet whom Victor Jara had met on one of his field expeditions to gather folklore. Victor Jara's setting of the verses to his own guitar arrangement became a prize-winning hit:

Voy a hacer un cigarrito
acaso encuentro tabaco
y si no hallo de a'onde saco
lo más cierto que no pito

estribillo:
ay ay ay, me querís?
ay ay ay, me querís
ay ay ay

Voy a hacer un cigarrito
con mi bolsa tabaquera
lo fumo y boto la cola
y recójalo el que quiera

estribillo:
Cuando amanezco con frío
Prendo un cigarro de a vara
y me caliento la cara
con el cigarro encendido (J. Jara Vol. 1)

"The Cigarette"
I'm gonna roll me a li'l cigarette
maybe I'll find some tobacco
and if I don't find nowhere to get it
I won't have a smoke

chorus:
ay ay ay, do ya love me?
ay ay ay, do ya love me?
ay ay ay

I'm gonna roll me a l'il cigarette
with my tobacco pouch
I'll smoke it and toss the butt
and whoever wants it can have it

Refrain:
When I wake up feeling cold
I light up a long one
and I heat my face
with the lit smoke.

This song also marked the beginning of a trend in recording that Joan Jara refers to as a "musical polarisation," since the traditional music performed in the *Peña* was considered to be authentic in contrast to commercialized, "easy listening" renditions of folklore (86). The lyrics of *"El cigarrito"* are reminiscent of Pablo Neruda's *Odas elementales* [Elemental Odes], a collection of equally simple poems each of which sings the praises of such basic pleasures of life as onions, fish stew, or a pair of woolen socks. Despite the absence of any political message, the popular verses of *"El cigarrito"* obviously originate in poverty where even tobacco is scarce and one might consider picking up a tossed butt to light up for want of a fresh cigarette.

Not all of Victor Jara's songs, however, were so ideologically uncompromising. And he soon got himself into a great deal of trouble by singing *"La beata:"* "one of Victor's repertoire of comic folksongs with typically Chilean double meanings which poked fun at the passion of *'La beata'*—an excessively pious lady—for the priest to whom she confesses her sins. It had a Chaucerian kind of humour" (J. Jara 86-87). The musical polarization mentioned by Joan Jara assumes more general and ominous dimensions with this incident. Once it was played on radio, all hell broke loose: "Many radios banned the record. The Information Office of the Presidency requested its withdrawal from the shops and the destruction of the master. Father Espinoza, head of the monastery of San Francisco, made a statement to the press ...," quoting Christ: "'He who commits scandal would be better not to have been born'" (J. Jara 87). It is hard to determine whether the draconian reaction was provoked by the popular, anonymous lyrics or because the song was performed by a leftist musician. One thing is certain: the climate of hostility and the power of aligned institutions to censure and scourge is the backdrop against which we must read the lives and deaths of Violeta Parra and Victor Jara.

When interviewed by the press for his response to the scandal, Victor said: "I never imagined that an absolutely authentic and ancient folk-song, collected in the region of Concepción, could cause such a reaction. People who consider a picaresque and witty folk-song like this one to be insolent and irreverent are denying the decency of the people's creativity which is the very basis of our traditions…" (J. Jara 87). It may even be argued that people have every right to be insolent and irreverent without being denied their decency. And further, that their sense of humour, expressive of their critical resistance to indoctrination, should be appreciated in a more fundamental way than the scientific study that Jara claims to disseminate in his own defense, of having sung the lyrics as they were passed on to him.

While Victor Jara's commitment and dedication to promoting popular culture and defending human rights is unquestionable, Joan Jara's accounts of the relationship between the urban poor and the intellectuals based in the *Peña* suggest that despite the best intentions, the intellectuals assumed a didactic role in relation to the poor. On the one hand, there appears to be an awareness of the dangers inherent in patronizing the poor (in what Victor Jara says to fellow artists in 1971). On the other hand, the vision of organizing and giving them their cultural roots is not sufficiently problematized: "In every place where we perform we should organize, and if possible leave functioning, a creative workshop. *We should ascend to the people*, not feel that we are lowering ourselves to them. Our job is to give them what belongs to them—their cultural roots—and the means of satisfying the hunger for cultural expression that we saw during the election campaign" (196). One wonders why the *nueva canción* groups did not incorporate or collaborate more with native musicians from outside the urban, university milieu. A simplistic and generalizing concept of "the people" may in part explain the belief held by intellectuals that their mission was to teach the urban poor their own culture. There is little distinction made between the urban proletariat—who are bombarded with musical hits from the United States via radio and are therefore increasingly alienated from their own regional culture—and the rural and primarily indigenous communities. This is a significant oversight since those indigenous communities are the very source of musical inspiration, instrumentation, and compositions for these *nueva canción* musicians and self-appointed cultural educators.

There is also little distinction made between recuperating cultural memory and values, and promoting ideology along clearly delineated party lines:

> The majority of Victor's friends in the *población* [slums] were instinctive supporters of the Communist or Socialist Parties, and voted for Allende, but in those early years of the sixties few of them were politically active. As far as I could see, the average shanty-town dweller had an almost passive acceptance of suffering. The activists seemed to be those who were slightly better off, and at this period many of them were Christian Democrats. (J. Jara 89)

Victor Jara in Chilean shanty-town
(From Victor: An Unfinished Song, Joan Jara, London: Jonathon Cape, 1983, p. 182)

To say that the poor are instinctive supporters of the Communist or Socialist Parties is to operate under the naïve assumption that people who live in poverty cannot and do not conceive of community based ways in which to improve their lives. While it is plausible that people who have been deprived of an education and are illiterate may have a harder time dealing with governmental offices on their own terms, it is nevertheless obvious that such people do imagine and organize effective ways of resisting systemic oppression. And that when they are terrorized and suffer retaliations from the government, it is not because they weren't smart enough to join the Socialist or Communist Parties, but because undemocratic governments act with impunity towards all citizens who do not belong to the dominant class, regardless of party affiliations. There is also a peculiar logical reversal at work in the above quotation suggesting that the two parties named are de facto organic outgrowths of popular need, even when Joan Jara represents "the people" as resigned to passive suffering and political inactivism.

Returning to the "*Peña de los Parra,*" it is telling that Violeta Parra herself felt uncomfortable in its intellectual milieu. She made clear distinctions between academics and administrators, whom she despised for their arrogance and narrow-minded élitist cultural agendas, and the students who, even if they came from a different social class from hers, had ethical ideals. Most importantly, she admired their courage and enthusiasm to fight for opening up a cultural space in which to promote human rights. Joan Jara also acknowledges that "the *Peña* was not yet really connected with the outside world. It had no links with the labour movement or the working-class as such, although the key figures there were all of working-class background and very faithful to that. It remained an experimental laboratory with a small, rather élite audience" (J. Jara 104). It is not clear why music, and especially popular music, would not have attracted both working-class musicians and audience from the day the *Peña* opened its doors to the public. Clearly, there was something in the atmosphere, maybe the predominance of educated people or their overt political agenda, that created a clique-like clientele who, despite having working-class roots as Joan Jara observes, no longer functioned in those circles.

Violeta did try to cultivate leftist connections by attending the meetings organized by "*El Comité de la Paz*" (Committee for Peace). But, according to her biographer Fernando Sáez (65), her limited participation was motivated by the need to gain some recognition in a society where she felt constantly ridiculed and pushed aside. As soon as it became clear that the politically motivated intellectuals wanted something from her that did *not* include facilitating her access to exhibitions and performances and that they moved as slowly and blindly as the worst bureaucrats, she lost interest in university affiliations. Although music functions as a collective repertoire for historical memory and an expression of hope for fulfilling human rights, the institutionalization of music put to the service of a political agenda ends by dissipating the potential power of popular music. The main assumption of Mattern's *Acting in Concert* is that "music embodies common memories and meanings" and that "this public, common quality gives music its

communicative capacity, which, in turn, may support the development of community by enabling the sharing of experience" (17). But Mattern, as we shall later see, does not adequately
distinguish specific communities and their direct participatory politics from political processes
that have nationalist objectives like those of the political parties that supported Popular Unity.
His interpretation of popular music in Chile also lacks the necessary historical contexts to understand the social structures that have divided Chile (like all colonized countries) along lines that
are so deeply antagonistic that the whole notion of "acting in concert" becomes unthinkable.
Furthermore, Mattern turns to the concept of the enabling power of music to share experience,
extrapolating from a community-based model to a nationalistic agenda that necessarily institu-
tionalizes cultural activity. He fails to ask whether institutions can ever really be democratic in the
sense that his view of sharing implies.

Cultural Polarization and the Impossibility of Democracy

In one of the many anecdotes that reveal how disengaged the universities and other cultural institutions were from popular culture, Alfonso Alcalde tells how Violeta had gathered and recorded hundreds of stories and song lyrics in the countryside. She then brought these to the
highest spheres of the University of Concepción where, as Violeta herself recalls:

> una vieja descocada le dijo con desprecio que a ella le cargaban los viejos. Son muy
> aburridos, le bostezó como un caballo. Así también se perdió para siempre el esfuerzo
> de muchos años de investigación y sacrificio. Las cintas magnéticas fueron borradas
> como más tarde borraron su incipiente Museo Popular desdeñando las cerámicas, las
> pinturas, los instrumentos parchados de los pobres músicos chilenos. Lo reemplazaron
> por cerámicas cultas y composiciones de más alcurnia. (Alcalde 43-44)

> a crazy old woman told her with contempt that the old songs bugged her. "They're so
> boring," she yawned like a horse. That is also how the efforts of so many years of re-
> search and sacrifice were irretrievably lost. The magnetic tapes were erased, the same
> way that later on her growing Popular Museum was erased, in an act of scorn for the ce-
> ramics, paintings, the patched up instruments of poor Chilean musicians. They replaced
> it all with high-class ceramics and compositions of "better lineage."

It is especially revealing that world-renowned writers like Pablo Neruda and José María Arguedas
acclaimed Violeta Parra's artistic creativity and integrity, while cultural institutions treated her as
an outcast.[13] The institutional mentality of the leftist circles duplicated this prejudice, seemingly
rejecting Violeta because she was simply one of the people instead of being engaged in party
politics in order to be a representative of the people. In general terms then, Chilean politics are
polarized between right wing parties that exclusively defend the interests of the moneyed ruling
class, and left wing parties that challenge the power structure and defend majority interests.
Party politics do not, however, involve all segments of society, and even alienate portions of the

working-class who, like Violeta Parra, distrust politicians and institutions. This distrust is mainly due to the belief or insight that ultimately all parties end up defending their own interests once they are in power regardless of where they fall on the political spectrum. On the other hand, political polarization was so acute in Chile that many people deny that there was any form of social consciousness possible beyond the left/right dichotomy. According to a Brazilian medical student who had been an eyewitness to the coup, "what happened in Chile is that there really were only the *momios* and the left. So every neighbor was either a potential ally or a potential enemy. We had neighbors who were in the state intelligence service" (Yglesias 53).[14] Still, those who speak in these terms tend to belong to the educated segments of the urban population, and one wonders whether the left/right dichotomy of party politics is too reductive a model to adequately account for social and cultural processes nation-wide. One feature shared by many indigenous communities across the Americas is to conceive of their bonds in transnational terms, given that the borders were drawn by national governments that do not represent native interests. The native Mapuche culture is also at odds with Chilean patriarchal society (reflected in the male-dominant *nueva canción* groups) in that their shamans (*machis*) are women, who play the sacred drum (*kultrún*) in religious ceremonies.[15]

Alfonso Alcalde draws explicit connections between all realms of hegemony in Chile when he says: "*Es que en Chile por esos años y por muchos más el arte estaba en manos de unos pocos. Como la tierra y la banca. No había espacio para la hija de una campesina y un profesor primario*" (47) [In Chile during those years and for many more, art was controlled by a few hands, like land and money. There was no space for the daughter of a peasant and a grade school teacher]. Alcalde goes on to point out the irony of Violeta's exposition at the Louvre where she had an entire hall to exhibit her art in all its diversity. The Chilean upper class and culture managers ignored the huge international successes of their own artists while importing everything, including ideas from France: "*Fue un balde de agua incluso para la crítica oficial que en Chile condenó rabiosamente a Pablo Neruda y también a Gabriela Mistral, nuestros dos premios Nobel. Después del honor hasta llegaron a escribir otros libros, pero ahora a favor*" (48) [It was a kick in the teeth for the official critics who in Chile had rabidly condemned both Pablo Neruda and Gabriela Mistral, our two Nobel Prize winners. After the honour, the critics ended up writing other books, this time in favour].

The numerous accounts of the extreme polarization of Chilean society puts into question the generally accepted assumption that Chile distinguished itself among Latin American nations as a democracy until Pinochet seized power. This assumption is challenged by Violeta's song lyrics about social injustice and dire poverty dating back as far as anyone can remember (and even further, when native people recount their experiences). That Chilean history was exceptional in its democracy is a gross overstatement, and should be qualified to mean that the army had never before turned against the government and the constitution. The army had even sided with the government to put down the *tancazo*, as the aborted coup of June is referred to. But surely democracy implies more than regular elections and unity between government and army. Parra's lyrics are an indictment against the false official history that glorifies the past, which she contradicts by circulating popular memory to set the record straight.

Violeta Parra wrote *décimas* throughout her life, eighty-two of which have been published as her autobiography in verse.[16] In *"Muda, triste y pensativa"* [Silent, Sad and Lost in Thought], Violeta replies to her brother's suggestion that she express all that she knows about popular culture *"a lo pueta" (sic.)* [as a poet].[17] To which she answers: *"si tengo tanto trabajo, / que ando de arriba p'abajo / desentierrando folklor. / No sabís cuánto dolor, / miseria y padecimiento / me dan los versos qu'encuentro; / muy pobre está mi bolsillo / y tengo cuatro chiquillos / a quienes darl' el sustento"* (29) [I have so much work, / running back and forth / unearthing folklore / You have no idea how much pain, / misery and suffering / the verses that I find give me; / my pockets are empty / and I have four little ones / to provide for]. The hardships that she faced personally mirror the widespread misery expressed in the popular verses that she gathered; autobiography is inextricable from its collective context. Her plight as a single mother living in poverty is not even fully comprehended by her own brother, judging from his suggestion that she become a poet.

Violeta's so-called autobiography reveals how her own mother struggled to make ends meet, while the simple verses describing a woman's fight to support her family simultaneously imply inequality and exploitation at the hands of landowners:

"Aquí empiezan mis quebrantos"
Diez bocas siempre pidiendo
lleva mi maire el problema,
vestidos, botas y medias,
panes al mes son seiscientos.
Pa'no andar con lamentos
remienda noches enteras,
cosiéndole a Valenzuela
y al dueño 'e la propiedad,
pero esta plata, en verdad,
por el arriendo descuentan. (54)

Ten mouths always begging
give my mother her problems,
clothes, boots and stockings,
bread in a month adds up to six hundred
To hush the complaints
she spends full nights mending,

sewing for Valenzuela
and the landowner,
but really that money
is just deducted from the rent. ("Where My Breakdowns Start")

In more explicitly political attacks, Violeta's lyrics represent President Ibáñez *"tan cruel como el león"* (80) [as cruel as a lion], and clearly call his government a dictatorship in *"Por ese tiempo el destino"* [Destiny at that Time], another "simple" *décima* describing in great detail the terrorist effects of the oligarchic, military government on people from all walks of life. Economics over human rights is clearly the operative paradigm that Violeta identifies as corrupt and undemocratic: *"Explica el zorro ladino / que busca la economía; / y siembra la cesantía"* (79) [The sly fox explains / that he's looking for economy; / and he sows unemployment].[18] Even the death of Violeta's baby brother is attributed to God and the president with equal rage, in an implicit metaphorical contraction that equates patriarchal power with gross negligence. Violeta expresses how, as a young child, she had understood that her brother had died when she heard her mother's anguished cries and curses: *"maldice al Omnipotente / por destinarl' este mal, y maldice al otro animal / de oficio de presidente"* ("Por ese tiempo se enferma" 84) [She curses the All Powerful / for this evil destiny, and curses that other animal / holding presidential office [The Time he Took Ill]. One of the most striking features of these verses is their popular, poetic quality, free of any officious or propagandistic tone. The emotional/intellectual (*sentipensante*) power of these verses depends on the uncompromisingly individual/collective force of expression and the fact that such expression resists narrow partisan co-optation, at the same time as it is embarrassing and therefore unappealing to the moneyed.

Contrary to the independent and non-aligned nature of these lyrics, those musicians who worked as cultural and political ambassadors for Allende's government, as part of a project called "Operation Truth," necessarily sought to communicate facts in response to the massive disinformation campaigns launched by the opposition and U.S. interests. Mattern describes the committed nature of revolutionary music after Allende's election when "Jara began setting up music and theatre groups among trade unions in Santiago and in the countryside. Songs during this period saluted Allende's policies and characterized their likely results, transmitted electoral propaganda, and denounced opponents of Allende and the Popular Unity" (49). Mattern criticizes the *nueva canción* musicians for their satirical lyrics against opponents or lukewarm supporters of Popular Unity on the basis that these did not bridge differences but fomented polarization. He goes as far as to suggest that these musicians contributed to Pinochet's takeover: "it is possible that self-criticism, conciliation, and compromise among *nueva canción* musicians might have helped avert the military coup and the subsequent bloodshed" (52). Before arguing the case that Mattern's evaluation of the *nueva canción* musicians constitutes slander, I will consider his own account of what pre-Allende democracy in Chile amounted to, in order to show how right-wing supporters had more in common with German Nazis than with American Republicans. How Mattern or anyone else could speak of compromise with fascists then becomes the challenge to Mattern's central thesis.

Mattern's vision of democracy conforms to the American view that economic factors—oligarchic land ownership and extreme poverty (with the inevitable violence needed to maintain that state of affairs)—do not disqualify a country from being considered democratic: "Between 1830 and 1973, Chileans governed themselves democratically except for a brief interruption of military rule in 1924. The parliamentary system was relatively open and representative with a well-developed system of political parties, although controlled in large part by wealthy landowners and commercial and industrial businesspeople" (37). Clearly, oligarchic hegemony is acceptable in Mattern's view of a "well-developed system." But as soon as the Marxist party comes on the scene he charges it with polarizing the system, as if Chilean society had not been polarized before: "By the 1930s, however, with the rise of a Marxist left within a highly unionized and politicized labor force, the party system became highly polarized, covering the full ideological spectrum and producing a vacuum at the center of political life" (37). Again, it seems acceptable to have extremist right-wing elements, but damaging for "political life" to have a unionized and politicized labour force. The limited information in this introductory paragraph to the chapter on popular music and democratic politics is enough to show that Mattern's tolerance of fascism and intolerance of Marxism is unequivocally in line with U.S. foreign policy.[19]

Countless testimonies reveal that the dominant class in Chile was far from moderate, and was characterized by extreme racism against people of African or indigenous background as well as suspicion of all foreigners who were not of Germanic descent. One of the many Latin American refugees who sought asylum in Chile from a fascist dictatorship remembers:

But the bourgeoisie, the people who were connected with North American and international capitalists, saw the political refugees as human monsters and waged a direct campaign against them as soon as they arrived. This persecution was not official, but was manifest in the streets, in the clubs, as if we were Jews in Germany during the time of Hitler. It was that way for the Argentines, Peruvians, and Bolivians. The Chilean bourgeoisie has a particular racial prejudice against the Bolivians who have always lived there; they were the most outcast.[20] (Yglesias 85)

The reference to Hitler's Germany is not just a loose comparison, for several reasons. Chilean newspapers published rabidly anti-Semitic articles, and fascists even attacked businesses owned by Jews. According to Joan Jara "during the war, Lanalhue, like other areas of the south of Chile, had been a centre for the activity of the local Nazi party, as some of the original families showed where their sympathies lay. And still, every summer, fascist youth camps which specialised in paramilitary training were held in a remote inlet of the lake" (93). Presumably this kind of extremist political activity has a legitimate place in Mattern's view of a "well-developed system," as long as elections are held and fascists democratically voted into office. He does not, however, maintain a coherent argument. First he laments the fact that *nueva canción* musicians did not seek to bridge differences and work towards common goals with those who hold all power and money. After that he concedes that it would be difficult to negotiate with the same people who made sure that nobody but themselves had access to the mass media and who launched a vicious campaign of misinformation against anyone supportive of majority interests. The truism that "the pragmatic form of acting in concert might have enabled Chileans to discover or create common ground among their extensive differences—for example, shared interests in economic prosperity, peaceful coexistence, and averting military rule" (Mattern 52)—rings unrealistically hypothetical. History consistently shows that Latin American oligarchies have never shown any (except perhaps strategic) interest in sharing power or prosperity.

The next chapter in Mattern's book, dealing with resistance and redemocratization after the 1973 coup, completely abandons the thesis argument in the previous chapter. He asserts in the opening paragraph that "the confrontational form of acting in concert remained central, in part because musicians had no choice: their strategies for political action were largely defined by the political context of extreme repression" (55). This rupture between pre-coup and post-coup in Mattern's interpretation assumes that the extremist fascists suddenly appeared out of the woodwork. His account of the extreme repression exercised in all imaginable forms by the Junta disregards the fact that these are the same people with whom Mattern thinks the *nueva canción* musicians should have been collaborating prior to the coup. He goes as far as to say that "it is hard to imagine how musicians could have found common ground for collaboration with a military regime intent on brutally imposing its will across all political differences" (77). But he does not acknowledge that the privileged class of Chileans had always been characterized by that same brutality. Once there is no longer any hope (or danger, from the U.S. point of view) of forging a truly democratic society and only the ashes remain, Mattern attributes positive value to the musical conservation of memories: "By preserving memories of a democratic Chile, musicians helped preserve its history; and by preserving its history, they helped preserve remnants of a democratic identity" (59). Small consolation!

Adding insult to injury, Mattern pushes his myopic view of peaceful democracy to the extreme of arguing that once music stopped protesting, it could be enjoyed equally by fascists and intellectuals with democratic pretensions: "by appealing to students and professionals from the upper and upper-middle classes and by purging their music of explicit political themes, *canto nuevo* musicians began to add Pinochet supporters to their audience…this shift can be considered a failure because it weakened ties to the democratic left. But it also indicates that *canto nuevo* played a modest role in bridging left and right in the Chilean political landscape" (64). Mattern's "reconciliatory" view actually forces a violent interpretation based on his naïve and dehistoricized understanding of social forces and class relations. His interpretation of "acting in concert" in this particular context is degraded to mean a minority of privileged Chileans passively listening to sanitized and commercialized folkloric music in an expensive *peña* that common people could not afford to attend. Before this kind of commercialized, colonized, and non-oppositional folklore emerged in privileged circles, Pinochet had actually prohibited the playing of indigenous instruments like the panpipes (*sikus* or *zampoñas*), notch flutes (*quena*), and small guitars (*charango*) associated with the protest movement and *nueva canción* (Olsen 90).

While the concept of authenticity is theoretically problematic in any discussion of art, Alcalde's use of the term signals the opposite cultural phenomenon to the commercialized folklore hailed by Mattern. Referring to the legacy of Violeta Parra, Alcalde distinguishes between Allende's cultural policies and the Junta's brutal erasure of culture:

> El Gobierno Popular del Dr. Salvador Allende la [Violeta Parra] recuperó al darle al folklore su calidad de ciencia popular. Cambió las masacres del tiempo de Frei, González Videla y de Alessandri por la investigación científica a todos los niveles. Hoy, de nuevo todo eso se borró no de una plumada, sino con la bota. Un folklorista auténtico puede ser tan peligroso como un patriota con el fusil en la mano, dicen los militares. (45)

> The Popular Government of Dr. Salvador Allende recuperated her [Violeta Parra] upon recognizing folklore's quality of popular science. Allende halted the massacres, characterizing the governments of Frei, González Videla and Alessandri, and encouraged scientific investigations on all levels. Today, once again all this has been erased not by the stroke of a pen, but rather by the boot. An authentic folklorist can be as dangerous as a patriot holding a gun, says the military.

While Alcalde's enthusiastic use of the term "scientific" sounds dated and misplaced in the context of art and culture, he is unequivocal in his assertion of the truly subversive force of music when it speaks truth to power, as Edward Said describes the role of the public intellectual. In sharp contrast to this politicized vision of the freedom of music to criticize and to envision another possible reality, Mattern limits his supposedly political interpretation to abrasive song lyrics, which he criticizes for being confrontational, types of instruments played, and a simplistic and elitist notion of community.

Revolutionary Music, Rebel Music, and Freedom

In "Sounds of Resistance," Robin Balliger warns that thinking about music in terms of such binary oppositions as spirituality versus pleasure, politics versus pleasure, or spirituality versus entertainment, results in an artificial construct arbitrarily dividing the body from the mind, when music moves both. Citing Susan McClary's and Robert Walser's critique of how the traditional

Left and musicology are positivist and "Enlightenment-driven," "systems designed to reinforce norms rather than liberate," Balliger identifies the central problem of the Left generally as "a desire to find explicit political agendas and intellectual complexity in the art it wants to claim and a distrust of those dimensions of art that appeal to the senses, to physical pleasure. Yet pleasure frequently is the politics of music-pleasure as interference, the pleasure of marginalized people that has evaded channelization" (21). The evasion of "channelization" associated with pleasure is a difficult position to maintain in the face of a fascist coup, and yet Balliger's insight about the non-aligned spirit of freedom cannot be ignored, even in extreme situations. This insight leads us out of the misguided distinction between art that is deemed to be universal and timeless, and activist art that sets its sights on current circumstances and local, regional, and community concerns. A more meaningful distinction within the context of rebel music and social justice would be the artist's commitment to a freedom that cannot tie itself to any organization, like government, that inevitably ends up protecting its own interests and institutional survival.

The advice given by Violeta Parra to the writer and composer Patricio Manns speaks to the exploration of creativity as a search for freedom especially relevant to music: "*Escribe como quieras, usa los ritmos como te salgan, prueba instrumentos diversos en el piano, destruye la métrica, libérate, grita en vez de cantar, sopla en la guitarra y tañe la corneta. La canción es un pájaro sin plan de vuelo que jamás volará en línea recta. Odia la matemática y ama los remolinos*" (Alcalde 39) [Write however you want, use rhythms as they come to you, try out different instruments on the piano, destroy metre, free yourself, shout instead of singing, blow into the guitar and strum the horn. Song is a bird without a flight plan, that will never fly in a straight line. It hates mathematics and loves whirlwinds].[21] Violeta Parra's poetic vision of the relationship of music to freedom suggests that musical freedom is born of experimentation and that music also liberates the spirit and the imagination. While in this particular piece of advice she does not explicitly address the relationship between the musician's flight to freedom through creativity and the power of "contagion" through which visions of freedom are transmitted to listeners and other participating musicians, her song lyrics tend to intertwine personal and public significance.

Joan Jara, on the other hand, draws a distinction between the private and the public spheres, suggesting that social justice can only be pursued in the public sphere:

> Victor's motives for singing and composing were gradually becoming less intimate and personal. The mainspring of his songs was a profound sense of identification with and love for the underprivileged people of Chile, in both the cities and the countryside; a very deep awareness of the injustices of society and their causes and a determination to denounce those injustices in the face of indifference and censorship...and also to try to do something to change them. In that sense Victor's songs were "political," but in these early years only indirectly so. (98)

The injustices suffered by Jara himself were not limited to indifference and censorship. In a typically pathetic and infantile attack on Victor Jara by the right-wing supporters of the National Party, their newspaper *La Tribuna* ran a story of how Jara "had been caught at an all-night homosexual party with little boys, 'dancing a perverted cueca'" (J. Jara 171). While this kind of homophobic slander is not restricted to the right wing, it is interesting to note that the intentionality here is to connect *cueca*—traditional rhythm and dance—to leftist politics, further associated with sexual perversion or feminization, and debauchery. In a published response to this article, Jara declares his membership in the Communist Party, which he represents as "the principal enemy of the reactionary forces of the country" (J. Jara 172). A troubling detail in his response is a reference to "the monolithic character of my Party," the term "monolithic" used as a positive attribute, which Jara assumes is envied by the desperate rightists. While he may have wished to convey the idea of unity and strength, his pride in the monolithic character of his party casts doubts on what kind of freedom such politics would envision and enact. A further consideration is what kind of musical and social freedom monolithic politics can generate.

Victor Jara singing to children in a shanty-town outside of Santiago
(From Victor: An Unfinished Song, Joan Jara, London: Jonathon Cape, 1983, p. 182)

Both Victor Jara's and Violeta Parra's lyrics reveal that even prior to the coup the human rights of the majority of Chileans were not protected, if by this we mean the right to life that is not a painful struggle for (not so) simple survival. Beyond the lyrics dealing with the plight of exploited and often massacred workers and peasants, their experiments with autochthonous forms of music also reveal a true commitment to bridging different communities through intercultural expression. In fairness to Victor Jara, any assessment of his musical production should take into account the different motives he saw as crucial to acting for democracy. While he accepted the responsibility of disseminating information through his music, given the critical political climate of imminent fascist take-over, the same songs that may be qualified as propaganda due to their explicitly partisan lyrics can also be considered as speaking truth to power. Nonetheless, even in more peaceful moments when Jara did not feel compelled to represent reality in terms of a life or death situation, the imagery seems borrowed from songs dedicated to armed struggle. While *"Canto libre"* does not express the confrontational attitudes with which Mattern charges *canción nueva* musicians, the metaphoric language is ambiguously militaristic:

El verso es una paloma
que busca donde anidar
estalla y abre sus alas
para volar y volar
mi canto es un canto libre
que se quiere regalar
a quien le estreche su mano
a quien quiera disparar
mi canto es una cadena
sin comienzo ni final
y en cada labor se encuentra
en canto de los demás
sigamos cantando junto
a toda la humanidad.
Que el canto es una paloma
que vuela para encontrar
estalla y abre sus alas
para volar y volar
mi canto es un canto libre (V. Jara Vol. 3)

Poetry is a dove
searching for a place to nest
it bursts out spreading its wings
to fly and fly

my song is a free song
that wants to give itself
to whoever shakes its hand
to whoever wants to shoot
my song is a chain
with no beginning or end
and in all works is present
in the song of others
let us go on singing together
with all of humanity
Song is a dove
that flies searching
it explodes spreading its wings
to fly and fly
my song is a free song.

Despite the absence of overt militancy in these lyrics, the Spanish verbs *"disparar"* and *"estallar"* are associated with weapons, the former with an explosive going off and the latter with the shooting of a rifle. While they also connote a "bursting forth" in reference to song or flight, the militaristic connotations are present and produce a strange tension between aggression and the image of the dove, connotative of peace and freedom.

Another parallel between Jara and Parra suggests itself in the *"Ars Poetica"* of lyrics dealing explicitly with the significance of song. Parra's best known composition *"Gracias a la vida"* [Thanks to Life] can be defined as a hymn to life in which she typically balances references to truth, beauty, and justice with her love for a particular man.[22] Each stanza opens with the singing of praises to some aspect of life and a giving of thanks for how it has blessed Violeta personally. Each stanza then closes with an image of the beloved giving an intimate tone to a song that nevertheless celebrates the gifts of the senses that Violeta connects to consciousness and the capacity to envision social justice:

Gracias a la vida que me ha dado tanto.
Me dio dos luceros, que cuando los abro
Perfecto distingo lo negro del blanco,
Y en el alto cielo su fondo estrellado
Y en las multitudes al hombre que yo amo.

Gracias a la vida que me ha dado tanto.
Me ha dado el oído, que en todo su ancho
Graba noche y día grillos y canarios;
Martillos, turbinas, ladridos, chubascos,
Y la voz tan tierna de mi bienamado.

Gracias a la vida que me ha dado tanto.
Me ha dado el sonido y el abecedario,
Con él las palabras que pienso y declaro,
Madre, amigo, hermano y luz alumbrando
La ruta del alma del que estoy amando.

Gracias a la vida que me ha dado tanto.
Me ha dado la marcha de mis pies cansados,
Con ellos anduve ciudades y charcos,
Playas y desiertos, montañas y llanos
Y la casa tuya, tu calle y tu patio.

Gracias a la vida que me ha dado tanto.
Me dio el corazón que agita su marco
Cuando miro el fruto del cerebro humano,
Cuando miro al bueno tan lejos del malo,
Cuando miro el fondo de tus ojos claros.

Gracias a la vida que me ha dado tanto.
Me ha dado la risa y me ha dado el llanto,
Así yo distingo dicha de quebranto,
Los dos materiales que forman mi canto,
Y el canto de ustedes que es el mismo canto
Y el canto de todos que es mi propio canto. (Alcade 133-134)

Thanks to life which has given me so much.
It gave me two shining stars, and when I open them
I perfectly distinguish black from white,
And high in the sky its starry depths
And in the crowds the man I love.

Thanks to life which has given me so much.
It has given me ears, which in their breadth
Record night and day crickets and canaries;
Hammers, turbines, barks, downpours,
And the tender voice of my beloved.

Thanks to life which has given me so much.
It has given me sound and alphabet,
With this the words I think and declare,
Mother, friend, brother, sister and light illuminating
The path of the soul I am loving.

Thanks to life which has given me so much.
It has given me the walking of my tired feet,
With them I wandered through cities and puddles,
Beaches and deserts, mountains and plains
And your house, your street and your patio.

Thanks to life which has given me so much.
It gave me my heart which moves its frame
When I look at the fruits of the human brain,
When I look at good so far from evil,
When I look into the depths of your blue eyes.

Thanks to life which has given me so much.
It has given me laughter and it has given me weeping,
This is how I distinguish luck from loss
The two materials that form my song,
And your song which is the same song
And everyone's song which is my own song.

The emphasis on the ability to distinguish good from evil, truth from falsehood, joy from misery, is reminiscent of the song "I Sing Difference" quoted in the epigraph to this essay. The striking feature of both song lyrics is the art with which Violeta Parra interweaves personal experience and feeling with her own place in community, even when that place constantly eluded her, leaving her in solitude. Fernando Sáez's interpretation of *"Gracias a la vida"* stresses the negative, perhaps as a result of concentrating too closely on the autobiographical dimensions of Parra's work: *"compuesta luego del intento de suicidio de enero del '66, que lejos de ser un himno a la vida, es un recuento poético de sus pérdidas"* (159-60) [composed shortly after attempting suicide in January of '66, far from being a hymn to life, it is a poetic recounting of her losses]. The fact that this song belonged to a collection that Parra chose to name *Las últimas canciones de Violeta Parra* [Violeta Parra's Last Songs] seems to support Sáez's interpretation (even though *"últimas"* can also mean "last" in the sense of "latest"). The title foreshadows Violeta's determination to end her life and solitude when and how she decided.

Both of the song lyrics cited in the epigraph to this essay suggest that the desire for peace and truth animate human creativity and resistance. But I also wonder if it isn't significant to consider that Jara's hymn to peace hails Ho Chi Minh as a triumphant leader whose political example is celebrated from a leftist internationalist perspective. By contrast, Parra's lyrics start with a proclamation of her own integrity after which each stanza denounces the military government's abuse of all poor people in Chile, though Parra represents them as concrete individuals with specific circumstances and stories. Besides identifying the government as military and anti-popular, Violeta Parra also positions nation—state, army, and church—against the people, who in Parra's verses are never represented in abstract terms as "the masses" but as individuals, especially women and children who, in many cases, are directly named. The most telling aspect of Violeta Parra's social criticism is that it could be leveled at any corrupt or inept government regardless of its position on the political spectrum.

As I write this essay during an academic exchange term in Cuba, the war in Iraq is officially over, the fall of Baghdad assured. I remember how well informed I felt watching Cuban television coverage of the beginning of the war, which focused almost entirely on the hundreds of thousands of protestors who poured into the streets of major cities around the world. Then, I thought that if I were watching the news in Canada, this focus on the extent of the global outcry against this war would largely have been lost. Now the tables turn. I realize my good luck at being in a hotel for a week where we have access to international television channels. (Not that I usually rely on TV for news, but there are no international newspapers or magazines in Cuba with the exception of a few spots in Havana). The American CNN shows crowds of rioting, jubilant Iraqi men (not a single woman in sight) celebrating the downfall of Saddam Hussein's brutal dictatorship. Suddenly, Cuban news shuts down; no more images from international sources. The news is limited to roundtable talks discussing the injustices of war and U.S. imperialism. There is not a single image of the mobs gone wild—ransacking stores, museums, palaces, occupying spots to which, for mysterious reasons, common people had been denied access. The images of men sitting on statues of Saddam Hussein beating his head with shoes, sticks and stones cannot be shown to Cubans. Is it because some Iraqis hold up signs thanking the Americans for "liberating" them? (They do not thank them for having placed Saddam Hussein in power in the first place). Why were the human rights abuses of the Iraqi regime tolerated for so long by the United States? Why does the Cuban government never mention these abuses, and even represents Saddam Hussein as a hero? Clearly, governments cannot commit themselves to social justice beyond the ulterior motives involved in justifying their own undemocratic actions, their own sustaining self-interest.

The war has been a media circus on both U.S. and Cuban television, although the Cuban coverage maintains a staunch intellectual approach to "discussion" that includes writers, artists, political analysts, and guest speakers from other Latin American countries. The variety of viewpoints is misleading, given that everyone seems to be in perfect agreement on all aspects of the situation. Criticism must be limited to enemy states, while identical cases of injustice by the state and its allies are "overlooked" through censorship on all sides. I feel compelled to take this detour because my surroundings and my limited contact with the outside world strike me as being completely relevant to my wondering about the substantive, critical differences between revolutionary and rebel musics. Revolutionary politics represents itself as complete once the victory has been won; all that remains is to ensure that nothing can undermine the revolutionary state, its leaders, its apparatus. Rebellion, on the other hand, does not posit an end, and therefore represents itself as an ongoing process of critical evaluation and material action.[23] Political parties have a hard time upholding rebellion because rebellion is a force that evades institutionalization and demands freedom, like song which, as Violeta Parra said, "is a bird without a flight plan, that will never fly in a straight line. It hates mathematics and loves whirlwinds" (Alcalde 39).

Violeta Parra's lyrics are universal, not in any transcendent or metaphysical sense, but in their freedom to attack meanness and stupidity *wherever* they are manifest, in concrete, material terms. Given that she did not tolerate hypocrisy within her own populist circles, her integrity would have made it difficult for her to integrate herself wholeheartedly into any "monolithic" party. This does not mean that she distanced herself from the collectivist activities, even those organized by government; before the rise of Popular Unity, Violeta Parra was already actively involved in voluntary work, distributing food to the poor from centres organized by the Frente Popular [Popular Front].[24] Despite the distance she kept from party affiliations, her lyrics make assertions about being a Communist and even summon guerrillas to fight for justice. "*Los hambrientos piden pan*" [The Hungry are Asking for Bread] closes with the verses "*Por suerte tengo guitarra / para llorar mi dolor, / también tengo nueve hermanos / fuera del que se m'engrilló, / los nueve son comunistas / con el favor de mi Dios, sí*" (Alcalde 120) [Luckily I have a guitar / to express my pain, / I also have nine brothers and sisters / besides the one that they shackled, / all nine are Communists / with God's blessing, yes]. Interestingly, Parra involves God in her ethical vision of social and political justice. The lyrics of "*Hace falta un guerrillero*" [A Guerrilla Fighter is Needed] express the desire to have a son worthy of the name Manuel Rodríguez, whom the mother would teach to defend her country from those who would sell it as if it were a pin. These explicitly political and revolutionary references appeal to the ethical basis of Leftist values and respond to personal adversity (the arrest of Parra's brother) and the collective memory of a hero of Chilean independence.

In the song "*Yo canto la diferencia*," Parra derides *comandos importantes* [important commandos], who swear allegiance to the flag, and *señor Ministro* [Mr. Minister] and *el señor Vicario* [the Vicar] for their hypocrisy in pretending to be patriotic while ignoring and even working against the people. She then asks the Vicar in an ironic tone "*¿Podría su majestad /oírme una palabrita? / Los niños andan con hambre. / Les dan una medallita / o bien una banderita*" (Alcade 123-24) [Could your majesty / listen to one little word of mine? / Children are hungry. / They give them a little medal / or a little flag]. In the next stanza, a woman named Luisa is giving birth, but nobody pays attention because while her screams reach the sky, they are drowned out by the *fiesta nacional* [festivities of the national holiday]. Parra inserts herself into the song as midwife and witness to Luisa's miserable conditions:

No tiene fuego la Luisa
ni una vela ni un pañal.
El niño nació en las manos
de la que cantando está.
Por un reguero de sangre
va marchando un Cadillac.
Cueca amarga nacional... (Alcade 124)

She doesn't have fire Luisa
a candle or a diaper
The child was born into the hands
of the one who is singing
Along a trail of blood
a Cadillac passes.
Bitter national cueca...

The last ambivalent verses of this stanza juxtapose the blood of the birth with bloodshed, perhaps as a result of violence represented obliquely as being committed by the rich who pass by in a Cadillac. Modifying the national song of Chile as bitter, and in the final verse of the song as "*Cueca larga militar*" [Long military cueca] expresses, in highly condensed language, the appropriation of popular music typically trotted out by

Popular Unity supporters celebrate their election victory

the government only in the month of September during Independence Day celebrations. Fernando Sáez observes how traditional music and the social recognition of the cultural value of folkloric musicians were limited to the official holiday:

> Septiembre es el único tiempo donde los artistas del folklore son requeridos por radios y lugares nocturnos y cuando se escuchan tonadas y cuecas que difícilmente se trasmiten el resto del año. Por eso no resulta difícil ver por esos días los atuendos de los huasos y los trajes repolludos de las mujeres, subiendo y bajando de taxis que transportan arpas y guitarras para ir de un lugar a otro, en el apuro de aprovechar esos pocos días para cumplir con todas las oportunidades posibles. (108)

> September is the only time when folkloric artists are required by radio stations and nightclubs, and when one can hear *tonadas* and *cuecas* which are rarely transmitted during the rest of the year.[25] This is the reason why during those days you can see peasant costumes and the full layered skirts of women getting in and out of taxis that also carry harps and guitars from one place to another, in a mad rush to take advantage of the few days in which to fulfill as many opportunities as possible.

The social marginalization of musical traditions is symptomatic of an artificially concocted and controlled culture. This kind of institutionalized display of music and dance conveys that the nation's indigenous roots are celebrated as a salute to the past. Indigenous culture and existence is represented as a picturesque vignette lifted from a historical reality with no relation to the present, or to the continued survival and resistance of native people in the future. Clearly, any musician dedicated to gathering, recording and performing traditional music in such a cultural climate would be engaged in an uphill battle to validate and disseminate musical forms that the dominant class deem to have little cultural currency. The polarization resulting from the institutional control of popular culture inevitably leads to political confrontation.

Postlude

While Violeta Parra and Victor Jara differed in their responses to this polarization—Parra by railing against functionaries, bureaucrats, and politicians, in short, against government, and Jara by opposing the ruling class through organized party politics—both fought to defend cultural survival, recognizing that social justice and human rights must be defined and defended within popular culture. The difficulty of judging Victor Jara's position and the necessity of questioning artistic affiliations with political institutions are addressed in what Robin Balliger says about the performative aspects of music:

> popular music can be a site of counter-hegemonic activities…performance and commodification of music products are not clearly bounded and how musicians and audiences negotiate these spheres varies in every situation. There is no correct strategy here…music and resistance are shaped in the moment of their coming into being, a musical/political praxis that is negotiated by social actors in particular spatial and temporal locations. As fixity itself is increasingly recognized as a necessary condition for the deployment of power, performative practices like music and dance suggest forms of resistance that produce experience in ever changing forms. (25)

Victor Jara believed that democratic values could be protected by a democratically elected government representative of the majority, which supposedly includes the most marginalized and impoverished. His faith in a revolutionary government led by a populist party did not take into account the inevitable fixity that institutions require for the deployment of power, as Balliger asserts. Jara gave the following reason for devoting most of his time to music, despite his reputation in the theatre:

> I am moved more and more by what I see around me…the poverty of my own country, of Latin America and other countries of the world; I have seen with my own eyes memorials to the Jews in Warsaw, the panic caused by the Bomb, the disintegration that war causes to human beings and all that is born of them…But I have also seen what love can do, what real liberty can do, what the strength of a man who is happy can achieve. Because of all this, and because above all I desire peace, I need the wood and strings of my guitar to give vent to sadness or happiness, some verse which opens up the heart like a wound, some line which helps us all to turn from inside ourselves to look out and see the world with new eyes. (J. Jara 98)

This connection of voice to ears to eyes, the potential of music to enter our ears and to give us new eyes relates to counter-hegemonic practice in a profound way, Jara's optimism in government aside. In the case of Violeta Parra, we would have to modify Jara's vision to read: "But I have also seen what love can do, what real liberty can do, what the strength of a woman who sings her unhappiness can achieve..." Both had the capacity to give new eyes through their song, giving witness to the cultural richness and democratic promise that Jara's last song represents as germinating in the midst of terror and annihilation. In this sense, Victor Jara's assertion that the Communist Party is "the principal enemy of the reactionary forces of the country" (J. Jara 172) is also his blind spot. The annihilation of the Communist Party and even of the elected government of Salvador Allende did not extinguish the desire for social justice and freedom in Chile. The idea that such desires could be circumscribed within a political agenda would indeed be "like tying the sea to a stick" (Alcade 39).

Far from the lukewarm "*ni chicha ni limoná*" politics and music of the post-coup *peñas* cited by Mattern, acting in concert does not depend on intellectuals looking for bridges with the powerful and the guilty, bridges that lead nowhere.[26] Such interaction has only consolidated the social acceptance and the rule of those who violated human rights on a massive scale with impunity. They have reaped the benefits and the rewards for acting in concert with U.S. and multinational business interests for long enough. Violeta Parra's affirmation of the ubiquity, depth, and constant renewal of popular musical culture in Chile is the true source of hope.[27] That constant regeneration implicit in Parra's affirmation is also alluded to in Jara's final words: "*lo que he sentido y lo que siento / hará brotar el momento...*" (V. Jara, n.p.) [What I've felt and what I'm feeling / Will germinate the moment...]. The promise contained in the movement from personal adversity to envisioning a future moment as a germination beyond the self is further echoed in Pablo Neruda's elegy to Violeta which he entitles "*Elegía para cantar*" [Elegy for Singing]. The closing verses express both a farewell to Violeta and an invitation to the shared performative aspect of song, a promise of the contagion of rebel music:

Bueno, Violeta Parra, me despido,
Me a mis deberes.
¿Y hora es? La hora de cantar.
Cantas.
　　Canto.
　　　　Cantemos. (Parra 13)

Well, Violeta Parra, I'll say goodbye,
I'm going off to my chores.
And what time is it? Time to sing.
You sing.
　　I sing.
　　　　Let's sing.

NOTES

1. In the biography of Victor Jara entitled *Victor: An Unfinished Story*, his wife Joan Jara relates how Jara tried to communicate his social views musically on the campuses of Berkley and UCLA, and how despite the hippies' sympathy towards the problems of Latin America, they were most concerned with the war in Vietnam and protesting the draft; "they had their own fight and their own cause. Victor felt that politically they tended to be very naïve, that they would never achieve a revolution, not even of 'flowers'—the drugs would take care of that, defusing what might have been a powerful movement of rebellion" (J. Jara 111). This view of the spoiled, self-centred, and politically naïve citizen of the United States is commonly held by Latin Americans who believe that all potentially rebellious activity is effectively co-opted in the United States through commercialization. Victor Jara himself commented on what he referred to as "commercial tripe" that "with professional expertise they have taken certain measures: first, the commercialisation of so-called 'protest music'; second, the creation of 'idols' of protest music who obey the same rules and suffer from the same constraints as the other idols of the consumer music industry—they last a little while and then disappear. Meanwhile they are useful in neutralising the innate spirit of rebellion of young people" (J. Jara 121).

2. Throughout this essay all translations from the Spanish are my own.

3. Violet Parra was believed to have been born in the city of Chillán, but in reality her birthplace was the small village of San Carlos on the road to Chillán, where her family did eventually settle for a time. I interpret this reference to singing "a la chillaneja" as an idiomatic expression that relates her style to her roots and regional traditions.

4. The *cueca* is danced to a lively rhythm by partners who do not hold on to each other, and is especially popular in Chile and Argentina.

5. As José Yglesias specifies "the guests invited were representatives of both the former Allende government and the militarists, Reverend William Wipfler of the National Council of Churches, and Professor James Ritter" (Yglesias 15).

6. Renato Trujillo, an exiled Chilean writer, expresses dissatisfaction with human relationships in his new country by playing on the linguistic challenges of learning English. In a poem entitled "Unsolicited Mail" he slips from asserting the greatness of the ambiguous territory named "Amerika" to one of its significant lacks: "Amerika is great. In every respect. / But for some reason / I have trouble with that word 're-spect'… / I don't think I conjugate that verb / often enough. I don't think they do, either." After taking inventory of all the material benefits and opportunities that he has gained by emigrating to North America, the poetic subject addresses the woman to whom he directs the poem/letter: "I'm not trying to dissuade you / from coming up here, Rosita, no. I'm only trying to tell you about / the pleasure one can find here and / also tell you that everything / has an end. (For some peculiar reason / these two seem to go together; / it's hard to distinguish between them.) But most importantly, / I am trying to tell you about all those things we leave behind" (231-32).

7. In the first vignette "Promise of America" of the second volume of Eduardo Galeano's trilogy *Memory of Fire*, the myth of an apocalyptic revolution envisioned by the Guaraní (shared by numerous indigenous tribes across the Americas) attributes the desire for radical transformation to the earth itself:

The blue tiger will smash the world. Another land, without evil, without death, will be born from the destruction of this one. This land wants it. It asks to die, asks to be born, this old and offended land. It is weary and blind from so much weeping behind closed eyelids. On the point of death it strides the days, garbage heap of time, and at night it inspires pity from the stars. Soon the First Father will hear the world's supplications, land wanting to be another, and then the blue tiger who sleeps beneath his hammock will jump. (3)

This belief is repeatedly referred to by the Uruguayan writer who also spent many years in exile and writes incessantly about his and others' visions of social justice. See Fischlin and Nandorfy.

8. Both Parra and Jara used the term "folklore" in a positive sense and considered themselves to be "folkloristas" in a movement that was dedicated to recuperating indigenous cultural roots. This term has since been problematized for connoting a lesser cultural value than other forms of institutionalized music, especially of European origin.

9. Referring to the Second Festival of New Chilean Song held in August 1970, Joan Jara observes that since the election was approaching, "there was none of the relative political tolerance of the previous year. Any performer known to support a candidate other than Allende was whistled off the stage" (145).

10. While "comrade" is the most literal translation of "*compañero*" in a political context, the Spanish word is connotative of the more intimate and friendly "companion." Therefore, the term sounds less officious and more expansive in Spanish.

11. The Mapuche Indians of Chile (also referred to as Araucanians) forced the Spaniards to withdraw from their territory during the conquest of South America, managing to keep them at bay for approximately ten years. Mapuches continue to suffer persecution at the hands of landowners but have organized themselves in peasant unions since 1928 in order to resist exploitation and demand basic necessities for their communities like drinking water supplies and electricity. Victor Jara was asked by a Mapuche community to represent their history and the terrible massacre that took place in their community six years after forming their union and attempting a rebellion. Joan Jara relates how "Victor was taken to the place where the river Ranquil converges with the great Bio-Bio, a rocky gorge which the peasants had named 'the slaughter house' because it was there that, one by one, their leaders had been shot, their bodies falling straight into the icy water below" (201). Unfortunately, Jara did not live long enough to realize this project. As recently as 2002, the Mapuches have struggled against government forces, and continue to fight for longstanding land claims.

12. In his biography *La Vida Intranquila* [An Agitated Life], Fernando Sáez addresses the difficulty of being accepted into an indigenous community and how Violeta overcame the reticence and suspicion of the Araucanos, which she never managed to do in the non-native context:

Siempre había que disponer de un tiempo largo, propicio para alcanzar la entrega. Una canción de ella, cantada por ella, o el intercambio de conocimientos podían bastar. Hasta llegó a usar la vieja costumbre del trueque para resolver su cometido, así lo hizo para entrar en los reductos araucanos, llevando una maleta con ropa que cambiaba por canciones. Así eran los primeros contactos que casi siempre terminaban en una amistad sincera, porque con todas estas gentes Violeta tenía la calidez de los que la conocían bien, quedando postergados y cuidadosamente reservados su mal humor y sus rabietas para quienes no lograran entender lo que ella hacía y representaba. (60)

A long time always had to be dedicated to getting them to "deliver." In some cases, one of her songs, sung by her, or the exchange of information would be enough. She went as far as to use the old custom of barter to gain access into Araucanian territory, taking a suitcase of clothes to exchange for songs. These first contacts almost always developed into sincere friendships, because with all these people Violeta showed the warmth that she gave freely to those who knew her well, saving her bad moods and fits of anger for those who did not comprehend what she was doing and what she represented.

13. The Peruvian novelist José María Arguedas suffered similar circumstances to Violeta Parra's in that he was traumatically torn between indigenous and white culture and committed suicide while writing a novel entitled *El zorro de arriba y el zorro de abajo* [The Fox from Up Above and the Fox from Down Below] which deals precisely with the cultural violence rooted in class and racial differences. Arguedas said about Violeta that she was "lo más chileno de lo más chileno que yo tengo la posibilidad de sentir; sin embargo, es al mismo tiempo, lo más universal que he conocido de Chile" [the most Chilean of Chileans that I had the opportunity of listening to; she is, at the same time however, the most universal of Chileans] (Alcalde 49).

14. The term *"momio"* literally means "mummy" in the Egyptian sense as Joan Jara explains: "In my mind I always associated the term with a character in a play by Raul Ruiz which Victor had directed some time before…an ancient landowner who appeared to be disintegrating in his wheelchair, attended by a servant as decrepit as himself. He would call querulously for his binoculars and peer out over the audience, as though over the vast expanses of his estates, a symbol of the decaying yet petrified oligarchy, jealously protecting their lands and privileges. *Momio* was becoming the popular term for anyone with a reactionary position" (98).

15. The song "El Guillatún" from *Las últimas canciones de Violeta Parra*, lyrically describes the ceremony referred to in the title, one of the most important seasonal ceremonies (also known as "nillipún" and ngillatún), which is presided over by a machi: "primarily a supplicatory ceremony, it takes place after harvest, but it can be performed during unfavorable meteorological conditions or in times of calamity. It lasts four days and follows a complex ritual. Throughout, music is important" (Olsen 308). Parra's performance of "El Guillatún" includes the beat of the kultrún and the rhythm of ritualistic song.

16. *Décimas* are poems or songs made up of five stanzas, each consisting of ten verses of eight syllables rhyming *abbaaccddc*. *Décimas de Violeta Parra* was published by the Spanish press Editorial Pomaire in 1976, nine years after her death. Her *décimas* and a selection of other songs are presented with poetic introductions by Pablo Neruda, Violeta's brother Nicanor Parra (a well known poet in his own right), and the poet Pablo de Rokha.

17. The erratic spelling, contractions, and grammar of these verses reflect the oral speech of the working-class and the dialect of Spanish spoken in the regions of Chile where Violeta Parra recorded popular songs.

18. While I translate "ladino" to the most general meaning of "sly," that word can also mean "mestizo" [mixed race] in which case calling Ibáñez a "ladino" would suggest that the perspective of this critical song is native, since that community would distinguish itself from the more privileged *ladinos* of partial European heritage with their accompanying power and wealth.

19. One quick example of this one-sided view of balance would be the open-armed welcome afforded to all Cuban exiles (including common criminals) and the highly suspicious attitude exercised towards exiles escaping from fascist regimes. Those who accept the theory that there are no more fascist dictatorships in Latin America should take into consideration the genocide practiced by the Rios Montt government in Guatemala, and the fact that this perpetrator of crimes against humanity (specifically Mayans) is not only free and unpunished, but poised to once again assume the presidency in the near future. Clearly his open-door policy with regards to Guatemala's richly biodiverse environment is so important to U.S. interests that the massacre of Mayans does not even merit news coverage, let alone serious criticism or sanctions.

20. The Bolivians would have suffered the most prejudice due to the predominance of the indigenous population in Bolivia. This same Brazilian eyewitness comments on how a black student was stoned by women in Providencia, a wealthy section of Santiago, a bastion of racism, classism, and extreme-right ideology.

21. This representation of song as freedom of movement and sound liberated from its conventional source to produce an orgy of synesthesia is strongly reminiscent of both García Lorca's artistic vision and language. For instance in the poem "Standards and Paradise of the Blacks," Lorca describes their vision in the same love/hate terms: "They hate the bird's shadow / on the white cheek's high tide /… / They hate the unbodied arrow, / the punctual handkerchief of farewell, / … / They love the deserted blue" (25).

22. It is interesting to note the significant differences between those songs of Parra and Jara that have been referred to as hymns. In Parra's case, "Gracias a la vida" has often been referred to as a hymn to life and love, while in Joan Jara's words, Victor's "Venceremos" [We Will Win / We Shall Overcome] "became the 'hymn' of Popular Unity" (145).

23. The distinction between "revolutionary" and "rebel" is not maintained in Cuba, and yet the allure of the term "rebel" is not lost on the propagandists; the name of one of the television channels is "TV Rebelde," and slogans painted on walls proclaim that Cubans are "Rebeldes."

24. In a chapter entitled "Ayudar a los necesitados" [Helping those in Need], Alonso Alcalde remembers how much time and energy Violeta Parra sacrificed whenever her help was required: "El Partido fue el que le dio esa tarea y ella se levantaba antes que apareciera el sol y ya abría su almacén y les vendía a esa gente a precio de costo, sin ganar ni un centavo. Porque eso es lo que le dictaba la conciencia de ella. Ayudar, ayudar a los más necesitados, sobre todo cuando la soberbia de los poderosos se ensañaba contra los pobres, contra los más indefensos como era ella misma" (31) [The Party assigned her this task (to run some of the food distribution centres) and she would get up before sunrise to open her shop and sell to people at cost, without earning a cent for herself. Because that is what her conscience dictated to her. To help, help the most needy, especially when the arrogance of the powerful was leveled against the poor, against the most helpless people like herself]. There are numerous accounts of how Violeta Parra would literally give all her clothes to poor women who came begging at her door, and that this generosity was one of the factors in her own poverty and her rundown appearance. These testimonies of her active involvement in helping others jive with the ethical tone of her lyrics, which express Violeta Parra's commitment to participatory politics and activism.

25. While the term "tonada" originally meant "tune" in Spanish, in the 1990s in Chile it refers more specifically to "a song performed by one or two singers in parallel thirds in nasal style" (Olsen and Sheehy 386). Due to the German influence in Chilean music, often the tonada is accompanied by accordion.

26. Victor Jara's song "Ni Chicha ni limoná" is cited by Mattern as an example of confrontational lyrics that undermines what he considers acting in concert. In this song, Jara ridicules those who sit on the fence calling them neither chicha (a fermented corn beverage) nor lemonade. The same term could be applied to Mattern's seemingly apolitical stance, which in fact reveals a strong ideological bias in line with U.S. interests.

27. Commenting on the different rhythms and forms of Chilean music, Violeta Parra observes: "La temática literaria abarca todo el mundo interior del hombre de mi pueblo. Los temas son infinitos. Se canta la tristeza y la alegría. La cueca, misma, por ejemplo, refleja todo eso, con la innúmera variedad de especies que se escuchan a lo largo de mi patria." (Alcade 55) [The literary themes encompass the whole internal world of my people. The themes are infinite. They sing of sorrow and joy. The cueca, for example, reflects all this with the countless variations of styles heard throughout my country]. She goes on to explain the different folkloric forms: "El folklore de Chile se halla dividido en canto a lo humano, canto a lo divino,

cuecas, tonadas, parabienes, danzas campesinas, cantos con influencia europea, esquinazos y cantos de Navidad. Pero grande es la variedad a través de las distintas zonas de mi patria. Yo he recogido una canción que se llama 'Tú eres la estrella más linda' con doce versiones diferentes en su melodía y en su letra. Se podría hacer un libro con una sola canción" (Alcade 67) [Chilean folkloric music is divided into human (prosaic) song, divine song, *cuecas, tonadas*, congratulatory songs, peasant dances, songs with European influences, *esquinazos* and Christmas songs. But there is great variety in the different regions of my country. I have found a song entitled "You are the Loveliest Star" with twelve different versions of its melody and lyrics. You could write a book based on just one song]. These comments leave little doubt as to how popular culture is an inexhaustible source of music, even in a country where it was ignored and held in contempt by the cultural institutions run by the élite. The endless variations mentioned by Parra also attest to the dynamic nature of popular music, the traditional base of which does not imply static repetition, but the power of cultural memory to sustain itself through continuous adaptation and experimentation.

WORKS CITED

Alcalde, Alfonso. *Toda Violeta Parra*. Buenos Aires: Ediciones de la Flor, 1975.

Balliger, Robin. "Sounds of Resistance." *Sounding Off!: Music as Subversion/Resistance/Revolution*. Eds. Ron Sakolsky and Fred Wei-han Ho. New York: Autonomedia, 1995. 13-26.

Fischlin, Daniel and Martha Nandorfy. *Eduardo Galeano: Through the Looking Glass*. Montréal: Black Rose Books, 2001.

Galeano, Eduardo. *The Book of Embraces*. Trans. Cedric Belfrage. New York: W. W. Norton and Co., 1991.

—. *Memory of Fire: II. Faces and Masks*. Trans. Cedric Belfrage. New York: Pantheon, 1988.

—. *Memory of Fire: III. Century of the Wind*. Trans. Cedric Belfrage. New York: Pantheon, 1988.

García Lorca, Federico. *Poet in New York*. Ed. Christopher Maurer. Translated by Greg Simon and Steven F. White. New York: Noonday Press, 1988.

Jara, Joan. *Victor: An Unfinished Song*. London: Jonathan Cape, 1983.

Jara, Victor. *Victor Jara: Para Tocar con Guitarra*. Vol. 1-3. Santiago: Lusic y Asociados Ltd., no date.

—. *Victor Jara: Biografía, Discografía, Estadio Chile*. Vol. 4. Santiago: Lusic y Asociados Ltd., no date.

Mattern, Mark. *Acting in Concert: Music, Community, and Political Action*. New Brunswick and London: Rutgers UP, 1998.

Olsen, Dale A. and Daniel E. Sheehy, eds. *The Garland Handbook of Latin American Music*. New York and London: Garland, 2000.

Parra, Violeta. *Décimas de Violeta Parra: Autobiografía en Versos*. Intro. Pablo Neruda, Nicanor Parra and Pablo de Rokha. Barcelona: Editorial Pomaire, 1976.

Sáez, Fernando. *La Vida Intranquila: Biografía Esencial*. Santiago: Editorial Sudamericana, 1999.

Said, Edward. "The Public Role of Writers and Intellectuals." *The Nation*. Sept. 17/24, 2001: 27-36.

Trujillo, Renato. "Unsolicited Mail." *Making a Difference: Canadian Multicultural Literature*. Ed. Smaro Kamboureli. Toronto and New York: Oxford UP, 1996.

Yglesias, José. "Introduction." *Chile's Days of Terror: Eyewitness Accounts of the Military Coup*. Ed. Judy White. New York: Pathfinder Press, 1974.

Timothy Brennan

8 / Global Youth and Local Pleasure: Cuba and the Right to Popular Music

"The emergence of the independent African states...was destined to produce young intellectuals [who wanted] an art that would reach the people...as popular as the Impressions or the Miracles or Marvin Gaye." —Amiri Baraka[1]

TIMOTHY BRENNAN is Professor of Cultural Studies & Comparative Literature and English at the University of Minnesota, and also the Director of the Humanities Institute. He is the author of *Salman Rushdie and the Third World: Myths of the Nation* (Macmillan, 1989) and *At Home in the World: Cosmopolitanism Now* (Harvard UP, 1997). He recently introduced, co-translated, and edited *Music in Cuba* by Alejo Carpentier (U of Minnesota P, 2001), and has just completed a book titled *Cultures of Belief*.

There is a joke told by certain Miami Cubans, who, when they are not closing down radio stations, picketing concerts of Cuban artists, hijacking aircraft, or violating Cuban airspace, pass the time pondering the destruction of Fidel Castro. According to the joke, in one of Fidel's famously long speeches in the Plaza de la Revolución, he implores the assembled to affirm their serious social tasks. Reaching a crescendo at one point, he thunders: "*Compañeros, no somos pachangueros*" (comrades, we Cubans are no silly dancing party-animals). And in a great swell of approbation, the followers timidly repeat in unison: "*No, Fidel, no somos pachangueros*" (No, you're right, we're no silly party-animals). And then again, to drive the point home, Fidel repeats, "*compañeros, no somos pachangueros*"; and they once more prove equal to the task: "*no, no somos pachangueros*."

And so the teller of the joke gradually begins to prolong the syllables, now syncopating them so that the people's antiphon becomes the call-and-response of salsa. Soon, the back-and-forth makes the words "*no, no somos pachangueros*" take the form of the tapping of a conga. Before long, in the joke-teller's rendition, one can see the crowd rocking to the words' rhythms, riffing on their sound, unable to resist the beat of syllables that only a moment before had been inappro-priate to the pleasures of the dance. The joke is trying to teach us that Cubans, try as they might, want only to break free of revolutionary puritanism. They are *pachangueros*.

In a certain social vision—call it the culture of Miami—this is a very useful joke. Cuba can be neatly dispensed with as comic-book socialism or worse: militarized altruism and vacuous, sleepwalking conformity. But even satirical jabs have a logic. In this case the humor falls flat be-cause it describes something not simply distorted as in caricature, but the exact opposite of the truth—not only false but false in a neatly symmetrical way.

Cuban popular music was never promoted so vigorously as after the July 26th movement came to power in 1959. In two decades, more serious scholarship on Afro-Cuban musical forms and religious expression found its way into print than had appeared in all of Cuban history up to that point. Afro-Cuban culture enjoyed a massive respectability in *official* circles for the first time. In the early years of the revolution, artists wrote jubilant *guarachas* and *mambos*, enthusiastically performed as signature elements at political gatherings. These were not enlisted as forms for the instrumental purpose of persuasion alone, but at least in part out of ecstasy for political transfor-mation. With official encouragement, popular movements set out to redefine Cuban identity as black, white, young, and mixed—in their own minds realizing what the nineteenth and twenti-eth-century independence movements had always chiefly been about.

Cuban socialism did not launch Afro-Cuban popular music, of course, but the intellectual movement of Afro-Cubanism in the 1920s and 1930s (mirrored later in the vast network of afi-cionados, chroniclers, and publicists who continue to make the music thrive) were central to the independence movements whose leaders directly inspired the July 26th movement (indeed, those who lived long enough to bridge the two eras—the era of the rise of the *son* and the era of the Sierra Maestra—saw only a seamless continuity). The revolution of 1959 was, in short, the consummation not only of the work of the nineteenth-century anti-Spanish revolutionaries José Martí and Antonio Maceo, but of Fernando Ortiz, Nicolás Guillén, Lydia Cabrera, and Alejo Carpentier—the great exponents of Afro-Cubanism in the 1920s and 1930s.

The sentiments of the early movements against Spanish, and later North American, occupa-tion most closely allied with the work of Martí (who advocated an inclusive Cuban identity), were finally coming to realization. Government speeches for the first time held up popular cultural forms, largely Afro-Cuban, as advertisements, if you will, of the new Cuba. Curricular changes in the art and music schools reflected an unprecedented valorization of a cultural creation from be-low, in which wholesale folkloric recovery work was conducted to learn about the sources, and heroes, of such musical forms as the *cha-cha-chá*, the *danzon*, and the early *septeto* combos. It would not be putting it too strongly to say the new government *identified itself* with a national musical, and Afro-Cuban patrimony, helping to drive home that already disintegrating division be-tween high and low culture that had been a part of Cuba's cultural past and its national struggle.

More than any other Latin country before or since (the competition is not even close), it is so-cialist Cuba that promoted popular music, studied its development, preserved its fragile records, and continued to encourage it with scarce public funds. What is more, the innovations within Cuban music have not flagged since 1959. Most of the great performers, with the exception of Celia Cruz, Osvaldo Farrés, Willie Chirino, La Lupe, Albita Rodriguez and others, chose to stay in Cuba—sometimes freely traveling abroad to perform without any hint of wanting to live any-where but the Island. The cream of the musical crop—including many who benefited directly from the warm commercial reception in the United States and Europe—found their creative sources in Cuba, and their support for the post-1959 social changes were often ardent.

But discussion around music, especially the music of the nightclubs and the dancehalls, is an especially effective arena for political persuasion. Cuba has been a favored target of this political strategy of alienation and censure by U.S. opinion-makers who have mastered the art of political othering. As such, the issue of Cuba's sovereignty (including, as we shall see, the control over its own musical contributions) emerges, and it is here that popular music becomes an issue of hu-man rights. I would like to explore the violation of Cuba's rights accomplished by denying the possibility of non-market pleasures and by employing music—and the idea of popular mu-sic—to conquer the sensibilities of "youth": indeed, to claim youth as the private property of U.S. mass culture.

Given Cuba's role in inventing many of the most globally successful leisure products of the last century, the irony of claims that it cripples the pursuit of pleasure is redoubled. As recent film and concert tours have reminded the American public, Cuba's cultural influences have been found all over U.S. popular music and theatre for a century and a half—from the *habanera*'s penetration into the American heartland via Mexican military bands in the 1880s to the Mario Bauza—and Beny Moré—led *mambo* crazes of New York in the 1940s and 1950s. The success of mambo (captured in Oscar Hijuelos' novel, *The Mambo Kings Play Songs of Love*) only re-peated the impact on U.S. popular culture of Latin hits (invariably from Cuba) like "La Paloma" in the 1870s, and "Cuban Song" from the Broadway play *The Idol's Eye* in 1897, or in the academy award-nominated film music of Ernesto Lecuona, whose work was very widely heard in Holly-wood and on the radio from the late 1930s to the 1950s.

Cuban performance of the popular is so overdetermined and so obvious it almost seems im-pertinent to mention it. The island nation was home to the golden age of 1970s poster art; pro-duced the theory of Julio García Espinoza's "imperfect cinema"; launched the so-called *filin* songs of the 1960s, and exported *nueva trova*—a music at once romantic, poetic, and politi-cal—and a form of troubadour modernity influential throughout Europe and Latin America for almost two decades. Ulf Hannerz in his helpful revision of the centre/periphery construct points out that there are actually many regional centers in the global layout of states: Qom as a major religious hub, for example; Bombay as a distribution source for a style of musical film that

touches most of Asia; Cairo for Arabic publishing, and so on. For Latin America and the Caribbean, Cuba has clearly acted as that sort of centre. The Havana film festival and the Casa de las
Americas awards in literature have prompted a regional creativity in explicitly Latin American
forms undirected by North American audiences. Among these forms was the *testimonio,* whose
early practitioners and theorists included Miguel Barnet and Margaret Randall, then resident in
Cuba. *Testimonio* was arguably a Cuban export. Nor does this begin to appreciate Cuba's visible
role as spokesman for the Non-Aligned nations—a role filled dramatically at the Rio Summit in
what can only be called an audacious confrontation with the United States over the *environment*—an issue not typically recognized as socialist.

Only a peculiar kind of insensitivity could pass over these contributions without comment, or
fail to observe that Cuba had also excelled in an even more popular form of cultural expression—*sport*, the activity claiming hours of working-class free time, a vast stage for the enactment of dream and desire (is it surprising that the German playwright and communist Bertolt
Brecht found sport the dramatist's teacher?). As the victor in the Pan American games of the
early 1990s, Cuba, facing a vanquished United States, demonstrated that sport was not merely
an exportable cultural message or national brag, but one whose style and modes of funding
tended to signify socialism itself, a spectacle of teamwork, state sponsorship, clean-living, and
broad accessibility.

In Cuba, socialist culture refers not only to the system as system, naming its heroes, devising
its myths, but to practices that predate the revolution and are still encouraged, as in the now decade old issue of the Union of Cuban Writers and Artists' official journal, *La Gaceta*, with its essay by Radamés Giró, "Everything You Wanted to Know About Mambo," the international
rumba festivals in Matanzas, or the Havana '94 "*encuentro*" (meeting) bringing musicians and
aficionados from around the world to celebrate Afro-Cuban music.[2]

It is startling, however, to chart the extent to which otherwise valuable popular music theory
suppresses the kinds of examples offered above in deference to a U.S. cover story on Cuba as a
devastated, frightened society walking in lockstep. Most popular music criticism in the United
States has no obvious relationship to the *cordon sanitaire* set up around the Island by its former
northern masters who resent the colony's impudence. But even among the clued-in critics of
rock magazines and hip publishing houses like Routledge, the view is still trotted out with surprising frequency that Cuba is an enemy of Dionysian freedom, and that Cuban kids live in a
straightjacket woven from the idealist dreams of their now-aging '60s parents. Because these
views—entirely mainstream—are coming from the "underground" or resistance cultures of music theory, they carry a special weight.[3]

There is no space here for a general review of the literature, but to get a sense of the tone of
the war, it might be useful to examine a single case. *Situating Salsa,* a recent anthology edited by
Lise Waxer, represents what may be taken to be a prevailing political sentiment accentuated for

being, on the surface, cultural and not political at all. There is no question that the anthology is very well-done—informative, smart, well-researched, forward-looking. Its musicological detail is especially valuable, offering graphic accounts of the actual structures of orchestral forms and arrangements as well as mapping the career of salsa in countries other than Cuba, Puerto Rico and the United States. But at times subtly, at others not, the volume falls into the trap of retelling an American "official story" that obscures the narrative of Cuba's musical contributions.[4]

Perhaps without intending to, the anthology demotes the cultural role of Cuba in Latin music, particularly after the revolution. Instinctively, its focus is fixed on *salsa* understood as a non-Cuban, pan-Latino form of U.S. vintage. On that cue, the volume places a special stress on the few well-known Cuban performers of *guaracha* and *son* who emigrated to the United States, neglecting to mention that most of the more accomplished musicians gave no thought to emigrating. They remained in Cuba, where most of the innovations to that pan-Latino complex known as "salsa" still emerge, and from where they are "borrowed" (often without acknowledgement) by international studio and dance musicians who pay no royalties to the Cubans whose work they copy, on the grounds that Cuba does not participate in copyright laws. *Pachanga, timba, songo* are only some of the examples from this more recent constellation. One of its chapters on women salsa performers, for example, restricts itself to U.S.-based singers, either transplanted or native, as though women only flourished in exile, and as though feminism were an exclusively metropolitan affair. A Venezuelan percussionist is quoted at the start of another chapter to the effect that "Cubans cannot play salsa. There is not a Cuban salsa group, it does not exist" (23)—an interesting point, and of course true provided one carefully restricts one's definition of salsa in order to make it true.[5]

But the conventional rhetoric of music theory about Cuba is best seen in the volume's essay "Salsa and Socialism," written by a justly praised younger musicologist, Robin Moore, known for a fine book on Cuban music and the national movements.[6] The essay is, in the end, filled with important information, and it stakes out a territory of intended balance, accounting for the successes and failures of socialist cultural policy. In other words, from its own point of view, the author's essay is crafted precisely to wring concessions from the enemies of Cuba by forcing them to grant that Cuba continues to thrive in the field of music.

But the case it presents is odd, and strangely irreversible. On the one hand, we find the *de rigueur* untruths: "people interviewed on the island," we are told, "are often reluctant to speak openly with researchers about issues that could be construed as critical of the government" (51). In my own experience, and in that of researchers I know (some of them having lived in Cuba for years at a time), this point is simply fiction. It is exceedingly easy to find people—almost anyone in fact—who will brashly say the most unflattering things about the government without blushing (in marked contrast, say, to a situation like Guatemala in the mid-1980s, which was truly a terror state).

More common, however, are those comments in the essay that, although true, distort through misdirection. Discussing the role of Cuba's National Culture Advisory in January 1961, for example, the author tells us that "privately controlled establishments" of the arts were ominously replaced by "monolithic state enterprises" (53) as though fewer rather than more people's opinions were expressible under this latter arrangement, and as though the private were by definition more open—a very counter-intuitive assumption. We are further told that the government closed down segregated cabarets of the 1950s primarily because their entertainment was "apolitical" and "escapist." Leaving alone that escapist cultural fare has always thrived in Cuba just as it has everywhere else (through *romántica* songs, soap opera, and nightclub comic routines [with their satirical *choteos*]), the claim is amazingly indifferent to a fact that almost everyone knows about pre-Castro Cuba (even if they know nothing else). Who would seriously deny that the cabarets were closed down because they were well-known money-laundering operations for the mafia as well as centers of prostitution—that is, not apolitical, but socio-pathological—the playground of the arrogantly well-heeled?

Above all, the essay reduces complexity, transforming it into a manageable credo of paranoid value. Every constraint on freedom—and life is filled with them, after all—is cast as the conspiratorial work of an oppressive socialism. We are told, for instance, that the system of musical production in Cuba "marginalizes many aspiring artists who are unable to receive official recognition," and that these pressures "influence the types of music they perform" (56).

What is remarkable here is not that such a statement is untrue, only that it assumes an irreversible condition. Are we supposed to believe that in the United States official recognition is not denied aspiring artists even more extravagantly and peremptorily? Think only of the closed networks of small-minded producers, rapacious lawyers, tyrannical distributors allergic to ideas, who artificially produce scandals and insure that youth music is kept antiseptically mindless or driven by the fake rebellions of "Grammy rap." A market-driven music industry is more dictatorial than anything one finds in the comparatively lavish system of rewards given artists in Cuba.

Globalism and Youth

The discourses of pleasure are political. If on the one hand, peripheral countries are popularly depicted in either the drab tones of destitute barrios or in the carnivalesque colors of mayhem, starvation and war, the entertainment industries of the major industrial nations ensure that the pleasures of travel must, like an MTV special, be either about tourism or distanced spectatorship. Weaker countries are kept weak by assaults on their resources, by debt interest, and by a barrage of images of enticement, which together form a powerful claim that technological prowess implies a metropolitan monopoly on pleasure itself. By way of well-equipped recording studios, the special-effects of film, and satellite transmissions, musical forms of entertainment are so mobile and ubiquitous that their political subtexts are particularly telling. Conventional wisdom, like the joke above, casts alternatives to the mass market in the role of an alien.

Socialism, needless to say, in the universe of the commercial, is genetically humorless. The grim grey apartment complexes of Poland come to mind; the tawdry, ill-made shoes of the Czech worker; the Moscow apartment-dweller's diet of potatoes and cabbage. In each image there is only colorlessness and tedium—no hint that some poorer countries fending for themselves without benefit of empire actually take the trouble to provide housing, clothing, and food for people who would not otherwise have them. Today's Cuba may not correspond to an image of the suburbs or Times Square on a Saturday night, but it is a far cry from rural destitution or, for that matter, inner-city Detroit, which is far more desperate and frightening than anything found in the third world. In North America's political religion of state, socialist pleasure is not just elusive but banished from above. Saying the word 'socialism' turns out the light of the mind. It does not have to be defined. As if by law, socialism must not be defined, only held up as an embarrassment.

When we consider global popular culture, it is good to remember that globalization attained its widespread use only after the fall of the Soviet Union and the Eastern bloc. The rise of the one accompanied the fall of the other. Along with the decline of a coherent, geopolitical space outside the market came the collapse of a set of international alliances that once appeared as a viable rival to a coercively exported U.S. way of life. In Mozambique, West Bengal, Kerala, China, and Cuba, for instance, the term "socialism" tended throughout the 1970s to mean little more than an official resistance towards unrestrained capital penetration. Although a highly charged, even tainted, word in U.S media renditions, socialism for these countries meant primarily local autonomy, political sovereignty, literacy, and development—all seen as the minimum basis upon which the invisible populations of those countries might approximate the quality of life outlined in the UN's Universal Declaration of Human Rights (1948). On the global periphery in these years (a period that did not conclude, really, until 1989), freedom from the market was typically considered a precondition for sovereignty. It hardly needs to be said today, after a series of externally dictated and disastrous structural adjustment programs in the Ukraine, Argentina, and Poland, or after the most recent round of neo-colonial invasions in Iraq, Afghanistan, and Colombia, that these countries had a point.

Globalization—taken in some circles to signify the inexorable emergence of an exciting world culture—can also be seen, less invitingly, as a mass global conversion. Particularly at this kind of juncture Cuba arises as a decisive case for testing the claims of globalization as a whole, not least because of the utility of the trope of exile both in globalization discourse and in the quarantining of Cuba by U.S. opinion-making. Exiles are the proper adjunct, one could say, of global culture—a world of supposedly diasporic wanderers, a human bricolage of adopted and adapted tatters of taste and foreign inspiration. But it does not take long for this sense of the term to seem overly jubilant and false when exploring Cuban art. One recalls, for instance, the scene at the airport in one of the early moments of Tomás Guttiérez Alea's *Memories of Under-*

development, when the protagonist Sergio surveys the departing bourgeois minions in bouffant hairdos and nervous smiles with something like bemusement. This image of a class whose "classness" is exposed only finds it way to the North American heart with difficulty, not wanting to be romantically swayed by ideals, and therefore going over to the extreme of allowing any discussion of class whatsoever to wither. In the rote responses of the official U.S. line so carefully prepared by our educational systems and press, the critic always errs on the side of cold-hearted expertise, eager to demonstrate awareness of the many sides of any issue.

And yet the character of the Cuban emigration after 1959 is lost in the discourse of a tropical Cold War. Unlike the Latin economic refugees of recent decades, the first wave of Cubans were overwhelmingly white, highly educated, and to the plantation born. It is only recently, caught in the vice of the U.S. encirclement of Cuba on the one hand, and intimidation of Cuba's potential allies and trading partners on the other, that a true economic flight has emerged. By contrast, the first generation was one in which the connection between exile and foreign travel had been blurred for generations. They were fleeing a country, it should be remembered, not only set to regulate their profit-making and restrict their inherited privileges, but whose image of itself was about to become officially Afro-Cuban as well as Spanish and creole—as Martí had proposed in the 1880s. Associating Cuban exiles with a boat people driven by the quest for political asylum makes nonsense of the history of movement to and from the Island. There had been a non-stop flow of Cuban exiles for over a century *before* the revolution: to the Tampa cigar-rolling centers, the New Orleans music halls, and the New York and New Jersey metropolitan areas.

The haze of the multiculturalism debates in the United States has, in this sense, clouded the contribution of Cuban socialism to racial diversity—a connection that is rarely made in celebrations of American pluralism in the United States. Even before the ouster of Battista, the long-brewing revolt of color against Cuban high society—marked both by a colonial servility and a country-club snobbery captured in Nicolás Guillén's poem, "No me dan pena los burgueses vencidos" ("I don't spend time worrying about the rich after they've lost power") and later set to song by Pablo Milanés—stamped itself on the character of the revolution throughout the decades of de facto U.S. rule. The revolution, in short, was always largely about *race,* which is one reason why the revolution is still disproportionately supported by black Cubans. A prominent, if not universal, aspect of Miami Cuban culture was disgust at Cuba's "vulgar" promotion of black culture after 1959, and the new prominence that Afro-Cubans came relatively to enjoy. At the same time, as in the United States itself, Afro-based expression in painting, sport, dance, and music were the most culturally attractive products disseminated abroad.

As an instrument of globalization, popular culture is almost by definition about marketing, whereas the demands of marketing dictate a certain structure of playfulness that affects pleasure. It is remarkable, though, how seldom questions are raised about the degree to which a market can be pleasurable. Since we are discussing *global* popular culture, one might be driven to explore those places where the popular is inimical to the market, but where, at the same time, popular culture is still produced before being consumed globally. This kind of consideration brings one inevitably to Cuba.

At the outset one would suppose that a meditation on desire and pleasure would immediately raise the issue of entertainment. But how much is this really so? Much of the criticism on the day-to-day life of the entertainment industry in the United States suggests that little pleasure is wrung from the arduous task of being entertained. Think only of the title of Neil Postman's memorable book, *Amusing Ourselves to Death*; or Andrew Goodwin's study of MTV: *Dancing in the Distraction Factory*, to take only two more or less recent studies of what the *Nation* magazine calls the "entertainment state." The economy—and by extension, private fortunes, peripheral poverties, and a number of seemingly unrelated government policies–is built on a foundation whose supposed product is distraction, release, relaxation, enjoyment. But as any executive will tell you, it is very hard to find joyful release with one eye on the clock. Or to put it another way, with so many serious things riding on the game of pleasure, or with so many business interests wanting a cut of the action of our supposed carefree moments away from work, pleasure itself is being harnessed for someone else's game. While appearing to be a service for us, the product of this entertainment state might be said to be, by contrast, simply *us*. That is, *we* are the product they are creating, a certain we who consumes. We are produced to consume.

La Peña de Sirique (The Sirique Club)

The consumption of desire, moreover, prompts an elaborate network of image-makers for outreach. When reading the research of managerial specialists and advertising experts, one quickly learns that one of their principal targets is youth. The concept of market research as well as of identifying youth as having a special place within it is the explicit invention of the United States, and dates from the 1920s.[7] Youth is key to the concept of a global popular culture for a number of reasons. Youth is considered by market researchers to be a standardized group. Advertisers are statistically confident that their responses to stimuli are predictable in whatever culture they appear, regardless of significant differences in the way that predictability is expressed. In the blunt mode of address that managerial theorists adopt when talking to one another, two aspects of youth above all are considered crucial by them: First, youth carry their patterns of preference far into adulthood. Thus, if their behavior is modified early, it remains throughout their lifetimes. Second, if one can reach youth, one has in effect reached the rest of the family as well. Parents and siblings are forced to conform to the drive and urgency of the young who determine the "now-ness" of all trends. Youth, in short, is not simply the young; it is the ideology of youth.

Youth, then, is perceived in these circles as the wedge, arbiter, and force of revolutionary dislodgement. There is no globalization without the idea of youth, which is the group whose friendliness towards the new gives it the power to issue calling-cards to foreign capital, or provide openings for next year's documentaries on a new wave of twenty-something entrepreneurs. Their experimentalism and novelty—which supposedly comes from having thought less along the rutted paths of their elders—can be moved by inches to the concept of entrepreneurship (as it is in today's quintessentially postmodern images of the computer hacker, the New Age environmentalist clothing designers, the Silicon Valley nerds). The well-known colonial contest between civilizations where capitalist technologies and dynamism on the one side are pitted against traditional religious or rural life on the other, is here recast in a macro-contest between youth and age. As the managerial specialists would have it, at any rate, capitalism is for youth. Capitalism *is* youth.

It is in this spirit that the young author, Thomas Frank, in *Commodify Your Dissent*, has issued a declaration to corporate advertisers refusing to play his assigned role:

> You snicker that our identities are little more than a patchwork of lines remember[ed] from episodes of the TV programs we watched as children...We refuse to accept your central historical/televisual myth...To us the idiocy, depravity, and soul-crushing cruelty of your human machine is so obvious, so plain and undisguised, that we set ourselves in opposition to it as a matter of course...The business of business is our minds. (31-45)

Apparently, *National Geographic* understood this formula perfectly in its special issue on global culture some years ago. On the magazine's cover an upper-class Indian mother dressed in a sari sits beside her Anglicized daughter, dressed in shiny patent leather. There, crudely symbolized, sit two poles: the traditional (age) vs. the modern (youth). The mother's admiring maternal glance stands in counterpoint to the daughter's steely, unsentimental and ambitious stare. As if parodying Gandhi's *swadeshi* movement against British imperialism (in which Gandhi counseled his countrymen to make homespun cloth in order to boycott British manufacture), the insouciant daughter wears a tight black jumpsuit of "her own design." Even as the mother projects quiet professional dignity, the daughter intimates a subtle, and therefore acceptable, sexual availability by her slightly parted legs. Youth, sexuality, and entrepreneurship are inextricable. The photograph, in short, is a pander. Beneath the make-up and the created desire (which depending on the viewer might involve sex, fashion, or the exoticism of India, now whittled down to size), the shibboleths of globalization are sold—hybridity, opportunity, diversity, untrammeled contact, brave new creative forms, and technological wonders.

Mother and Daughter

Systems of Desire and Pleasure

So far, then, one would be dealing in codes that are familiar enough—even depressingly familiar to the forced consumers of the metropolitan countries. But, again, since our topic is *global* culture, what would one find if one explored the possibilities of a non-market pleasure, which Cuba, at least on the surface of the matter, would seem to provide? If there is a specific pleasure to socialism, it would amount to more, presumably, than mere altruism or the solemn comforts of justice. In a system outside the zero sum contest of competitive individualism with its perpetual wrangling over spoils, would lie, for example, the pleasures of a slower pace. In a society not calculated to push its citizens anxiously on the road to mindless acquisition, one would not have to hurry up to die. Sharing would extend not only to resources, one would think, but to enjoyments as well. That is, spectatorship would take place live,

jointly, and in public places—in squares, plazas, parks, and the street. Criticism of art and politics would be both a personal matter and one that took place in the presence of others rather than as a lonely gawker at that televisual gift delivered from the corporate on-high.

More of life would take place face-to-face. If the mass ownership of cars were no longer a requirement of economic health (mass ownership of cars would be, on the contrary, too expensive and irrational with available mass transportation) city life would thrive by way of a series of non-internetted personal encounters. The relative paucity of commodities—at first glance an anti-pleasure—would actually allow a less extreme division of labor, freeing one from illusory consumption "choices" and the mental overload of advertising, as well as a greater (if not absolute) freedom from the tyranny of things. The body would become more than an identity-corkboard, resuming its status once more as a "person"; and the person would, in turn, assume his or her political identity as a citizen, leaving behind its preferred late capitalist designator, the "subject," with all the intentional ambiguity of that term (vassal or lord?).

What, by contrast, can one say then about capitalist desire? Given the need to sell products, the most compelling desires under capitalism are compelled: the choices, paradoxically, that one *has* to make because a society of choice tends towards a world without choices: owning a car in Los Angeles, for example, employing Qwest as one's phone service in a market where only Qwest offers phone service, switching from vinyl records to compact discs, from cash to credit cards, from slower to faster internet access. Desire amounts to a constantly delayed satisfaction. It is present as either a set of demands to seek what cannot be found or as addiction (video game, cigarette, valium, sitcom). Desire, moreover, in its capitalist forms involves libidinal terror-

ism—the conquest of the libido by incessant repetition, the splicing of sexuality and hunger onto the attractions of inconsequential purchases. It involves the making of all value quantifiable where the question "how much" replaces "how good"? Q: which film was the most creative, the most off-beat? A: *The Blair Witch Project* only cost $100,000 and made over $40 million; Q: Will it be fun? A: Yes, it will not take much time. Q: How old is this fashion model? A. She is the youngest ever to be on the cover of *Talk* magazine.

Socialist pleasure as community exchange does not exist purely or apart from the more dominant, and coercive, form of market desire based on unfulfillment and addiction. The latter, with its powers of mass-media dissemination, tourist visitations, and military conquest, seeps into the former, blending with it to make a disorienting hybrid. Let us examine an actual case—one with immediate effects for the issues of youth, pleasure, and global culture.

Marketing Youth: Las Jineteras and the Plaza

> In Cuba they say 'We are exporting mothers,' which means we are exporting even mothers to get cash. But it also explains two other things: 1) why there are so many mother-fuckers and 2) why so many Cubans are sons of bitches. —Sonia Baez (official with Cultural Ministry)

In the early 1990s, on Havana's meandering seaside boulevard, the Malecon, with wind-swept hair the women known locally simply as "*las chicas*" lure tourists on warm nights to cruise slowly in taxis driven by panders. Exceedingly young—between sixteen and twenty years old—the women are not professionals in the usual sense, although their display on the waterfront makes a mockery of Carlos Puebla's early song "Y en eso llegó el Fidel" [Fidel Arrived]: "The fun and games stopped cold when [Fidel] arrived to say, "Enough!" The government cleaned up the gambling and prostitution of the mafia 1950s only to see it revive unofficially under the edicts of tourism in "the special period"—the local term for the time after 1989 when trade with the Soviet Union and Eastern Europe first collapsed.

As of January 1993, food rationing had not plummeted to the degree where Cuban teenagers would be driven by hunger to "date" foreign visitors for payment. The economic indicators were nevertheless severe. In addition to the decline in production brought by drastically curtailed oil imports, Cuba suffered three devastating tropical storms in March, May and November of 1993. The one in March—the so-called storm of the century—might have been the worst Cuba ever experienced. Asked by prospective clients, the women themselves would simply bear out what much of the 1993 American press had been reporting—that prior to the new currency laws allowing citizens to hold U.S. dollars, the likelihood was faint that teens would procure such things as makeup, pumps, dance dresses, and cosmetics without visitor largesse.

The new Cuban prostitution, flagrantly illegal but also officially tolerated, was therefore not about survival nor the creation of a class of professional prostitutes. The motive in this case—only slightly less depressing—was about style, nightlife, frills, the taste of liquor, being bad, being on the town. For some time in the bootstrap mode, the real Cuba confronted a three-fourths decline in its standard of living over a four-year period; malnutrition began to set itself upon the poorer barrios of the larger cities with the appearance of a mysterious eye disease as one of its probable effects. The Torricelli bill, passed in this period by the U.S. congress, promised to deliver more of the same.[8]

But these statistics of misery overlook other sorts of deprivations—the deprivations of excess itself that have to do with less obvious forms of desire as depicted in the collision of the myth surrounding two social systems, with its placard-like Cold War clichés. With no other way to enjoy the clubs, women might spend one night every week or two with a strange tourist drinking, flirting, and coasting the dance floors. The not always implicit promise would be to sleep with him at the evening's end, although the difference between this and dating could always be rationalized as relatively small in the final analysis. From the point of view of the government, this was the logic of the market on full display, and a cancellation of the *type* of improvement it thought it had always stood for. There was a dictator on the island, and it was foreign currency.[9]

Some of the drama of the Malecon arises in Cristina García's novel *Dreaming in Cuban*, which formulaically characterizes Cuba as suffering a rift between the generation of *playa giron* (the Bay of Pigs) and the generation of Michael Jackson: " 'We're dying of security!' [Felicia] moans when [her mother] Celia tries to point out the revolution's merits. No one is starving or denied medical care, no one sleeps in the streets, everyone works who wants to work. But her daughter prefers the luxury of uncertainty, of time unplanned, of waste" (117). Uttered significantly in a private space, this criticism by youth assaults the materialist project of satisfying needs even as in quite another, more colloquial, sense it is about "materialism"—the superfluous or excessive consumption which attracts people of any class for its intimations of small-scale luxury. To be rich, after all, is to be able to throw things away, to pass time idly, to buy clothes for looks rather than the weather.

Historically, the socialist movement knew and knows all about this, from Paul Lafargue's late nineteenth-century tract, *The Right to be Lazy*, to Henri Lefebvre's remarkable study "Renewal, Youth, Repetition" from his *Introduction to Modernity*. The Italian communist, Antonio Gramsci, cleverly observed in 1918 that socialism itself depended on selfishness—a selfishness that, as it were, could not be selfish but only collective—the only resort of the plebs. One did not join political groups, form CDCs, or trade unionize because it was moral to share, but because one could not get one's own any other way. As anyone who lived through adolescence knows, among people's many needs is the need to be bad, to be lazy, to be useless—a sentiment expressed eloquently in the socialist tradition by Bertolt Brecht's early play *Baal* and by the Soviet poet Vladamir Mayakovsky's "A Cloud in Trousers." Cuba has not always understood this, a socialism teetering abroad between images of the uniformed primness of the Young Pioneers and images of the *pachanguero*.

At the feverish height of libidinal drives, youth supposedly has no hankering for the New Man. And yet, widely if not universally, the *chicas* of the Malecon are referred to by a term that uncomfortably summons associations with an oppressive past overthrown by the revolution. They are called *jineteras*—a word derived from an image of a plantation foreman on a horse, and popularly used for con-men and cheats who prey on naive strangers. Far from this attempt to retain what is most wholesome, and drawing on the assumption that youth's instincts cannot be wrong, the advertising voices of America divert what is really a theoretical contest between competing strategies of organizing production into, say, a glossy magazine picture, or the color monitor screen of a PowerMac—items, at any rate, of an extendable series of unanswerable arguments for the superior attractions of what Ministry officials still call (in what some will think an act of foolishness and envy) imperialism. Expensively produced propaganda by the United States is unnecessary for tempting the libidos of the Cuban consumer. In the special period at least, something as simple as shampoo was a luxury, and plastic slippers were finagled only in a complex protocol of (usually sexual) give-and-take with tourist "friends."

If the Malecon announces the market as it enters Cuba in full splendor, the official celebrations that outsiders automatically associate with gatherings in the Plaza de la Revolución may be taken as one, but only one, of the more traditionally socialist refusals of the market. On New Years Day, tens of thousands of Havana residents—most of them teenagers—gather to watch a well-organized open-air concert featuring the country's most popular musicians. With a comparable billing in local terms to that of Britain's Band Aid concert, the events are free. They demand payment only in the listening to a speech. The ponderous address on one evening in 1993 was given by the leader of the Communist Youth in the presence of Fidel, who stood patiently to the side of the podium in full view of the crowd.

A mass of nattily dressed teenagers, uncannily sober, leaned casually on bikes, small-talked, or bought soup from the event's only hawker of wares. But with the exception of the thousand or so waving banners at the base of the stage, they were not paying attention to the Youth leader's speech, and the crowd's hum was reaching the audible registers of a distraction. Most in attendance were there for the smooth *salsa romántica* of teen idol Carlos Varela. Others had come to see the all-women's group Anacaona (now in its third generation), or to watch the tightly engineered light show, which moved the audience gaze from stage to stage in a set up that allowed abrupt shifts between acts (from the acoustic lyricism of Silvio Rodriguez on one stage to the big band electric brass of Los Van Van on the other) without causing a tiresome delay. Already an hour into the preliminaries, Fidel's turn at the mic prompted a speech of unexpected brevity. Cocking his head, he spoke simply about the need to have fun.

Later that evening on television, he chatted with two Cuban journalists (a man and a woman) who were dressed informally in open shirts and who sat on some outdoor patio overlooking Havana's city lights, prodding him with candor about the shuffles and murmurs of the crowd during the Youth leader's protracted oratory. As striking as this patter was between reporters and a head of state (a White House press secretary would certainly have filtered out any embarrassing comments, for instance), even more striking was the concessionary response. People, especially young people, he answered, are sick of speeches about sacrifice during a period of sacrifices. "I cut my comments short because I did not want to burden the crowd. It is a difficult time" (Castro interview).

Somewhere beyond this acknowledgement of the need for a space of leisure outside politics lies the nightlife of the *jinetera*, which is also a fixture of Cuban life but much more fatal to its moral property. The point that arises in this juxtaposition, then, concerns a cross-wiring of two cases of socialism and the popular. One of them is found in the principle of tolerance.[10] The other case would point to a tolerance towards social forms that are allowed because of economic exigency, violating the principles of the society one is trying to build. So the government, cast repeatedly in U.S. accounts as a police state, is then ridiculed for, of all things, its excessive permissiveness, which is taken to be hypocrisy. In the warped vision of the Cuban cover story, one is simply not allowed to wonder whether this permissiveness is simply the creeping power of capitalist desire exerting its tyranny over the Island's emerging market.

Cuba: Some Reflections on the Music Now

The invocations of youth—especially virulent now—have repeatedly launched predictions of Cuba's imminent free-market transformation, where angry layabouts in torn jeans are said to be waiting for the arrival of Miami, and wanting nothing so much as a quiet place to play their rock guitars. It is true that there is a division in *popular* music between the classical Cuban forms of *son/rumba/mambo,* extolled and played by an older generation (captured so well for foreign audiences by the *Buena Vista Social Club*) and the rock/rap/reggae of a younger generation, richly displayed in the immensely innovative recent Cuban fusion groups like Buena Fe, Triángulo Oscuro, Moneda Dura, and Azúcar.

Just as in New York or Paris, the art scene has been taken over by popular culture, which is, however, made more complicated by the attempt to define oneself as Cuban under the shadow of a popular culture that often signifies American for international audiences. However, it is important to notice that in Cuba, several bands of enormous popularity (and immense longevity, with thirty-year careers in some cases) blend Latin jazz, Afro-Cuban traditional music, and North American rock into a distinctive sound with contemporary—often politically critical—lyrics. These very bands—among them, Irakere, Los Terry, the avant-garde pop N.G. La Banda ("N.G." standing for *nueva generación* [new generation]), and dissidents like Charanga Habanera—are thoroughly mainstream, appearing in public often, at events official and unofficial, and widely followed.

The investments made in the United States for winning Cuba over from socialism through youth confuses rebellion against socialism with the rebelliousness of youth against age. Latin America has a unique relationship to these questions. Its history of development directly affects its role now in a global popular culture. First, it is that part of the underdeveloped world that is, for a variety of reasons, most Europeanized in its cities. It is the third world whose intellectuals have historically been most saturated by Europe and European culture. But it is also the place where the largest pockets of indigenous peoples with their own languages and cultures still survive, creating a two-tiered culture at the level of individual nations or regions, with the one side mimicking dominant culture and the other side rather hopelessly outside and contemptuous of it. Finally, consider the proximity of the United States as imperium, with Latin America its special domain. From the time of the early radio experiments of the WWII era, Latin America has been a captive audience for American popular cultural marketing in a more intensive sense than elsewhere—and within the framework of a common New World, which is to say, in a context that facilitates its dispersion.

But Latin America has also, paradoxically, been the place where the greatest hope of countering the world market, and its forms of desire, can be found. Eduardo Galeano, in his wonderful *The Book of Embraces*, speaks of the natural socialism of the indigenous peoples there:

> Community—the communal mode of production and life—is the oldest of American traditions, the most American of all. It belongs to the earliest days and the first people, but it also belongs to the times ahead and anticipates a new New World. For there is nothing less alien to these lands of ours than socialism. Capitalism, on the other hand, is foreign: like smallpox, like the flu, it came from abroad.

Galeano observes one of the reasons, apparently, why so many metropolitan intellectuals looked to Latin America as an escape from the Georgian and Second-Empire staidness of Europe, inspired by its histories of upheavals and novel social experiments in Mexico (1912-1929), Peru (1935-1940), Chile (1970-1973), Cuba (1958-Present), and Nicaragua (1979-1986). One hopes that the Brazil of Lula da Silva and the Venezuela of Hugo Chavez will emerge as the next members of this attractive tradition. Cuba is best seen as belonging to a more general Latin American aversion to the suffocations of the market.

This sense of experimental freedom permeates its art. For Cuban music is largely a party music, a music set in nightclubs and for lovers, whose origins and current meaning is, at the same time, a secularized devotional expression of Afro-Cuban religion. N.G. La Banda's "La Expresiva," to take one example, is a dance song about nightlife that—because it is about nightlife—praises African deities, and systematically calls out with pride the names of the neighborhoods of Havana, each for its own character and style of play. While the corporate sector of U.S. opinion-making spins its fantasies about a generation raised solely by TV, a youth they insult by considering them pliable and clueless, many U.S. young people have learned to see the utter falseness of these revered institutions. It is time to pool resources, and by learning from Cuba's leads, to challenge this establishment political correctness.

En el Liceo (In the Lyceum)

NOTES

1. Baraka 367. In his account on the outcome of this search, Baraka describes how the Black Arts Movement "had huge audiences, really mass audiences, and though what we brought was supposed to be avant and super-new, most of it the people dug" (379).

2. See Radamés Giró, "Todo lo que usted quiso saber sobre el mambo..." *La Gaceta* (Noviembre-diciembre 1992) 13-17.

3. See Elena Perez Sanjurjo, *Historia de la musica cubana* (Miami: Moderna Poesia, 1986); John Beverley, *Against Literature* (Minneapolis: U of Minnesota P, 1993); Marc Cooper, "Semper Fidel," *Village Voice*, May 1, 1990, 20-3. See also the informative, but tendentious video, *Son Sabroson,* directed by Hugo Barroso, (Miami: HBM Productions, P.O. Box 33255-8811) which tells the story of *son* entirely through Miami-based exiles or now dead earlier artists such as Miguel Matamoros and Rita Montaner. For a much fuller and more accurate account of the rise of *son,* see *The Roots of Rhythm,* an excellent documentary narrated by Harry Belafonte (Directors/Producers Howard Dratch and Eugene Rosow, KCET Television, Cat. NVG 9436, 1994).

4. Not all recent work on Cuba succumbs to these temptations. For a brilliant recent anthology that does not partake of the U.S. cover story see Lisa Brock and Digna Castañeda Fuertes, eds., *Between Race and Empire: African-Americans and Cubans before the Cuban Revolution* (Philadelphia: Temple UP, 1998). The essays by Rosalie Schwartz, "Cuba's Roaring Twenties: Race Consciousness and the Column 'Ideales de una Raza,'" and Geoffrey Jacques, "CuBop! Afro-Cuban Music and Mid-Twentieth-Century American Culture," are particularly good.

5. On this point, there is a relevant moment in *The Roots of Rhythm.* In one of the documentary's interviews, Celia Cruz exclaims "I don't like communism, so I learned that what I sing has another name: it's called 'salsa.' But it's not a new rhythm. It's Cuban music by another name."

6. The work of Robin Moore is justly well-regarded for its in-depth research and knowledge of musical form. He writes, moreover, not merely as an historian but a musician. His book *Nationalizing Blackness* admirably recounts for North American audiences the kind of story found in earlier Cuban musical historians such as Carmen Valdes, Maria Teresa Linares, and before all of them, Alejo Carpentier. The point is that many critics are forced against their instincts into a routine set of observations that distort the portrait of Cuban creativity after the revolution. The rules of the game, apparently, are that charges of constricted freedom can be leveled against state-run enterprises, but never the leveling and censoring decision-making bodies of the U.S. corporate music industry.

7. This uncontroversial, although startling, fact is registered, for example, in Marieke de Mooij, *Global Marketing and Advertising: Understanding Cultural Paradoxes*; Stanley C. Hollander and Richard Germain, *Was There a Pepsi Generation Before Pepsi Discovered It? Youth-based Segmentation in Marketing*; Alfred L. Schreiber with Barry Lenson, *Multicultural Marketing: Selling to the New America: Position your Company Today for Optimal Success in the Diverse America of Tomorrow*. For a critique, see Theodore Roszak, *The Making of a Counter Culture: Reflections on the Technocratic Society and its Youthful Opposition*.

8. Raymundo del Toro, president of the Cuban American Committee for Peace based in Linden, New Jersey, attested to the effectiveness of the embargo when he reviled Torricelli for "a policy of genocide that seeks to create a Somalia in Cuba."

9. For a typical and, if anything, uncommonly honest example of the genre as it appeared in voluminous quantities in the Winter of 1993, see Georgia Pabst's four-part series, "Revolution in Ruins," *Milwaukee*

Journal, August, 1993. Still alive a decade later, the revolution has so far confounded the apocalyptic pre-dictions of its imminent collapse—an issue not unrelated to its successes in creating and disseminating popular culture.

10. Tolerance, in cultural circles, expressed itself most clearly in earlier artistic debates over realism vs abstrac-tion in socialist societies, where the tolerant view among the stalwarts was that artistic abstraction (like Dionysian excess) is no enemy of socialism. This is, after all, the position of the Cuban leadership itself, as few notice or seem willing to grant. In the early 1960s, Fidel flatly announced to his East European allies: "Our enemies are capitalists and imperialists, not abstract art." Quoted in David Craven, "The Visual Arts since the Cuban Revolution" (80).

WORKS CITED

Acosta, Leonardo. (1993) *Elige tú, que canto yo.* La Habana: Letra Cubanas.

Baez, Sonia. (official with Cultural Ministry). Interview with the author. Havana, January 1993.

Baraka, Amiri. "The Black Arts (Harlem, Politics, Search for a New Life)." *The Leroi Jones/Amiri Baraka Reader.* New York: Thunder Mouth, 1991.

Beverley, John. *Against Literature.* Minneapolis: U of Minnesota P, 1993.

Brecht, Bertolt. "Emphasis on Sport." *Brecht on Theatre: The Development of an Aesthetic.* Ed and trans. John Willett. New York: Hill and Wang, 1964.

Brock, Lisa and Digna Castañeda Fuertes, eds. *Between Race and Empire: African-Americans and Cubans Before the Cuban Revolution.* Philadelphia: Temple UP, 1998.

Carpentier, Alejo. *Music in Cuba*, Edited with an Introduction by Timothy Brennan. Minneapolis: U of Min-nesota P, 2001.

Castro, Fidel. Interview with Fidel Castro on Cuban Television. Havana, Cuba, December 30, 1992.

Cooper, Marc. "Semper Fidel," *Village Voice*, 1990: 20-23.

Craven, David. (1992) "The Visual Arts since the Cuban Revolution," *Third Text* 20 (Autumn 1992): 76-102.

Frank, Thomas. "Why Johnny Can't Dissent," *Commodify Your Dissent: Salvos from the Baffler.* Eds. Thomas Frank and Matt Weiland. New York and London: North, 1997: 31-45.

Galeano, Eduardo. *The Book of Embraces.* Trans. Cedric Belfrage with Mark Schafer. New York: W. W. Norton, 1991.

García, Cristina. *Dreaming in Cuban.* New York: Ballantine, 1992.

Giró, Radamés. "Todo lo que usted quiso saber sobre el mambo ..." *La Gaceta* (Noviembre-diciembre, 1992): 13-17.

Goodwin, Andrew. *Dancing in the Distraction Factory: Music Television and Popular Culture.* Minneapolis: U of Minnesota P, 1992.

Gramsci, Antonio. "Margins" *History, Philosophy and Culture in the Young Gramsci.* Eds. Pedro Cavalcanti and Paul Piccone. St. Louis: Telos, 1975: 41.

Hannerz, Ulf. *Transnational Connections: Culture, People, Places.* London and New York: Routledge, 1996.

Hijuelos, Oscar. *The Mambo Kings Play Songs of Love.* Perennial, 1999.

Hollander, Stanley C. and Richard Germain. *Was There a Pepsi Generation Before Pepsi Discovered It? Youth-based Segmentation in Marketing.* Chicago: American Marketing Association, 1992.

Lafargue, Paul. *The Right to Be Lazy and Other Studies.* Chicago: C. H. Kerr & Company, 1907.

Lefebvre, Henri. "Renewal, Youth, Repetition." *Introduction to Modernity: Twelve Preludes 1959-1961.* Trans. John Moore. London and New York: Verso, 1995.

de Mooij, Marieke. *Global Marketing and Advertising: Understanding Cultural Paradoxes.* Thousand Oaks, CA: Sage, 1998.

Moore, Robin D.G. "Salsa and socialism: dance music in Cuba 1959-99." *Situating Salsa: Global Markets and Local Meaning in Latin Popular Music.* Ed. Lise Waxer. New York and London: Routledge, 2002. 51-74.

Pabst, Georgia. "Revolution in Ruins." *Milwaukee Journal.* (August) 1993.

Perez Sanjurjo, Elena. *Historia de la musica cubana.* Miami: Moderna Poesia, 1986.

Postman, Neil. *Amusing Ourselves to Death: Public Discourse in the Age of Show Business.* New York: Penguin, 1985.

Puebla, Carlos. "Y es eso llegó Fidel." *Soy del Pueblo* ASIN B000054A04 Egrem Records, October 16, 2000.

The Roots of Rhythm (Video). Directors/Producers Howard Dratch and Eugene Rosow, Harry Belafonte, narrator and host. Cat. NVG 9436, KCET Television, 1994.

Roszak, Theodore. *The Making of a Counter Culture: Reflections on the Technocratic Society and its Youthful Opposition.* London: Faber, 1969.

Schreiber, Alfred L. with Barry Lenson *Multicultural Marketing: Selling to the New America: Position your Company Today for Optimal Success in the Diverse America of Tomorrow.* Lincolnwood, IL: NTC Business Books, 2001.

Son Sabroson (Video). Dir. Hugo Barroso. Miami: HBM Productions, 1998.

del Toro, Raymundo. "Law on Cuba Trade Starves the Babies." *New York Times.* 20 Jan. 1994: A20.

Waxer, Lise, ed. *Situating Salsa: Global Markets and Local Meaning in Latin Popular Music.* New York and London: Routledge, 2002.

Ajay Heble

Take Two / Rebel Musics: Human Rights, Resistant Sounds, and the Politics of Music Making

In May 1952, when the United States government prevented Paul Robeson from crossing the U.S. border because of his active participation in worldwide struggles for human rights, the singer and activist stood one foot from the Canadian border on a makeshift stage at the back of a flat-bed truck and delivered the now historic Peace Arch concert to some 40,000 people.

AJAY HEBLE is Professor of English at the University of Guelph, author of *Landing on the Wrong Note: Jazz, Dissonance, and Critical Practice* (Routledge) and co-editor (with Daniel Fischlin) of *The Other Side of Nowhere: Jazz, Improvisation, and Communities in Dialogue* (Wesleyan UP, forthcoming). Artistic Director and Founder of The Guelph Jazz Festival, he is also a pianist. His first CD, a live recording of improvised music with percussionist Jesse Stewart, was released on the IntrepidEar label.

To introduce the concert, Robeson declared, "I stand here today under great stress because I dare, as do you—all of you—to fight for peace and for a decent life for all men, women, and children" (Robeson, *The Peace Arch Concerts*).

Robeson's lifework as a singer and an activist—indeed, the two were largely inseparable for him—was dedicated to taking a stand against oppression and injustice, and to creating opportunities to express hope for a more just world. The labour songs and spirituals that he performed during that 1952 Peace Arch Concert expressed solidarity with aggrieved peoples, and culminated in a defiant rendition of "Ol' Man River." Instead of the scripted "Git a little drunk an' you'll land in jail," Robeson sang, "You show a little grit and you land in jail," thus countering centuries of misrepresentations of African-American people by changing the "crime" from drinking to resistance (Heble 93).

Indeed, as many commentators have noted, Robeson, throughout his career, made several changes to the lyrics of "Ol' Man River," beginning with a recital at Albert Hall in 1937, where, instead of "I'm tired of livin' and scared of dyin'," Robeson sang, "I must keep fightin' until I'm dyin'," turning a line about fate and resignation into a statement about stamina and protest. What Robeson's interventions into this popular showtune so compellingly make clear is not only the way in which music making can be a powerful force for troubling the assumptions of fixity fostered by dominant orders of knowledge production, but also the extent to which music can play a signally important role in cultivating resources for hope. If, as Mary Zournazi suggests in her recent book *Hope: New Philosophies For Change*, hope is "the force which keeps us moving and changing...so that the future may be about how we come to live and hope in the present" (274), then Robeson's example speaks directly to the risks we need to take in order to create opportunities for change, in order to envision a more hopeful, more just, world in the face of the injustices that beset us.

That sense of hope is registered in Robeson's ability to make do with the materials at hand. Once one of the world's most influential artists, and the man W.E.B. Du Bois called "the best known American on earth, to the largest number of human beings" (quoted in Brown x) in the 1950s, Robeson subsequently found himself blacklisted and persecuted by his own country because of his outspoken views on human rights and his communist sympathies. Branded a dangerous radical by U.S. authorities, Robeson was denied his rights as a citizen and prevented from working or performing. His passport was revoked and he was unable to leave the United States. Despite these restrictions, Robeson, as the Peace Arch concert made clear, refused to be silenced. Improvising with the materials at hand—in this case, a makeshift stage on the back of a flat-bed truck located just shy of the border he was not allowed to cross—Robeson created a stunningly original and enduring document of hope out of what might have seemed a hopeless situation. Similarly, his ability to improvise upon the scripted lyrics of "Ol' Man River" in order to insert a resistant presence into the heart of a popular showtune reveals a remarkable commitment to creating opportunities for hope and defiance: a song that might otherwise have fostered stereotypical portrayals of African American peoples is now known to have given rise to one of the more powerful examples of resistant creative practice in the recent history of music making.

This ability to cultivate resources for hope out of seemingly hopeless situations, to foster new structures of understanding, resounds in the history of African American creative practice. Ray Pratt, in his essay in this book, suggests, for example, that we should hear the blues in this context. And drummer Max Roach, in an interview with Frank Owen, puts it this way: "Every new generation of black folks comes up with a new innovation because we're not satisfied with the way the system is economically, politically and sociologically" (quoted in Owen 60). Roach continues: "Every new generation of black people is going to come up with something new until things are equitable for black people in society" (quoted in Owen 60). When asked by Owen (60) to riff on "the theory that hip hop is the new jazz, that there are profound links between what is happening in rap today and the bebop of the late '40s and '50s," Roach explains that "Hip hop is related to what Louis Armstrong did and Charlie Parker did because here was a group of young people who made something out of very little." "Hip hop," Roach argues,

Paul Robeson at the Peace Arch Concert, 1952

came out of the city's poorest area, out of miserable public education, out of miserable housing. They [the artists] didn't have instruments to learn on and take home and play, they didn't have rhetoric classes to learn how to deal with theatre, they didn't have visual arts classes. And yet these people came up with a product of total theatre. On the visual arts side they came up with something erroneously called graffiti. On the dance side they came up with break-dancing. And on the music side, because they didn't have normal instruments, they invented a way to create sounds with turntables...They joined the ranks of the Louis Armstrongs and Charlie Parkers because they created something out of nothing. No one gave them any kind of direction; they had to do it themselves with the materials they had available. (quoted in Owen 60)

All of these examples attest to the creative ways in which aggrieved peoples have responded to oppression. Particularly compelling is music's ability to enable a recognition that social change *is* possible, to sound the possibility of different, and more hopeful, ways of doing things.

The essays we've collected in this volume are written in a similar spirit of hope. Music, they show us, has always played an important role in animating public life with the spirit of dialogue and community. Indeed, in some of its most provocative historical instances, it has served as a catalyst for social engagement and a powerful agent in the creation of cultural awareness. In the face of diminishing opportunities for public dissent against global suffering and injustice, music making, as Robeson's refusal to be silenced makes clear, can encourage us to hear what Robin Kelley calls "life as possibility" (2). In this book, then, we've been, we hope, enlarging on Kelley's argument in *Freedom Dreams* about the roles that hope and the imagination have played (and will continue to play) as revolutionary impulses for social betterment. Kelley suggests that "the most radical art is not protest art but works that take us to another place, envision a new way of seeing, perhaps a different way of feeling" (11). It is our contention that music can (and does) enable us to document such expressions of hope: to take new risks in our relationships with others, to work together across various divides, traditions, styles, and sites, and to discover genuinely new ways of relating to the world around us.

Now, most discussions of music and resistance tend to focus on words, on the lyrics that artists use to articulate their noncompliance with—or, to borrow from Ron Sakolsky and Fred Ho, to "sound off" against—dominant orders of knowledge production. From Paul Robeson's interventions into popular showtunes, to Gil Scott-Heron's acerbic statements about American foreign policy in "B Movie" (or his linking, in "Johannesburg," of black oppression in South Africa *and* the USA), to Tracy Chapman's stirring "Talkin' Bout a Revolution," to Phil Ochs's songs about civil rights and the struggles of working people, to the Australian multi-ethnic group Yothu Yindi's songs about aboriginal land rights, to the "news poems" of Norman Nawrocki's Rhythm Activism, to Victor Jara's revolutionary songs, to Delvina Bernard's anthems of struggle, to Peter Gabriel's "Biko"—singers have relied on words to unsettle customary assumptions about the status quo and to raise awareness of human rights violations.

But we'd like, at least for the moment, to return to a question that's been broached in various ways in this book, and to look not so much at the lyric content of what we've been referring to as rebel musics, but rather at the ways in which sounds themselves might enable us to articulate and to envision new forms of social organization. After all, as Max Roach argues in that same interview with Thomas Owen, the political militancy of hip hop is in the sound, rather than simply—as many might be inclined to think—in the lyrics: "The rhythm [of hip hop] was very militant to me because it was like marching, the sound of an army on the move. We lost Malcolm, we lost King and they thought they had blotted out everybody. But all of a sudden this new art form arises and the militancy is still there in the music" (73).

We'll return to Roach's interview with Owen later in the essay. For now, though, let's acknowledge that any analysis of sound *in itself* is already problematic. For sound doesn't, we suggest, simply signify on its own. A chord or an interval, for instance, cannot, by itself, automatically signify as an expression of noncompliance against oppressions and injustices. Rather, resistant sound, as the diverse range of essays represented in this volume all suggest, needs to be considered in the broader context of a set of institutions and practices that serve to reinvigorate public dialogue about the injustices facing aggrieved populations and that facilitate the creation of oppositional sites, formations, and opportunities.

Our consideration of resistant sounds is predicated on the understanding that music cannot be discussed as a static object of inquiry; its meanings reside not in some understanding of the music in itself, but rather in the broader social and institutional contexts (of production, distribution, and reception) in which it takes place. In his book *Rebel Rock: The Politics of Popular Music* (one of the few books, along with Ray Pratt's *Rhythm and Resistance* and Ho and Sakolsky's *Sounding Off*, to inaugurate sustained discussion of music as a discourse of resistance), John Street makes a similar point. "Politics," he reminds us, "is introduced into the making, manufacturing and distribution of music, in the decisions about how music is to be marketed and sold" (2). And Christopher Small, in his book *Musicking: The Meanings of Performance and Listening*, is explicit on this point, suggesting that music's social meanings are not simply incidental: "the fundamental nature and meaning of music," says Small, "lie not in objects, not in musical works at all, *but in action, in what people do*" (8; our emphasis). Hence, Small seeks to replace the noun "music" with the verb "to music" or the present participle or gerund "musicking." A similar shift from from noun to verb has animated the work of a number of African-American critics writing specifically about jazz. Nathaniel Mackey, by way of Amiri Baraka's well known argument on white appropriation of black music in "Swing—from Verb to Noun" suggests that the movement from verb to noun "means, on the aesthetic level, a less dynamic, less improvisatory, less blues-inflected music, and, on the political level, a containment of black mobility, a containment of the economic and social advances that might accrue to black artistic innovation" (266). By contrast, suggests Mackey, privileging the verb "linguistically accentuates action among a people whose ability to act is curtailed by racist constraint" (268). Picking up on Small's notion of musicking, Samuel Floyd, Jr., in his book *The Power of Black Music*, points out that "aesthetic deliberation about African-American music requires a perceptual and conceptual shift from the idea of music as an object to music as an event, from music as written—as a frozen, sonic ideal—to music as making" (232).

How can music, then, be an active force for building a politics of hope? How can we best assess what it means for artists to be socially responsible? And how might that responsibility most purposefully and most creatively manifest itself in practice? These are the kinds of questions that animate the work of the essayists in this volume.

We are aware that in public perception, heavily reinforced by traditional models of musical education and by institutional protocol, music tends to be represented, taught, and talked about primarily as an aesthetic form distinct from issues of social responsibility. This tendency to neglect issues of social concern is, of course, especially the case with instrumental music which, again, tends to get institutionalized in the most formalist of terms. In traditional music education, students are taught technique and form, but they tend *not* to be taught what it might mean to be an artist *in the world*. In an attempt to counter this rather narrow focus on established practices and priorities in music education, we've sought, in this book, to open up questions about appropriate models of artistic responsibility. We make the case here that creative practitioners have long worked as catalysts for collective action and community development. Indeed, the essays in the volume provide direct examples of musicians who have made a difference in their communities, musicians who have used modes of working together (improvisation and collaboration) to envision new forms of social organization, and musicians who have a long history of involvement with struggles for social justice and human rights.

History provides no shortage of examples of musicians who have variously sought to construct an activist framework of understanding for their music. Often, these frameworks of understanding are articulated in public pronouncements which insist that the music be heard as a form of political action. Ranging from Fred Ho's suggestion that jazz is "fundamentally rooted...in the struggle to end all forms of exploitation and oppression" (137) to Thomas Mapfumo's insistence that his music is "a tool for change and we need a change very badly in Zimbabwe" ("Zimbabwe"), public statements from musicians (in interviews, in self-penned liner notes, in open forums and panel discussions, in essays, in films) have encouraged audiences to contextualize musical practices in relation to pressing issues of human rights, social justice, and the development of new networks of social interaction and responsibility.

In this context, Eric Porter's book *What Is This Thing Called Jazz?* provides a detailed and much-needed analysis of what African American jazz musicians have had to say about their own work. Citing the comments of prominent artists such as Archie Shepp, Cecil Taylor, and others (many of whom are discussed in Jesse Stewart's essay in this volume), Porter focusses on a number of issues germane to our discussion here. He takes a detailed look, for example, at the role that artists played in forming alternative institutions (such as the Association for the Advancement of Creative Musicians, the Jazz Composers Guild, and The Collective Black Artists), which insisted upon the social relevance of musical activity and countered the egregiously unjust conditions under which these artists worked (for more on alternative institution-building in the history of jazz, see Heble 69-71). Referring specifically to Shepp, Porter (207) suggests that many African American jazz musicians (especially in the 1960s and 1970s) were being encouraged "to do more than create a socially relevant art form." Far from being content with allowing the music to speak for itself, Shepp wanted his fellow artists "to become spokespeople and to engage in practical programs to address issues within and outside the jazz community." Shepp believed that "the music itself could only accomplish so much" (203). In Shepp's own words: "There are limitations—music has its limitations, especially in *intense* political times…At times simply to play is not enough…At times we must do more than play" (quoted in Porter 203; emphasis in original).

Shepp is right in suggesting that playing music isn't enough, that tangible results in real-world terms, especially when it comes to matters of human rights violations and struggles for social justice, are unlikely to be attained through acts of musical expression alone. Yet, as the essays in this volume demonstrate, music can also be about the power to dream, about creating new structures of hope and momentum, new opportunities for developing a community of concern, as well as for radicalizing the commitment to preserving a record—a kind of collective memory, if you will—of human suffering and survival. In their book *Free Spaces: The Sources of Democratic Change in America*, Sara Evans and Harry Boyte ask, "Where are the places in our culture through which people sustain bonds and history? What are the processes through which they may broaden their sense of the possible, make alliances with others, develop the practical skills and knowledge to maintain democratic organization?" (202). The contributors to this book would all likely agree that music offers one such site in our culture where aggrieved peoples can gain the hope to assert their own rights, to enhance our collective ability to see (and to hear) "life as possibility," to educate the public on abiding matters of justice and rights, and to advance the struggle for more inclusive frameworks of understanding. And all would, we think, agree with George Lipsitz who tells us that "we have much to learn from artists who are facing up to the things that are killing them and their communities. Cultural creators are," he suggests, "also creating new kinds of social theory. Engaged in the hard work of fashioning cultural and political coalitions based on shared suffering, they have been forced to think clearly about cultural production in contemporary society" (230).

In this context, the pioneering work of sound artist Bob Ostertag is particularly compelling. A musician, human rights activist, and social theorist in his own right, Ostertag uses digital sampling and found materials to create disturbing and powerfully moving testimonies of human suffering and endurance. His politically-charged works include *All the Rage* (1993), a piece commissioned by the Kronos Quartet using recordings from a San Francisco gay rights riot in which Ostertag participated; *Sooner or Later* (1991), which combines guitar work by Fred Frith with a recording of a Salvadoran boy burying his father slain by El Salvador's National Guard; and the more recent *Yugoslavia Suite*, a multimedia project on the Bosnian War which received its Canadian premiere at the Festival International Musique Actuelle in Victoriaville, Québec in 2000. In this latter piece, Ostertag mixes sound samples with images from video and computer war-simulation games, as well as with actual images from U.S. Army and Air Force training videos. *Yugoslavia Suite* is divided into two sections, "War Games" and "These Hands." As Fabrizio Gilardino explains in the programme notes from the Victoriaville performance, "The first part of *Yugoslavia Suite*...becomes a reflection on this new American way of conducting a war: aseptic and surgical, as CNN reporters were so pleased to define it during the Gulf War; whereas the second part brutally brings us back to reality, where being shot does not necessarily exclude the possibility of looking into the eyes of the shooter" (17).

In his book *States of Denial: Knowing About Atrocities and Suffering*, human rights scholar Stanley Cohen suggests that with "mass media coverage of atrocities and social suffering" (11)—exemplified in coverage of the Gulf War—an "entire language of denial has been constructed in order to evade thinking about the unthinkable" (11). Cohen's book addresses why organized atrocities—genocides, torture, massacres—are repeatedly denied, evaded, or neutralized: "people, organizations, governments or whole societies are presented with information that is too disturbing, threatening or anomalous to be fully absorbed or openly acknowledged. The information is therefore somehow repressed, disavowed, pushed aside or reinterpreted. Or else the information 'registers' well enough, but its implications...are evaded, neutralized or rationalized away" (1). Ostertag's intrepid spirit of sonic exploration suggests that while Shepp may be right in arguing that music making isn't always, in itself, a sufficient response to the atrocities of horrific proportions taking place all over the globe, it *is* the task of musicians to find new ways to radicalize public understanding. And in an era when, as Cohen's remarks on denial and Ron Sakolsky's essay in this volume both remind us, corporate control over media representations works to prioritize profit over people, and to put the struggles of aggrieved peoples at risk of being completely abandoned, this task gains a particular urgency.

Indeed, if one of the key issues for human rights activists and organizations involves finding ways to create conditions so information about atrocities and suffering is both acknowledged and acted upon (Cohen 249), then music can be a potent social force. "Campaigns against injustice," in Lipsitz's words, can draw "strength from the power of cultural expressions and ideas to forge alliances among people with distinctly different social roles and status" (232-33). Yothu Yindi's song "Treaty," for instance, is cited by Lipsitz as having secured "a power in the market that helped spark a successful struggle to force the Australian government to negotiate a new treaty between that continent's original inhabitants and the descendants of European settlers" (231). And the band's leader, Mandawuy Yunupingu, is explicit in his insistence that his music can play a role in struggles for social betterment. "When you talk about the revolutionary things that have happened in the world," he tells us, "it's always been connected with art and I think the Aboriginal people are in that process now. Our art is a mechanism for change" (quoted in Lipsitz 231). Like Joy Kogawa's novel *Obasan*, a text that not only helped create public aware-ness about the internment of Japanese Canadians during World War 2—something that was certainly omitted from textbooks when I studied history—but also played a role in bringing about reparations from the Canadian government, Yothu Yindi's music making provides an ex-emplary instance of the ways in which art can contribute to the processes of social change. If it is the task of intellectuals, as Edward Said has argued, to speak out against injustice and suffering, then musicians, too, have been engaged in powerful and resonant forms of social critique. Ev-ans and Boyte also ask, "What are the structures of support, the resources, and the experiences that generate the capacity and inspiration to challenge 'the way things are' and imagine a differ-ent world?" (2) Again, the essays collected here argue that music making can both unsettle insti-tutionally determined epistemic orders and help to foster alternative visions of human possibility.

Often, those visions are realized most powerfully and most innovatively not in the content of the music itself, but, as we've already implied, in the way in which the music is produced, distrib-uted, and promoted. The alternative institution-building strategies of musicians' collectives such as the Association for the Advancement of Creative Musicians and the Jazz Composers Guild, or independent record labels such as Sun Ra's Saturn or Ani DiFranco's Righteous Babe command our attention in this context. DiFranco, for instance, links her own musical and institutional prac-tices with broader issues of social justice. In content, the songs she performs often grapple head-on with issues of social justice and human rights. Her 1999 collaboration with spoken word artist Utah Phillips, *Fellow Workers*, might, for instance, be heard as a kind of alternative history lesson about workers' rights. The songs of struggle and remembrance—including the moving tribute to martyred trade unionist and mine organizer Joe Hill (a song that Paul Robeson frequently included in his repertoire and which he sang at the Peace Arch concert in 1952)—counter institutionalized interpretations of American history. And it's entirely fitting, then, that the liner notes should be written by radical historian Howard Zinn, the author of *A People's History of the United States*, a book explicitly named in the liner notes as providing "in-formation on the American history you didn't get in school." Zinn writes, "The songs on this disk, the stories told in Utah Phillips' extraordinary style, bring back the history, but even more, the feelings of people struggling together for a better life." He continues: "We need to remind everyone of what the Declaration of Independence promised, that all human beings, here and everywhere in the world, have an equal right to life, liberty, and the pursuit of happiness. And we will use our energy, our talent, to achieve those aims, with the good feeling that people have always had when they worked together for justice."

For Ani DiFranco, working together for justice seems to mean more than simply playing music. True, she's an artist first and foremost, but, like Archie Shepp, her activist orientations are also revealed in her extra-musical initiatives. The Righteous Babe website, for instance, boasts an "Action" page which declares that "our actions will define us." Containing links to alternative media sites and social justice organizations such as the Southern Centre for Human Rights, the "Action" page explains, "Our humble goal here is to share information and ideas, to suggest places you can look for alternatives to mainstream media coverage of world events, and to propose ways you can find and work with like-minded individuals and organizations around the planet and in your own neighborhood." Rather an unorthodox statement, this, for a record label, yet DiFranco's Righteous Babe is, of course, no ordinary or mainstream outfit. Committed to taking control over (and thus changing) unjust relations of production, DiFranco is at the forefront of contemporary efforts by artists seeking to build activist oppositional communities of concern and commitment not only in the content of their art but in decisions about how that art is to be marketed, distributed, and contextualized.

There are, of course, numerous and wide-ranging examples of musicians endeavouring through various extra-musical means to construct an activist orientation for their work. Many of these are discussed in the essays in this volume. Think, for example, of the causes with which musicians get identified: Artists Against Apartheid, Tracy Chapman singing at a concert to Free Nelson Mandala, Avant Jazz For Peace, Live Aid, or even the avowedly nonpolitical Thelonious Monk performing in 1963 for the Student Nonviolent Coordinating Committee (SNCC) honouring Southern Students' "Courageous, Dedicated and Persistent Struggle for Human Dignity and Freedom on the Third Anniversary of the Sit-Ins" (see Monson 189), and so forth. Consider, too, the example of artists performing instrumental soundtracks to films about human rights, such as Québécois guitarist René Lussier's music for *Chronique d'un Genocide Annoncé* (*Chronicle of a Genocide Foretold*), a documentary by Danièle Lacourse and Yvan Patry about genocide in Rwanda. The CD version of Lussier's soundtrack contains photographs of, and statements by, those who survived the massacre. Also included are comments from human rights activists such as Joseph Matata who explains, "This [the genocide] happened because no one has been held responsible for the atrocities of the past 35 years. We must react. Justice must be done so that people realize that you can't just take someone's life like that. Impunity must be stopped" (Lussier, liner notes). These comments about the need for responsibility are echoed in liner notes by Claire Julier: "The genocide was planned, it carries a precise date. The international community owns up to its cowardice but takes no action. Who is responsible? How should they be punished? It was children, women and men who were massacred in the name of hate. Were the ghosts of other crimes powerless to prevent it?"

Think also about how artists—even those performing purely instrumental music—can profoundly shape our understanding and interpretation of music through their choice of composition titles: John Coltrane's "Alabama," for instance, a piece in memory of the black school children killed by a bomb planted by white supremacists, comes to mind in this context. In discussing artists who linked their own experiences of inequities in the music industry to broader social issues, and who performed politically explicit material, Porter tells us that "for many musicians, activist orientations coincided with an internationalist perspective, which had been evident during the 1940s and early 1950s but became more pronounced in the late 1950s and early 1960s in the context of anticolonial struggles...John Coltrane, for example, made efforts to incorporate 'Eastern' melodic elements in his music; [Abbey] Lincoln, Roach, and Randy Weston used African rhythms and explicit references to African political and cultural issues in their composition and song titles" (195-96). And, as Daniel Fischlin notes in his first take on the complex and interconnected issues discussed throughout this book, rebel rock groups such as Rage Against the Machine are, like Ani DiFranco, explicit not only in their lyrical content, but also in listing resources and websites as part of their recordings, encouraging listeners to follow up and to take the next step and act for social justice.

But how, we're tempted to ask, does all of this translate into action? How precisely will it result in improvements in people's lives, in policy changes, in alterations in the distribution of power, in prevention of human rights abuses? True, these sorts of changes can (and have) sometimes come about because of the cultural work of the artists discussed in this book. But perhaps these are not quite the right questions. Better, perhaps, to try to understand how rebel musics bear witness to suffering and atrocities. Better to recognize how they give testimony and sounding to issues ignored in the mainstream press, and raise questions about positions which too often get institutionalized as unworthy of public attention. Better to understand that artists, as Lipsitz so rightly reminds us, have provided strength and inspiration for social movements. Better to focus on the hope and the opportunities for change that rebel musics articulate.

Indeed, as Juan Antonio Blanco puts it in a recent essay documenting urgent priorities conditioning the struggle for human rights, "The challenge is to bring together all the wisdom, imagination and hope needed in order to correct in a timely fashion the self-destructive direction of our social history...Advocates and activists for human rights...are often told to resign themselves to the understanding that no other future is possible" (47-8). Rebel musics, as we've seen in this book, are, by contrast, insistent in their sounding of other possible futures. They're insistent, too, in their efforts to create what Martha Nandorfy, in her essay in this book, calls a "repertoire of historical memory," in documenting and fostering critical consciousness of injustice and suffering. Again, let's recall Edward Said's argument here: "No one can speak up all the time on all the issues," says Said. "But, I believe, there is a special duty to address the constituted and authorized powers of one's own society, which are accountable to its citizenry, particularly when those powers are exercised in a manifestly disproportionate and immoral war, or in a deliberate program of discrimination, repression, and collective cruelty (98). Said, to be sure, is talking about the responsibility of intellectuals, but his comments also speak to the urgent need for creative practitioners to find compelling and innovative ways to enter the fray.

In his introduction to *Edward Said and the Work of the Critic: Speaking Truth to Power*, editor Paul Bové suggests that Said has jettisoned postmodernist worries about "what we can know" to argue that, "at the level of politics and history, we can know certain and often quite deadly things—massacres, cover-ups, and the suppression of human rights—and intellectuals must use their special training and knowledge to speak of these matters as they speak about race and stories"(5). Said says: "The first imperative is to find out what occurred and then why, not as isolated events but as part of an unfolding history whose broad contours include one's own nation as an actor. The incoherence of the standard foreign policy analysis performed by apologists, strategists, and planners is that it concentrates on others as the objects of a situation, rarely on 'our' involvement and what it has wrought" (99). Human rights activist and educator Sherene Razack makes a related claim in asserting that efforts to build critical consciousness and to develop blueprints for the achievement of social justice must find ways to "disrupt claims of innocence" (16). "My goal," she says, "is to move towards accountability, a process that begins with a recognition that we are each implicated in systems of oppression that profoundly structure our understanding of one another" (10). Too often, as William Warden argues in an essay published in the monumental anthology, *Human Rights in the Twenty-First Century: A Global Challenge*, people tend to conceive of human rights "as an issue in the wider world 'out there'—and not for 'me' in the here and now. Treated in this fashion, the result is more likely to be a dulling of sensitivity to abuses on one's own doorstep. Canadians, for example, prefer to focus on apartheid in South Africa, rather than confront burning problems in their own relations with aboriginal peoples" (985-86). Interrogating the assumption that struggles for human rights are someone else's issue (and that these struggles have little, if anything, to do with our own life-situations)—think, for example, of Gil Scott-Heron's insistence that "New York's like Johannesburg," "Detroit's like Johannesburg," ("Johannesburg")—necessitates that we put a fair bit of critical pressure on notions of individualism and autonomy, that we confront the networks of power and privilege that make innocence and self-sufficiency even thinkable.

We want to conclude by speculating about some of the ways in which rebel musics might support and advance the goals Said and Razack have in mind. If Warden is correct in suggesting that "probably the most formidable challenge today for the human rights community of activists is that of education," and if we take seriously his contention that "there is a fundamental need to translate the growing consciousness of human rights issues to the entire spectrum of human society" (989), then it behooves us, as artists, scholars, and citizens, to continue to reflect on how our practices and commitments can nourish people's capacity to participate in the transformation of unjust social relations. As we've already suggested, sounds in and of themselves are not likely to result in direct social change. But, to be sure, legislation, by itself, is clearly not enough either. Witness the barbarous and unchecked abuses of power that continue despite alleged adherence to international treaties and covenants. Here, it's worth bearing in mind that the United Nations human rights programme is founded conceptually upon a three-way relationship among legislation, implementation, and information/education (Martenson 928). In the context of that three-way relationship, education, surely, remains crucial, especially, as the essays in this book suggest, when global forces and the concomitant naturalization of corporate frames of reference threaten to put the rights of aggrieved peoples at risk of being completely abandoned. And let's recall, too, Bové's insistence, via Said, that justice matters, that "intellectuals must use their special training and knowledge" to speak out against human rights violations and social injustice. The argument we assert here is that it's not only scholars, theorists, and intellectuals who are positioned to raise pressing questions about systems of dominance. And often, the most common ways that such "speaking out" can take place within the context of music, is, indeed, through affiliation with an appropriate choice of subject matter, as well as through the encouragement and development of a public form of critical literacy and consciousness. But we need to remind ourselves that a renewed understanding of the place of human rights in the context of music making can only come about if we refuse to become complacent about our commitment to finding ways of being moved to action.

If the exercise of human rights becomes meaningful not only through the existence of rules and treaties but also as a result of the broader cultures of obligation that might help transform those rules into acknowledgement and action, then a radical reorganization of our priorities seems to be in order. " 'More of the same,' " Blanco warns us, "can only lead towards new totalitarianisms, social conflicts, famines, [and] massive uncontrolled migrations" (42). When policies and positions become entrenched, naturalized, and hegemonic, they close off alternatives, negate possible futures, and crowd out alternative frameworks of understanding. One way to counter such entrenchment is for Human Rights Education (HRE), in Upendra Baxi's words, "to commission a world history of peoples' struggles for rights and against injustice and tyranny" (142). Surely the rebel musics described in this book have an important role to play in helping to document (and raise public awareness about) such a history.

Music as Alternative History, Music as Education, Music as Community, Music as Witness and Remembrance, Music as Hope, Music as Other Possible Futures: however we choose to understand the power, the force, of resistant sound, one of the great lessons of rebel musics resides in the acknowledgement that listeners need to share responsibility for developing and nurturing a more prevalent culture of rights. Again, music by itself offers no simple cure for monumental global suffering and injustice. What it can provide, though, is an opening, an opportunity, a vision, for a sorely needed new cultural paradigm. The next step, then, is, by necessity, yours. What steps can you, as a listener, reader, and citizen take to respect and to advance the struggle for rights enshrined in international treaties such as the Universal Declaration of Human Rights? Sure, it's probably idealistic to suggest that there's a new form of cultural activism afoot, utopian to think that music making, whether through radical content, innovations in form, or various kinds of extra-musical affiliations with human rights causes, will result directly in a transformation of consciousness. Yet among the many artists and audience members we continue to encounter (and interact with) are those who clearly see it as a priority for musicians and listeners alike to build inclusive activist communities of concern and commitment. None pretend to have easy solutions. But many, if not most, offer their music (and their practices of listening) as a model (even if only indirectly) for new forms of social mobilization, new (and more just) ways of understanding, new kinds of relationships. Again, it's worth recalling Christopher Small's argument about the meanings associated with musicking:

> The act of musicking establishes…a set of relationships, and it is in those relationships that the meaning of the act lies. They are to be found not only between those organized sounds which are conventionally thought of as being the stuff of musical meaning but also between the people who are taking part, in whatever capacity, in the performance; and they model, or stand as a metaphor for, ideal relationships as the participants in the performance imagine them to be: relationships between person and person, between individual and society, between humanity and the natural world and perhaps even the supernatural world. These are important matters, perhaps the most important in human life. (13)

These are important matters, indeed. No wonder, then, that Max Roach, in the interview with Thomas Owen from which we quoted earlier, turns on his interviewer when asked whether the black militancy he hears in the *sound* of hip hop—recall Roach's argument that the militancy is in the rhythm—is somehow compromised by the fact that hip hop artists are sampling from non-black sources. Owen asks, "Is the black militancy you hear in L.L. Cool J's rhythms changed by the fact that some of those beats were sampled from John Bonham, Led Zeppelin's drummer, and the fact that hip hop often uses music from a wide variety of sources, many not obviously black: like Kraftwerk, Billy Squire, the Monkees, Elton John, Billy Joel, Mountain" (73). Roach's response: "Hip hop swings. I never heard Led Zeppelin swing. Jesus Christ, now hip hop comes from Led Zeppelin, you motherfucker" (73). As the exchange continues, the tension builds. "You're English and you come to this country and try to tell us that everything we got came from whites," Roach tells Owen. "You're telling me that Charlie Parker came out of a white experience." The interview ends abruptly with Roach closing off the possibility of further dialogue: "I know where you're coming from," he says to his interviewer. "I've had it with you, you motherfucker. Get out of my house" (73).

While this interview is frequently cited in critical work on contemporary music—especially for Roach's insight that the politics is in the sound—commentators have tended to stay clear of the controversial nature of the exchange between Roach and Owen, omitting to mention, for example, that the interview ends with Roach lunging at Owen from across his living room and demanding at the top of his voice that the interviewer "get the fuck out of" Roach's house. This is tricky territory, to be sure, but the very urgency of the encounter demands that we not ignore its implications, especially in the context of an argument about how musicking can model new (and more hopeful) social relations. Roach understands well what's at stake in the politics and assessment of black music. He knows that for too long, as George Lewis has documented in his landmark essay on afrological and eurological perspectives on improvised music, black music has been denigrated, dismissed, or contextualized, by white critics, as having white cultural precedents. Roach's point is well taken. But where, we need to ask, can his response to Owen lead us? How might his refusal, in this case, even to discuss the possibility of intercultural musical borrowings square with his profound commitment to the power and force of artistic innovation?

In asking these questions, we certainly intend no disparagement to Roach, who rightly detects, and takes issue with, more than a hint of racism in the interpretive frameworks that have historically served to belittle the achievements of black music. But Roach, it appears here, is only willing to push boundaries, to countenance innovative artistic practices, within the context of his own frames of reference. His unwillingness even to allow the discussion to continue is at odds with the spirit of hope and dialogue (and the other possible futures) that we've sought to locate in rebel musics. In the face of an urgent need for cultural paradigms that are inclusive, pluralist, dialogic, reciprocal, equitable, and ethically responsible, Roach's reaction problematizes the dialogue over how to achieve human rights—especially in relation to issues of how historical amnesia and interpretive frames for understanding musical contexts are so often complicit. Recall our earlier point, that as positions become entrenched, they crowd out possibilities for alternative frameworks of understanding.

The lesson here is that we mustn't allow our interpretive habits to settle into an orthodoxy. Or, better: let's take our cue from so many of the musics described in this book and continue to work on new resources for hope. Let's recognize that music can be (and has been) both a repository for history and a shaper of other possible futures, and that its power—symbolic or otherwise—resides precisely in its refusal to be aligned with any and all forms of reductive thinking. Yes, Roach is correct to urge us to understand that music is a matter of context, that it inhabits the cultural landscape in complex and often misunderstood ways. But music's power, as we've already argued in Take One, also extends beyond context. Music's capacity to unsettle fixed systems of understanding, we suggest, is precisely what enables hope and dialogue. And further: its rights dimensions, as a primary assertion of human expression and expressivity, as a force that keeps us moving, changing, dreaming, and imagining, are thus woven into the very nature of its being and meaning. After all, as this volume consistently demonstrates, out of dead-end situations, musicians have fashioned opportunities for hope and momentum in the here and now. The ability to create and to sustain such opportunities in the face of monumental global suffering and injustice surely ranks among the most inspirational and enduring artistic achievements of our time.

Thanks to Daniel Fischlin, Cory Legassic, Sheila O'Reilly, Jesse Stewart, Tim Struthers, and Ellen Waterman for sharing resources, recordings, and dialogue.

WORKS CITED

"Action: Our Actions Will Define Us." *Righteous Babe Records.* 2003. 2 June 2003 <http://www.righteousbabe.com/action/index.asp>.

Baxi, Upendra. "Human Rights Education: The Promise of the Third Millennium?" *Human Rights Education for the Twenty-First Century.* Ed. George Andreopoulos and Richard Pierre-Claude. Philadelphia: U of Pennsylvania P, 1997. 142-54.

Blanco, Juan Antonio. "Natural History and Social History: Limits and Urgent Priorities which Condition the Exercise of Human Rights." *The Poverty of Rights: Human Rights and the Eradication of Poverty.* Ed. Willem van Genugten and Camilo Perez-Bustillo. London: Zed Books, 2001. 40-48.

Bové, Paul. Introduction. *Edward Said and the Work of the Critic: Speaking Truth to Power.* Ed. Bové. Durham, NC: Duke UP, 2000. 1-8.

Brown, Lloyd. "Preface." *Here I Stand.* By Paul Robeson. Boston: Beacon Press, 1971. ix-xx.

Cohen, Stanley. *States of Denial: Knowing About Atrocities and Suffering.* Cambridge: Polity, 2001.

DiFranco, Ani, and Utah Phillips. *Fellow Workers.* Righteous Babe, 1999.

Evans, Sara, and Harry Boyte. *Free Spaces: The Sources of Democratic Change in America.* New York: Harper and Row, 1986.

Floyd, Samuel A., Jr. *The Power of Black Music: Interpreting Its History from Africa to the United States.* New York: Oxford UP, 1995.

Gilardino, Fabrizio. Programme notes. "Bob Ostertag: *Yugoslavia Suite.*" Festival international musique actuelle, Victoriaville, PQ. May 2000. 17.

Heble, Ajay. *Landing on the Wrong Note: Jazz, Dissonance, and Critical Practice.* New York: Routledge, 2000.

Ho, Fred Wei-han. "'Jazz,' 'Kreolization and Revolutionary Music for the 21st Century." *Sounding Off: Music as Subversion/Resistance/Revolution.* Ed. Ron Sakolsky and Fred Wei-han Ho. Brooklyn: Autonomedia, 1995. 133-43.

Julier, Claire. Liner notes. *Chronique d'un Genocide Annoncé.* By René Lussier. Ambiances Magnétiques, 1998.

Kelley, Robin D.G. *Freedom Dreams: The Black Radical Imagination.* Boston: Beacon, 2002.

Lewis, George E. "Improvised Music after 1950: Afrological and Eurological Perspectives." *Black Music Research Journal* 16 (Spring 1996): 91-122.

Lipsitz, George. *American Studies in a Moment of Danger*. Minneapolis: U of Minnesota P, 2001.

Lussier, René. *Chronique d'un Genocide Annoncé*. Dirs. Danièle Lacours and Yvan Patry. Ambiances Magnétiques, 1998.

Mackey, Nathaniel. *Discrepant Engagement: Dissonance, Cross-Culturality, and Experimental Writing*. Cambridge: Cambridge UP, 1993.

Martenson, Jan. "The United Nations and Human Rights Today and Tomorrow." *Human Rights in the Twenty-First Century: A Global Challenge*. Ed. Kathleen E. Mahoney and Paul Mahoney. Dordrecht: Martinus Nijhoff, 1993. 925-36.

Monson, Ingrid. "Monk Meets SNCC." *Black Music Research Journal* 19.2 (Fall 1999): 187-200.

Ostertag, Bob. *All the Rage*. Perf. Kronos Quartet. Nonesuch, 1993.

—. *Sooner or Later*. Sealand, 1991.

Owen, Frank. "Hip Hop Bebop." *Spin* 4 (October 1988): 60, 73.

Porter, Eric. *What is this Thing Called Jazz?: African American Musicians as Artists, Critics, and Activists*. Berkeley: U of California P, 2002.

Pratt, Ray. *Rhythm and Resistance: The Political Uses of American Popular Music*. 1990. Washington: Smithsonian Institution P, 1994.

Razack, Sherene. *Looking White People in the Eye: Gender, Race, and Culture in Courtrooms and Classrooms*. Toronto: U of Toronto P, 1998.

Robeson, Paul. *The Peace Arch Concerts*. Folk Era Records, 1998.

Said, Edward W. *Representations of the Intellectual*. New York: Pantheon, 1994.

Sakolsky, Ron, and Fred Wei-han Ho, eds. *Sounding Off: Music as Subversion/Resistance/Revolution*. Brooklyn: Autonomedia, 1995.

Scott-Heron, Gil. "Johannesburg." *The Best of Gil Scott-Heron*. LP. Arista, 1984.

Small, Christopher. *Musicking: The Meanings of Performance and Listening*. Hanover, NH: Wesleyan UP, 1998.

Street, John. *Rebel Rock: The Politics of Popular Music*. Oxford: Blackwell, 1986.

Warden, William. "From Analysis to Activism." *Human Rights in the Twenty-First Century: A Global Challenge*. Ed. Kathleen E. Mahoney and Paul Mahoney. Dordrecht: Martinus Nijhoff, 1993. 985-90.

Yothi Yindi. "Treaty." *Tribal Voice*. Mushroom Records, 1991.

"Zimbabwe." *Freemuse: Freedom of Musical Expression*. 2003. 2 June 2003 <http://www.freemuse.org/03libra/countries/zimbabwe/zimb01.html>.

Zinn, Howard. Liner notes. *Fellow Workers*. By Ani DiFranco and Utah Phillips. Righteous Babe, 1999.

Zournazi, Mary. *Hope: New Philosophies For Change*. New York: Routledge, 2003.

BOOKS of RELATED INTEREST

THREE MOMENTS OF LOVE IN LEONARD COHEN AND BRUCE COCKBURN
Paul Nonnekes

Examines the way in which these two artists, so different in style and temperament, approach the question of love and desire—in their art and in their life.

> An original and challenging study of two brilliant and idiosyncratic songwriters, whose work has never before been compared in such depth … essential reading. —Stephen Scobie, *winner of the Governor General's Award for Poetry*

PAUL NONNEKES, Ph.D., teaches Sociology in the Department of Humanities and Social Sciences, Red Deer College, Alberta.

> 192 pages, 6x9, photographs, bibliography, index
> Paperback ISBN: 1-55164-176-3 $19.99
> Hardcover ISBN: 1-55614-177-1 $48.99

THE ANARCHIST AND THE DEVIL DO CABARET
Norman Nawrocki

A travel diary of the cabaret band Rhythm Activism as they toured Europe, combined with short stories, real and exaggerated, filled with friends, lovers, and fellow travelers.

> Real events, tall tales … proving that fables speak truths. Clever. —*VUEWeekly*

> As a travel book it's quite a trip, man. —*Winnipeg Sun*

> This work is much more complex than simply a musician's chronicle of drinking his way across Europe. It is firmly rooted in socio-political concerns. —*Uptown*

> A gritty yet raucous account … true to his anarchist roots. —*Montreal Gazette*

As frontman/violinist NORMAN NAWROCKI has given thousands of shows, in hundreds of cities around the world, most recently at the prestigious Montreal Jazz Festival.

> 192 pages, 6x9, photographs, illustrations
> Paperback ISBN: 1-55164-204-2 $19.99
> Hardcover ISBN: 1-55164-205-0 $48.99

BOOKS of RELATED INTEREST

EDUARDO GALEANO Through the Looking Glass
Daniel Fischlin, Martha Nandorfy

Part political biography, part cultural theory—especially in relation to the telling of history and the relations between literature and human rights—this book is the first full-length, critical study of the life and work of Eduardo Galeano.

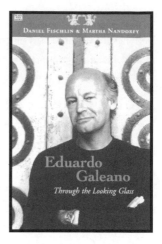

> Traces a magnificent path through the work of Galeano.
> —Enrique Dussel, *The Invention of the Americas*

> Skillfully guides us into the world of one of the finest writers of our time. —Ronald Wright, *Time Among the Maya*

> Neither straightforward biography nor ordinary literary criticism, this is a provocative study of rights, story, and memory. —Barbara Harlow, *Resistance Literature and After Lives*

DANIEL FISCHLIN is professor of English at the University of Guelph. MARTHA NANDORFY is an associate professor of Latino/a and Chicano/a Literature at the University of Guelph.

450 pages, 6x9, illustrations, bibliography, index
Paperback ISBN: 1-55164-178-X $24.99
Hardcover ISBN: 1-55164-179-8 $53.99

send for a free catalogue of all our titles

BLACK ROSE BOOKS

C.P. 1258, Succ. Place du Parc
Montréal, Québec
H2X 4A7 Canada

or visit our website at http://www.web.net/blackrosebooks

To order books
In Canada: (phone) 1-800-565-9523 (fax) 1-800-221-9985
email: utpbooks@utpress.utoronto.ca
In United States: (phone) 1-800-283-3572 (fax) 1-651-917-6406
In UK & Europe: (phone) London 44 (0)20 8986-4854 (fax) 44 (0)20 8533-5821
email: order@centralbooks.com

Printed by the workers of
MARC VEILLEUX IMPRIMEUR INC.
Boucherville, Québec
for Black Rose Books Ltd.